La Nueva California

La Nueva California

LATINOS IN THE GOLDEN STATE

David E. Hayes-Bautista

UNIVERSITY OF CALIFORNIA PRESS

BERKELEY   LOS ANGELES   LONDON

University of California Press
Berkeley and Los Angeles, California

University of California Press, Ltd.
London, England

© 2004 by
The Regents of the University of California

Library of Congress Cataloging-in-Publication Data

Hayes-Bautista, David E.
    La nueva California : Latinos in the Golden State / by David E. Hayes-Bautista.
        p.   cm.
    Includes bibliographical references and index.
    ISBN 0-520-24145-2 (cloth : alk. paper) — ISBN 0-520-24146-0 (pbk. : alk. paper)
        1. Hispanic Americans—California—Social conditions.   2. Hispanic
Americans—California—Statistics.   3. Hispanic Americans—California—Ethnic
identity.   4. California—Social conditions.   5. California—Population.
6. California—Ethnic relations.   I. Title.

F870.S75H385   2004
979.4'00468073—dc22   2004006949

Manufactured in the United States of America
13   12   11   10   09   08   07   06   05   04
11   10   9   8   7   6   5   4   3   2   1

To my wife, Teodocia María de Jesús, and to the young Latinos of today's California, including our daughter, Catalina Mercedes Ixcotl, and our son, Diego David Cuauhtemoc, who are daily creating the state's, and this country's, future

Human beings share a tradition. There is no creation without tradition. No one creates from nothing.

CARLOS FUENTES
"How I Started to Write"

CONTENTS

ILLUSTRATIONS

FIGURES

TABLES

PREFACE

Whither California? During three earlier demographic booms—the gold rush (1849–60), the railroad-facilitated boom (1890–1920), and the automobile-borne baby boom (1946–64)—California was not unlike the rest of America, only a bit ahead of the trends. The fourth population boom (1975–90), however, was largely driven by growth in the Latino population.[1] Indeed, since 2001 Latino babies have counted for more than half of all newborns in the state. This new boom has not met with the boosterlike enthusiasm that greeted past population shifts. Instead, this boom has spurred more than a little trepidation and resistance, notably in the form of emotionally driven state initiatives to limit immigration and eliminate bilingual education. The question underlying such responses is usually this: What will happen to American identity and society in California when Latinos become half the state's entire population?

1. "Latino" is used as the most comprehensive, generic term to refer to individuals whose origins are in the Latin American societies of the Western Hemisphere. It is roughly equivalent to the term "Hispanic," which has a specific definition given on page 63 but is purposely fuzzier around the edges. There are many Latino subpopulations, such as people of Mexican origin, Chicanos, Salvadorans, and so on. About 77.1 percent of Latinos in California are of Mexican origin; therefore, the Mexican portion of the Latino experience predominates in this book.

Since 1940, American society has developed images of Latinos as individuals from a culture of poverty and backward-looking traditions, which has spawned a dysfunctional minority urban underclass. The future of California, when framed by such images and viewed with the knowledge that the Latino population will continue to outpace other ethnic groups, appears grim, indeed. These images of Latinos, however, have evolved without significant Latino input and are not sustained by the data. To the contrary, from 1940 to 2000, Latinos have behaved more like members of the "American" middle class than middle-class "Americans" themselves have: Latinos exhibit the most vigorous workforce participation; the lowest public welfare usage; the strongest family structures; the fewest heart attacks; lower cancer rates and fewer strokes; the healthiest babies; and a five-year-longer life expectancy, compared to non-Hispanic whites and African Americans.

The purpose of this book is to bring these and other data to the public's attention, with the hope (*ojalá*, not in vain) that such information will inform the creation of contemporary—and accurate—images of Latinos, which could in turn inspire confidence in the future of American identity and society in a state that will be half Latino by 2040.

In my most optimistic moments, I am able to envision a cohesive, productive California in the year 2040, with the state continuing to function as the lead society for American culture in a globalized economy. In pessimistic moments, I can only see my home state in smoking ruins by 2040, an abject lesson in what not to do in the twenty-first century. The difference between the optimistic best-case scenario and the pessimistic worst-case one is a simple policy variable: the state's investment, or lack of investment, in the energies, dreams, and behaviors offered to the state by Latinos for more than sixty years.

The choice is ours to make.

PERSONAL BACKGROUND TO THIS BOOK

Normally, in my academic research I do not purposely inject myself into the written narrative, preferring instead to let the data speak. I realize that complete "academic objectivity" is largely a fiction, for the very nature of research, even very quantitative research—selecting a topic, feeling comfortable with one particular theoretical model out of many competing theories, limiting the questions on a survey to a precious few, selecting the variables for analysis—is driven very much by personal interest and biography, more so than by some immanent dictate of science. In brief peer-reviewed papers, however, the researcher tries to stand out of the way, so that the messy underside of research—the data collection truncated by lack of funds, the numerous blind alleys tried out before a flash of insight leads to a good analytic model, the constant struggle between trying to conduct the "perfect" research project and one that must respect timelines, funding dictates, and personnel issues—is not apparent. The topic I have chosen for this book, including a data-driven social history and a projection into the future, covers so many different data sets requiring so much interpretation, that I feel compelled to be more actively involved in the narrative than is my wont.

And, to be fair, it deals more honestly with the reader, for I have been a participant-observer for nearly all the history presented here. As a participant, I was born and raised in California, became involved in the Chicano movement in the late 1960s, have made my professional life as an academic in the University of California system (first at UC Berkeley, then at UCLA), have married and raised children here, have been a homeowner, and have been a relative, friend, fellow parishioner, and acquaintance of many fellow Californians. In short, I have lived a Latino California experience all my life, and it would be ingenuous to pretend that I have not.

However, I also have been a trained observer of the California scene, particularly that part touching Latino lives. As an undergraduate student at UC Berkeley in the late 1960s, when Latinos were a small minority in the state, I informed one professor whom I was working with that I wanted to study Latinos. He advised me to take a course in "rare population sampling"; there were so few Latinos then that special techniques would be required to undertake a believable population-based survey. Later, to a different professor, I indicated that I needed to find a theoretical framework that would help me understand Latino life, and he offered to let me into his seminar on the theory of deviance; being Latino, he informed me, was a "spoiled identity" and could be understood by learning about other deviant groups, such as drug addicts, prisoners, prostitutes, and criminals.

When I began my graduate work in medical sociology at UC San Francisco in 1970, as the first-ever bilingual graduate student in the program, I was asked to assist in fieldwork on Latino health beliefs. Nearly all the work on Latino health up to that time had been undertaken by anthropologists interested in the more exotic areas that seemed to illustrate how different and un-American Latinos were, especially when it came to health. My first project was to develop a typology of healing herbs supposedly used by Latinos. As I gathered interviews about the more exotic elements of Latino "folk beliefs" about health and medicine, I also inadvertently received quite a bit of information about Latino exasperation in trying to deal with an unresponsive health care system. Compared to the volumes of material I heard about the trials of dealing with the county hospital, trying to communicate with disinterested physicians, and attempting to enroll in Medi-Cal (California's Medicaid program), the information on healing herbs seemed rather marginal to the respondents' overall lives.

That same year, I also became the founding executive director of La Clínica de la Raza, a small, community-based clinic serving the Latino population living in the Fruitvale District of East Oakland. My day-job responsibilities were legion: securing funding to operate, identifying health professionals willing to work in spartan conditions for virtually no pay, holding together a vigorous volunteer staff, trying to bring a community board to maturity so that the members would not feel intimidated by providing policy direction to physicians and dentists, and grappling with county health department directives. My daily activities there took me into the policy arena, and I learned on the job about doing policy research. While academic research at that time focused on the more exotic "folk" aspects of Latino health, I needed hard data and information for program building and policy development. Because at the time there were virtually no studies of Latino patients, I undertook a federally funded study of Latino patient behavior, and the results became the basis for my first published papers.

Being by nature an inveterate organizer, I was one of the founders of the local Latino health sciences student group, Chicanos in Health and Education (CHE), and later of the National Chicano Health Organization (NCHO). I traveled from medical school to medical school in the Southwest organizing NCHO chapters and was struck by the nuances of Chicano identity with which the medical students were grappling. I wound up doing my dissertation on the personal and professional socialization of that first generation of Latino medical students.

Having developed some of that rarely encountered Latino health data, I have been asked in the course of thirty years to provide input to local, state, and federal policymakers. These efforts have ranged from the ragtag 1970s group called the California Raza Health Alliance, to federal agencies and private foundations. Clearly I have not been an outside, objective observer of things Latino, but rather have been quite involved in Latino daily life.

Yet while I obviously have my personal interests intertwined with my professional work, I do not think that I am a "biased" researcher, in that I do not purposely try to bias questions asked on a survey or "cook the data" to make an analysis fit my preconceived notions. I have been trained as a data-based researcher, and while I might ask questions that are new and different or might look into a data set and see a new way to understand it, my work is informed, indeed is driven, by the professional norms of my colleagues, expressed so well by my division chief, Martin Shapiro, whose guiding research principle may be summed up as: "Make sure the science is good, and everything else will take care of itself."[2]

Thus, both to constantly remind the reader that, while I am a conscientious researcher, I am also but a human being, and to provide firsthand accounts of various research projects, I am taking the liberty of injecting myself into the narrative.

In 1992, I established the Center for the Study of Latino Health and Culture (CESLAC) to provide a focus within the UCLA School of Medicine for research, teaching, and public service in the area of Latino health. The center has collected a large number of general data sets: the decennial censuses; the annual Current Population Survey; the Consumer Expenditure Survey; and the Survey of Latino-Owned Businesses. Given its specific health focus, the center has also included a number of health-related data sets: the annual California Summary Death File; the Summary Birth File; the Hospital Discharge File; the annual Behavioral Risk Factor Surveillance Survey; and others. In addition, the center has conducted a number of surveys, each one prodding from a different direction to understand the fabric of Latino daily life and the role of culture in forming it. In addition to this quantitative work, the center conducts from four to eight focus groups every month, as well as six to twelve individual interviews. The resulting qualitative data provide insights that cannot be captured in large surveys and that point to new directions for research.

This book, then, builds on years of data-based research. As I have studied the data, two conclusions have become clear to me. First, while non-Latino perceptions of Latinos, often driven by the eleven o'clock television news, have been that Latinos are largely illegal-immigrant, gang-banging, welfare-dependent teenage mothers, the reality in data is quite different. Latinos indeed have low incomes and poor educations, but they also have some of the strongest social behavior of any group: a high work ethic, low

---

2. Martin Shapiro, Division Chief of the Division of General Internal Medicine and Health Services Research, Department of Medicine, UCLA.

welfare dependency, strong family structures, beneficial health behaviors, and the like. The second conclusion is that there has been a major sea change in the way Latinos see themselves and their lives in California. Where once America—Atlantic America, to be sure—had defined Latinos, now Latinos are defining not only Latinos but the very nature of American identity and society as well.

Gradually, my research focus has expanded to look not at Latinos qua Latinos but at Latinos as the new generation of Americans who will create American society and identity for the twenty-first century. This book presents the data that have led me to this conclusion.

ACKNOWLEDGMENTS

Writing, like painting, is a solitary act that cannot be conducted by committee. However, while one can compose sentences in isolation, the content of a data-heavy book such as this one requires a rather large, long-term team effort. For more than a decade at the Center for the Study of Latino Health and Culture at the UCLA School of Medicine, I have been, every year, the principal investigator of at least one population based survey, of three to six secondary analyses of large public data sets such as the Master Birth File or the U.S. census, and four to six qualitative studies. Because I have used many of these studies to provide the data foundations for this book, it is appropriate that I acknowledge the participation of many. In particular, I wish to thank two key people who have functioned as "data field marshals" during this Long March.

Teodocia María de Jesús (everyone calls her, *simplemente,* María), my wife, has conducted or supervised the qualitative data collection undertaken by the center for the past decade. She brings to these efforts years of experience as a public health nurse in Berkeley, California, as well as a curiosity about her Latino culture and a natural gregariousness. These personal qualities have made her an ideal researcher to probe and question participants to give her their heartfelt perceptions about their lives rather than the "safe," expected answers; indeed, María's reputation for eliciting commentary from respondents is that "puede hacer que hasta las piedras hablen" [she can even convince stones to speak]. Her skill is such that she can relax non-Hispanic white respondents to the point of sharing their deepest fears of Latinos, forgetting that she is Latina. Throughout this book I have used quotations from her work on diabetes, arthritis, health perceptions, food-industry executives, and American identity. Under María's supervision, Valerie Talavera-Bustillo and Cristina Orcí conducted individual interviews for the Chicano Health Movement study. The center's office administrator, Virginia Gonzalez-Cornejo, supervised the transcription staff of Alejandra Martín, José Carlos Real, Patricia Ramirez, Marla Almazán, Juan Mejía, and María Nuño.

In a similar fashion, Paul Hsu has functioned as the centering person for the various quantitative data efforts. Originally trained as an engineer but diverted to epidemiology, he has been responsible for acquiring large public data sets, configuring them for the computing platform at the center, writing programs to extract the data, and preparing the documentation for each file. He has taken the time to train some premed students, among them Lucette Sosa, Aidé Pérez, and Cristina Gamboa, to participate in the quantitative analysis. Staffers Delmy Iñiguez and Mariam Iya Kharamanian have assisted in Paul's efforts.

My in-house editors have relentlessly reined me in through various iterations of this book. Avril Angevine Stewart has truly taught me the meaning of parsimony, showing me how to say twice as much by using half the number of words. Cynthia L. Chamberlin has straightened out my syntax and provided invaluable fact-checking.

A number of organizations and individuals provided information and support beyond the call of duty that helped to bring this book to fruition. I would like thank profusely: Steve Soto of the Mexican American Grocers Association (MAGA); Antonio Gonzalez of the Southwest Voters Registration Project (SWVRP); Raul Yzaguirre of the National Council of La Raza (NCLR); Antonia Hernandez of the Mexican American Legal Defense and Education Fund (MALDEF); Roberto Orcí, Hector Orcí, and Norma Orcí of La Agencia de Orcí (Roberto now of M3 Orcí); Lieutenant Governor Cruz Bustamante; State Senator Richard Alarcon; Saeed Ali of State Senator Richard Polanco's office; State Assemblymember Tony Cardenas; State Assemblymember Marco Firebaugh, Chair of the Latino Legislative Caucus; Max Espinosa of State Assemblymember Jenny Oropeza's office; and Los Angeles City Councilmember Antonio Villarraigosa.

Writing requires long periods of intense concentration. This is impossible in a busy office that fields scores of telephone calls and e-mails every day and handles numerous meetings with staff, students, faculty, and community organizations every week. Thus, for three years, I have imposed myself on others to provide the lengthy, isolated concentration I have required, and I would like to thank them publicly for not complaining about my obdurate presence. In order the write the first draft of this book, I had to flee to Paris, where my friend and colleague, the late René Pellat, former high commissioner of the Comission d'Energie Atomique, graciously allowed me and Paul Hsu, who had to analyze data under field conditions, to use his apartment near the Place d'Italie for a summer. Once begun, subsequent iterations of this book took shape over endless cups of coffee thanks to the indulgence of staff in many places: Café la Paloma in Guadalajara, Gran Café Gijón in Madrid, Cases Sant Jaume in Benissa, Hotel Venesia in Valencia, and the Hotel Marco Polo in Mexico City. Closer to home, I would like to especially thank the indulgent staff of Starbucks in Westwood and Beverly Glen Plaza and of the South Side Coffee Company in Lompoc, California, for allowing me to sit, think, and write for hours at a time, without a word of complaint about the need to give up the table.

Introduction

THE NARRATIVE OF THIS BOOK BEGINS IN 1940, when Latinos were a small minority and lacked political representation or public voice in California (see Figure 1). The Spanish language itself appeared to be on the verge of extinction in the state. Certainly schoolteachers prohibited the speaking of Spanish, even in the rigidly segregated "Mexican schools" to which Latino students were routinely assigned even if they knew how to speak English. Latino daily life was marked by a number of indignities, including housing covenants, which restricted their house occupancy to a few segregated areas; widespread employment discrimination, which defined the types of jobs that were "appropriate" for them; and social and racial barriers, such as having access to public swimming pools only on the one "colored day" per week. When the Latino presence in the state was noticed at all, it was viewed as a problem, the "Mexican Problem," that most public officials hoped would quietly go away.

But Latinos did not go away quietly. Instead, a combination of dynamics—war, labor needs, immigration, fertility, and mortality—created for Latinos a "second act" rare in American society. For, rather than fading away, Latino numbers surged and resurged after World War II, so that by 2000, one out of every three persons in California is Latino, as seen in the 2000 composition in Figure 1. Particularly in southern California, the number-one television and radio shows are routinely broadcast in Span-

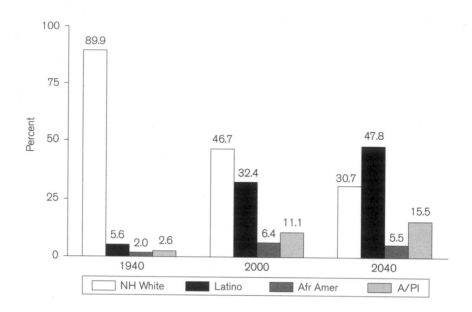

Figure 1. Composition of California's Population in 1940, 2000, and 2040.
Sources: 1940 (CA EDD 1986, 9, table 1); 2000 (U.S. Bureau of the Census 2001b,
table P8); 2040 (CA DOF, Demographic Research Unit 1998).

ish; billboards in Spanish announce tortillas, disposable diapers, and new
automobiles; music awards shows honor Latino artists whose verses are in
Spanish; and one of the largest, most powerful political groups in California is the Latino Legislative Caucus. Clearly, there have been changes
from 1940 to 2000.

Yet even more changes are afoot. Currently, one out of every two babies
born in the state is being raised by a Latino family. (See the California composition of births in Figure 35, on page 201.) And among the nearly ten million residents of Los Angeles County, nearly two out of every three babies
are the product of a Latino family (see Figure 35). When these children already in the state today become adults, Latinos will comprise by 2040
nearly half the population of the state of California (see Figure 1).

The road from demographic near-oblivion to demographic preeminence
is only part of the narrative of this book. Far more important than sheer
numbers is the question of what a Latino majority in California means for
the future of American society and identity. That is really the topic of this
book.

The fact of Latino demographic growth into the future should be considered, by now, a given. In 1988, when I published one of the first scholarly works on Latino demographic projections, *The Burden of Support: Young Latinos in an Aging Society* (D. Hayes-Bautista, Schink, and Chapa 1988), the notion that the Latino population could possibly grow to be nearly half of California's residents seemed unrealistic to most policymakers. After the release of this book, I was taken aback by the negative response to the idea that half the state one day might be Latino (I discuss this experience in greater detail in chapter 3, below). That negative reaction was not about the projections themselves, which were based on solid demographics and an unarguable methodology; the reactions were instead about the meaning of such projections for the future of California and the United States.

At that time (the late 1980s), the general public image of Latinos was one of failure and dysfunction. On magazine covers or on the eleven o'clock evening news in English, the images of Latinos making the news were inevitably of three types: the undocumented immigrant, the gangbanger, and the welfare mother (Leo Chavez 2001). These public images drove the concern about Latino population growth; after all, if they were true representations of Latinos, then soon half the state's population could easily consist of poverty-stricken, poorly educated, welfare-dependent, law-breaking people. The events of the 1990s seared those images in the minds of many: the Los Angeles riots of 1992, Proposition 187 with its repeated images of vast numbers of dark figures furtively sneaking across the border, and Proposition 227, which banned bilingual education. Yet these images were all wrong. I describe in chapter 3 my own intellectual development regarding the meaning of Latino population growth for the state, including my epiphany when I realized that sixty years of data on Latino behavior and values completely contradicted the popular public images that had driven so much of California's politics during the 1990s.

LATINO CIVIL SOCIETY

What I had not seen, even in my own research, prior to my sudden insight, was that Latinos were not the phenomenon described by all the policy models used until the present day: a racial group, a language group, a group locked into a traditional culture, a dysfunctional minority group, an urban underclass. All these models—which I had been taught as an undergraduate at the University of California, Berkeley, and as a graduate student at the University of California Medical Center, San Francisco—had missed the central dynamic that made Latinos so Latino: the continuing presence of a Latino civil society, dating in this state from April 1769 and continuing to the present. This Latino civil society, alive and functioning in the Latino families present in the state for more than two hundred years, provides to young children their initial introduction to the world of right and wrong, the desirable and the undesirable, duty and dereliction. Around the kitchen table, out in the garden, tucked into beds at night, through thousands of simple daily acts, Latino civil society provides Latino children with their first introduction to the social world, gives them their first notions of civic responsibility and their first hints of personal identity (see the discussion of this in chapter 7, below).

Beginning in 2019, half of the young adults who turn eighteen, and who will be able to express their opinion by registering and voting, will be Latino. Their choices of candidates, their preferences on issues, their decisions about their own education, about their families, and about the future of the state, all will rely to a great extent on the daily *dichos y hechos* (sayings and doings) their parents repeat to them thousands of times, unaware of the tremendous import of what they are doing.

Judging from sixty years of data of the Latino population, these children, once grown, will make many decisions that will benefit the state. They will most likely continue to be the hardest-working component of the state's labor force, with the highest rate of workforce participation, working far more hours per week, working far more in the private sector, and using welfare far less than any other population. They will continue to marry and form families with children at far higher rates than any other population. They will continue to have far fewer heart attacks, lower cancer rates, fewer strokes, a lower infant mortality rate, and a five-year-longer life expectancy than non-Hispanic whites. They will be proud to be Americans, and they will be disproportionately willing to fight and die in this country's wars. These behaviors are easy to project, because they are based solidly on sixty years of data-based Latino history.

For anyone using most current models of Latino behavior—the dysfunctional minority, the urban underclass, and the like—these behaviors seem surprising. But when one understands the presence and function of Latino civil society, these behaviors are not at all surprising; they are derived from the experience of the meeting of peoples in the Western Hemisphere since 1492, as Indians, Europeans, Africans, and Asians met and melded in most of the two continents known today as the Americas (discussed in chapter 7). The Mexican variant of this experience can be dated from August 13, 1521, with the fall of the great city of Tenochtitlan, and was brought to California with the first group of Mexican colonists to the region in 1769, who bestowed not only names famous around the country to the area—Los Angeles, San Francisco, San José, San Diego, Fresno, Santa Barbara, Sacramento—but also a Latino civil society, into which Latino babies have been born and children raised since that day.

A NOTE ON TERMINOLOGY

This book is a data-based recounting of the population whose primary socialization took place in Latino civil society from 1940 to 2004; it is also a projection into the future of the population's effects on American society and identity. As will be detailed in chapter 1, Latinos are not a simple racial or ethnic group; they are the product of a distinctive civil society. Yet the available data treats Latinos as the equivalent of a racial group; hence, I shall use the census bureau's groupings of data, and we shall speak of non-Hispanic whites (abbreviated as NH whites or NHW in the illustrations), African Americans (abbreviated as Afr Amer), Asians and Pacific Islanders (abbreviated as A/PI), American Indians (abbreviated as Amer Inds), and, of course, Latinos.

Given this book's interest in civil society, the racial groupings it must employ are only poor, surrogate measures what for really drives sometimes differential behavior patterns: the constellation of a group's values, images, and beliefs generated by historical experience. As I describe in chapter 7, it would be ridiculous to speak of "white civil society," because the genetic fact of being "white" has little to do with the emergence of civil society among that population. Rather than dwell on the putative genetics of a group, I will speak of a shared social experience communicated from parent to child, hence my term "Latino civil society." Although I will often refer to a generic national American society and identity, at times I will refer to a specific regional variant of the national society and identity as "Atlantic American." This regionally specific variant is grounded in the historical experience begun by predominantly British settlers on the North Atlantic coast of the United States (Fischer 1989), which has molded the socialization of people, irrespective of race or ethnicity, who are raised in that region. In a delicious irony, just as the U.S. Bureau of the Census announces on its charts that "Hispanic may be of any race," in my view an Atlantic American likewise may be of any race or ethnicity. A member of the Daughters of the American Revolution, an African American whose ancestors arrived on these shores before George Washington was born, and the descendant of an Italian immigrant who was processed at Ellis Island are all products of the Atlantic American civil society.

The future of American identity and society will be the result of the current encounter, on somewhat unequal terms, between Latino civil society and Atlantic American civil society. The racial categories of data we currently use will provide some notions of how this encounter is faring, but we must remember they are only surrogate, substitute indicators of the real phenomenon occurring: the emergence of a distinctive, regional civil society that will draw on roots in both the Latino and Atlantic American historical experiences.

The movement of Latinos from near-oblivion to a position of major social influence, and its implications for American society, is handled in eight chronological chapters. In 1940, non-Hispanic white America defined the public image of Latinos: who they were, what race they belonged to, what language they could speak, what their culture was like, what houses they could buy, what schools they could attend, what public facilities they could use. Although Latinos made up barely 2.4 percent of the state's population in 1910, revolutionary events in Mexico propelled twenty years of immigration; by 1930, about two hundred thousand Mexican immigrants lived in California and had started families. The state's major policy response to the Depression of the 1930s was to trim welfare rolls and provide jobs for "Americans" by deporting one-third of Mexican immigrants back to Mexico. The tactics used to isolate and repatriate Mexican immigrants created a decade-long climate of fear of appearing "too Mexican" in that deportation-era Latino population.

Officially, Latinos were a race, for census purposes, and race-based segregation limited Latino access to schools, public facilities, and real estate. Yet in 1940, the census bureau ruled that Latinos were white, and Latinos ceased to be counted as a separate entity on official forms, yet they were still subject to restrictive covenants that forbade sale of property to "members of the Mexican race."

The U.S. bipolar racial algorithm collided with the Latino racial dynamic, which has been one of intermarriage and *mestizaje* (ethnic mixing) of Indian, African, European, and Asian forebears. Subsequent censuses defined Latinos as a Spanish-surname group and as a Spanish-speaking language group. Anthropologists defined Latinos as a "traditional culture" group, characterized as suffering from fatalism and familism. The Zoot-Suit Riots of 1943 created public hysteria about the Latino presence by combining racial and cultural definitions of Latinos to paint a picture of an undesirable social element. During this period, America defined Latinos.

The Chicano generation, born in postwar America, grew up in still-segregated California, being told in many different ways that they were not quite American. They arrived at university campuses in the 1960s, breathed in the heady rebellious atmosphere, and began to protest the treatment accorded their parents and grandparents. As part of this confrontation, they actively rejected the definitions imposed on them by American society. Impelled by a sense of psychological bonding to a common movement, they burst forth from the campuses and the barrios to stamp their presence on society by creating organizations, political movements, service centers, and artistic expression, to present a bilingual, bicultural face to the world that their parents' generation had avoided. Tired of being rejected as Americans, they gladly embraced a new, emergent identity as "Chicanos." For all their claims of cultural vindication, however, few were fluent in Spanish, few had visited Mexico or other parts of Latin America, few knew any history and literature from south of the border. When some did manage to visit Mexico, they quickly discovered that they were not Mexican. They were considered American. And so they found themselves too Mexican to be accepted as American, and too American to be accepted as Mexican. Even as this generation defiantly rejected American definitions of Latino, they lived during a period of heated debate over what a "real" Latino was like.

Below the radar screen, the ending of the bracero program in 1964 coincided with changes in immigration law that allowed Mexican guest workers to change their status from temporary sojourners to permanent immigrants. The immigration wave returned to Latino barrios after a nearly forty-year absence. But these new immigrants were generally not involved in the Chicano movement and did not engage in debate over what a "real" Latino might do. Instead, unconsciously, or simply without reflecting, they asserted their cultural presence through their ways of living, which underpinned all their life decisions.

During the period of the "long, hot summers," when American cities burned every year from 1965 to 1969, Washington policymakers created the model of the "minority" population to guide public programs and expenditure. Drawing on research on the culture of poverty and the urban underclass, a model of minority dysfunction emerged to explain urban poverty and unrest. Minority-group poverty, unemployment, low education levels, and disintegrating families were considered to be the result of the absence of middle-class values and behaviors to be found in the rest of America. This absence was in turn perceived to be the result of racism and oppression. A "War on Poverty" was declared, and social programs were geared accordingly. Eager to be eligible for this federal largesse, many Latino groups willingly embraced the minority label. During the Reagan years, however, a "compassion fatigue backlash" set in, and the lack of socially acceptable behaviors was imputed to weaknesses inherent in minority groups. Out of this thinking emerged what can be called the "minority dysfunction" model.

I began my academic career being taught this particular model, but as data on Latinos became available, it grew more and more evident that it did not describe Latinos very well. In fact, in the health care arena, the minority dysfunction model was on a collision course with Latino health reality. In spite of high risk factors (that is, low income, poor education, and limited access to care), Latinos have far fewer heart attacks, lower cancer rates, fewer strokes, lower infant mortality, and live more than five years longer on average than non-Hispanic whites and nearly eleven years longer than African Americans. Moreover, while poorer than non-Hispanic whites and African Americans, Latinos have higher workforce participation, work more in the private sector, and rely less on welfare. Latinos demonstrate very middle-class values and behaviors, with very low income. While Latinos do not behave like one, Washington continues to define them as members of a dysfunctional minority group.

The first trickle of immigrant Latinos turned into a flood by the early 1970s. Immigrants accounted for nearly 60 percent of Latino population growth between 1970 and 1990. Latino immigrants had a heavy impact, due to the fact that they were concentrated in the young adult, young parent age group (twenty to thirty-nine); they rarely immigrated as children or elderly people. Thus, they arrived, joined the labor force, and started forming families. Compared to U.S.-born Latinos, immigrant Latinos have far higher labor-force participation and far less welfare dependency; they are far more likely to form a household composed of the classic married couple with children. These behaviors seem paradoxical, as immigrant Latinos also have far lower incomes and poorer educations, deepening the Latino Social Paradox explored in chapter 3. This is, however, evidence of the very middle-class values Latinos, especially immigrants, hold.

Such a vigorous population concentrated in a narrow age range has had a disproportionate effect on the economy; virtually any service or good important to young families with children quickly became reliant on this expanding consumer base. The food industry was first affected, as Latino consumers chose salsa rather than catsup, tortillas rather than white bread. Media in Spanish were given a tremendous boost with growth in viewers, listeners, and readers. Purchasing power grew and outdistanced the gross national product of Latin American countries such as Mexico. U.S.-born Latinos either became retro-assimilators, picking up their Spanish and reestablishing their cultural roots, or felt doubly alienated, now too American to be considered Latino by immigrants. The tremendous market impact of Latinos changed the nature of their relation to society, from a civil rights relation of a small minority to the large-scale market impact of an emergent majority. The important change was that Latinos were now defining what was Latino.

While both the non-Hispanic white and African American middle classes fled urban poverty in Los Angeles, immigrant Latinos were willing to move into emptying "ghetto" areas in South Central Los Angeles, to renovate the housing stock, thus keeping it active on the tax rolls rather than languishing as derelict property, and to reintroduce family and commercial life to these areas. When the 1992 riots erupted, because Latinos were the majority population where the unrest took place, they were involved in the action, first as victims of car damage, physical beatings, and shop lootings, and then, with stores closed and food in short supply, days later they became involved as furtive looters. But their behavior did not demonstrate solidarity with the largely African American, incendiary crowd. Nevertheless, images of Latinos looting stores led to the perception that Latinos were suddenly numerous and out of control, which in turn led to the formation of Proposition 187 as a state initiative for the 1994 ballot. This measure's existence was used by then-governor Pete Wilson to shore up his flagging reelection strategies, and he exultantly rode it to victory in a divisive campaign. It turned out to be a pyrrhic victory for him, however, because he awoke the political sleeping Latino giant, galvanizing it into action with his virulent attacks. Even years after Proposition 187, both U.S.-born Latinos and immigrant Latinos still feel bitter about the initiative. Subsequent initiatives to ban affirmative action and prohibit bilingual education led to a deeply polarized electorate, with about 80 percent of Latino voters rejecting the measures, and about 60 percent of non-Hispanic white voters approving them. Latinos felt rejected, but rather than shrinking into invisibility as deportation-era Latinos had done, they sprang into action. Along with the Chicano-era organizations, they responded by leading a legal and political charge against the measures. Immigrant Latinos became naturalized citizens and registered to vote in unprecedented numbers, then voted in record turnouts for Latino candidates. This political turnaround led to the emergence of the Latino Legislative Caucus as one of the most powerful groups in the state government.

In 1997, the Mexican American Legal Defense and Education Fund (MALDEF) wanted to create a message to counter lingering anti-Latino sentiments created by the Proposition 187 campaign. Focus groups were conducted with non-Hispanic whites to understand their concerns about Latinos. These participants defined being American not in cultural terms, as their parents did (for example, by language or food preferences), but by adherence to civic values, including patriotism, achievement, and rugged individualism. Their concern about Latinos was that attachment to Latino culture was perceived as political attachment to Mexico and Latin America instead of civic attachment to the United States, expressed by one non-Hispanic white participant as doubt about which side Latino soldiers might fight on if there were ever a war with a Latin American country. Focus groups were also conducted with Latinos to probe how they felt about being American. U.S.-born Latinos described feeling American as children, but being gradually excluded from that identity by non-Hispanic whites, who did not see Latinos as being fully American. Immigrant Latinos described the process of going from being recently arrived immigrants to having an emotional attachment and feelings of patriotism for the United States. Data from a 2000 survey corroborate that Latinos nearly unanimously feel proud to be American; only recently arrived immigrants show a less-than-unanimous feeling of pride, but this feeling develops over time as they make investments—economic, social, and emotional—in this country.

Based on these findings, MALDEF ran a thirty-second commercial, a "Message from Hispanic Americans," that aired on prime-time television in southern California for three months, showing Latino daily life: parents with children, buying a house, teachers in classrooms, soldiers returning from war, graduation. Follow-up focus groups about the commercial were held with non-Hispanic whites, who initially described feeling good, with a sense of hope and commonality of interest with Latinos. But then the serpent appeared in the garden: after repeated viewings, these images of achieving Latinos came to be thought too middle class to be believable. In their daily lives, these non-Hispanic whites saw Latinos in terms of failure, of inability to move ahead in spite of having a strong work ethic, of inability to do anything other than menial labor. Ultimately, they rejected the commercial on the grounds that Latinos were not as middle class as they were depicted in the TV spot.

Latino focus groups shown the commercial had a completely different reaction. U.S.-born Latinos were overwhelmed, seeing positive images of themselves for the first time in English-language media. Immigrant Latinos felt the commercial depicted them accurately, showing the daily activities of their lives. These middle-class images that were so shocking for non-Hispanic whites were seen by Latinos as so mundane as to be almost boring. Roberto Lopez, a *Los Angeles Times* reporter who had graduated from Belmont High School—the most dysfunctional high school in the dysfunctional Los Angeles Unified School District—persuaded his editor to do a follow-up survey of the class of 1989. To his surprise, the vast majority of his classmates had achieved, within ten years, very middle-class lifestyles, including a 28 percent college graduation rate and high levels of marriage, children, and home ownership.

Non-Hispanic white perceptions of Latino failure miss the "elevator effect" by which immigrants rise into the middle class. Public attention instead is focused almost exclusively on the recently arrived immigrant.

Adolescent development includes the emergence of notions of citizenship. Nearly half of all adolescents in California, and 62.4 percent in Los Angeles, are developing their notions of American citizenship in their families, influenced by their largely Latino peer groups. By sheer magnitude, Latino adolescents today are defining the nature of American identity and culture. They feel entirely American but are not at all self-conscious about speaking Spanish as well as English or listening to *rock en español* as well as to rap music. Even non-Hispanic white focus group participants felt that Latinos were reshaping American identity into a new complex, which will include large elements of what is today considered Latino culture: "They want to be American, as Latinos."

Being Latino is not tantamount to being un-American. Rather, it is like being a Texan; it is a distinctive way of being American. The quintessential Texas icon, the cowboy, is a regional identity figure, which itself developed out of the meeting and interaction of Atlantic American and Mexican cattle cultures and technologies in the early nineteenth century. The regional identity that is being created by young adults in California, half of whom are Latino, draws heavily on their early socialization in Latino civil society, which influences daily behavior and is rooted in the larger civil society that resulted from the cultural dynamics of Mexico and elsewhere in Latin

America, a true "melting pot" where Indian, European, African, and even Asian cultures have left their imprint and progeny. The viability of those patterns of civil society can be seen in the health beliefs encountered in current medical visits, for example concerning diabetes causation, prenatal care, and heart transplantation beliefs, which can be traced back to Mesoamerican cultures. Two general traditions in Atlantic American culture have different interactions with groups they perceive to be "different": Puritans, who have always had difficulty with any form of diversity, and Quakers, who have always embraced diversity. The Quaker variant of Atlantic American civil society and Latino-Catholic civil society will most likely provide the new underpinnings for a new regional identity.

The early traces of the new regional identity are seen in interpaternity patterns, in which non-Hispanic white, African American, and Asian mothers increasingly have Latino fathers for their children. Intermarriage patterns show "mixed marriages" but do not show unilateral assimilation patterns. As these marriage, paternity, and cultural patterns continue, California demographically and culturally points the way for the rest of America. Young adults in California are recreating the "Latin-Yankee" society that once held sway in the state. Such an easy cultural-racial blend may very well be the hallmark of Californians in the future.

At the end of this study, a "best-case" scenario for California in 2040 is presented. That scenario is of a culturally dynamic, economically vigorous state at the forefront of defining American society and identity. The entrepreneurial and professional energies of Latinos have been welcomed, invested in, and unleashed to provide impetus in various industries, ranging from music and film to high-tech businesses and international trade, making California the gateway to the surging economies of Mexico and Latin America, as well as the wellspring and epicenter of American society for the twenty-first century. A "worst-case" scenario for California of 2040 presents a *Blade Runner*-type image of a state whose economy has unraveled, and ethnic groups in the state are virtually at war with one another, as ethnic secessionist movements tear the state apart. Meanwhile, the neighboring country of Mexico has imploded politically, economically, and socially. The major difference between the best- and the worst-case scenario is the educational attainment of Latino children in the state's schools by 2015. The good news is that the educational attainment of U.S.-born Latinos has been rising quickly, far outpacing the attainment levels of the largely immigrant Latino parents. The bad news is that the state's public education infrastructure has crumbled and the admissions bar to the University of California has been raised, making college-level education more difficult for Latino students than it was for non-Hispanic white students during the baby-boom years. The Latino physician shortage is provided as a case history of the effects of the limited Latino presence in higher education. The decisions, public and private, made over the next ten years about investing in Latino potential will determine which of the two scenarios the state ultimately resembles.

———

The poet-laureate of Atlantic American letters, Walt Whitman, was asked in 1883 by the non-Hispanic white city leaders of Santa Fe, New Mexico, to address them on the celebration of their city's founding. Unable to travel to Santa Fe, Whitman nonetheless offered some written words in which he reminded the proud new leaders that they, unwitting or not, shared a cultural space with the Latino society that antedated them by centuries. "We Americans have . . . the notion that our United States have been fashion'd from the British Islands, only . . . which is a very great mistake. We do not begin to appreciate the splendor and sterling value of the Spanish stock of our Southwest" (Whitman 1907, 388–89). While, at the time of the request, British Protestant-based Atlantic American culture was on the upswing, Whitman presciently cautioned that Latinos were far from gone from the scene. He imagined a day, perhaps far in the future from his time, in which Latinos would once again be an important part of the culture of the region. "Who knows but that element [the 'Spanish stock'], like the course of some subterranean river, dipping invisibly for a hundred or two hundred years, is now to emerge in the broadest flow and permanent action?" (Whitman 1907, 389). At the beginning of the twenty-first century, Whitman's words are 120 years old, and, as if to make a prophet of the great American poet, Latinos have indeed emerged into public view, poised to become the majority population in major California cities over the next decade and slated to become the state's numeric majority within the next three to four decades.

ONE

America Defines Latinos

1940–1965

LATINOS REMEMBER BEING DEFINED

*My mother . . . is angry and hurt because they went through a lot. I
mean, she couldn't even go to the plunge [swimming pool] in Monrovia
on White Days. She had to go on Black Day. And my mother's lighter
than me. But because she was a Mexican, she had to sit in certain places
on the bus; she could only go swimming on certain days.*

CESLAC UW 1998, 3: U.S.-born Latinos, some college, 19

IN THE SUMMER OF 1998, the Center for the Study of Latino Health and
Culture at UCLA convened a number of middle-aged Latinos to help us
understand the changes that have taken place in Latino society in California during their lives. Born in the 1940s and 1950s, these participants grew
up in a world far different from the one they lived in by the late 1990s. They
were old enough to remember a much more segregated, much more rigidly
exclusionary society. Still expressing hurt and pain, they described growing
up in a situation in which being Latino was simply not validated. "Back
then [1950s] . . . who cares? You're just a Mexican, you're a 'beaner,' you
know, you're a 'greaser' " (CESLAC UW 1998, 3: U.S.-born Latinos, some
college, 90).

The postwar period was a time, these older participants remembered, when the Spanish language was not used in public. There was no television, very little radio, only one newspaper, and certainly no billboards or bus-boards advertising goods and services in Spanish. "It's real easy to live here now and speak Spanish. It wasn't when my mother was growing up; in the fifties and the sixties, I don't think it was" (CESLAC UW 1998, 3: U.S.-born Latinos, some college, 29).

Spanish may have been merely absent in the pubic arena, but it was actively rooted out in the public schools these participants attended. Many older respondents remembered being punished if they were "caught" speaking Spanish at school, which provided a disincentive to develop fluency in that language. "In high school . . . you wanted not to speak Spanish, and [teachers would] punish us. . . . I didn't want to hang around anybody that spoke Spanish" (CESLAC UW 1998, 7: Latino civic leaders, 37). The longer they stayed in school, the more this constant reminder that Spanish was somehow "bad" worked into the images these respondents had of their families, their culture, and themselves. Of course, the images were negative: if Spanish was bad, those who spoke it must be bad, and the culture they came from, by association, must also be bad. "[My] own language, in a way, for me was invalidated. We were punished if we spoke Spanish. So, as a kid, your values, all of a sudden is, 'What I have known—my parents, my grandmother, all these people that I've loved—were speaking wrong'" (CESLAC UW 1998, 8: Latino business leaders, 25). In the days before the emergence of Chicano studies on college campuses, a passive, studied ignorance of things Latino compounded this active invalidation. As a result, many older Latinos grew up knowing very little, if anything, about Latino and Latin American culture. "My great-grandma was born in Mexico, but I don't know anything about it" (CESLAC UW 1998, 1: U.S.-born Latinos, high school only, 20).

As a result, these older Latinos described growing up with a void in their identity. For some, particularly those who did not go to college and therefore missed out on the heyday of the Chicano movement, the void continued to the day of their participation in the 1998 focus group. "Supposedly I'm Mexican, but I don't know the background. I don't know anything about the Aztecs or anything, so I don't have anything to say 'This is me.' I don't know who I am, as far as culture" (CESLAC UW 1998, 1: U.S.-born Latinos, high school only, 21).

At its most virulent, this constant downgrading of things Latino led some to actively deny their Latino families and friends. "Yeah, I mean, I knew I was Mexican, but then I had my mother tell me here, because of her experiences, that '[When] people ask you, you tell them you are white. You're tall, you can pass for white, you're light skinned. Don't say you are Mexican' " (CESLAC UW 1998, 3: U.S.-born Latinos, some college, 89). From our vantage point in the first decade of the twenty-first century, we can understand their reactions given their experiences in school and in public life. At the time, they had few other options. It was their personal tragedy to have grown up in a unique historical moment in Latino California—a time that will never be duplicated. Theirs was the era of Latino invisibility, a time when Atlantic America defined Latinos.

DEMOGRAPHICS OF LATINO PRESENCE, 1910–1965

Latinos governed California from 1769 until statehood in 1850. They had run its economy, forged its culture, and established its cities. But when the gold rush attracted hundreds of thousands of new in-migrants to the state, they swamped the native-born Latino Californio population within a decade or two. By 1910, Latinos were barely 2.4 percent of the state's overall population, which was still heavily concentrated in the northern half of the state. In Los Angeles, Latinos were still nearly 15 percent of the population (Romo 1983, 29). In spite of an ongoing physical presence since 1769, Latino contributions were relegated to a mere colorful footnote in the prehistory of the state, romanticized in events like Los Angeles's "La Fiesta" and Santa Barbara's annual "Old Spanish Days."

When the Mexican Revolution erupted in 1910, it unleashed social unrest that had been festering for more than forty years under the near-dictatorship of Porfírio Díaz. As a result of the war, one-tenth of the Mexican population fled to its stable neighbor, the United States. The number of Mexican immigrants in California shot up, from 33,444 in 1910 to 86,610 in 1920, reaching a high of 199,165 by 1930 (U.S. Bureau of the Census 1952, 5–65, table 24). See Table 1.

Often forbidden by legal residential segregation to live in non-Hispanic white areas, these refugees settled in areas already largely populated by Latinos. Indeed, some of these barrios had been established by the Californios a century and more earlier. The immigrants brought to these well-established Latino communities a fresh infusion of language and customs. For nearly twenty years, immigrants from Mexico made the journey northward and began settling in, starting families, raising children, and buying small lots on which to build their houses and plant their gardens. Their arrival coincided with the post–World War I economic boom called

TABLE I
Number of Latinos in California, 1910–1960

Year	Immigrant Latinos	U.S.-born Latinos	Total Latinos
1910	33,444[a]	24,744[d]	58,188
1920	86,610[a]	34,566[b]	121,176
1930	199,165[a]	168,848[b]	368,013
1940	111,900[c]	262,100[c]	374,000
1950	189,800[c]	819,600[c]	1,009,400
1960	282,400[c]	1,174,500[c]	1,456,900

SOURCES: [a]U.S. Bureau of the Census 1952, 5–65, table 24; [b]U.S. Bureau of the Census 1933a, 90, table 35; [c]CA EDD 1986, 10, table 2c; [d]CESLAC estimate, 2003.

the Roaring Twenties, and their willingness to take dangerous, dirty, and low-paying jobs made the immigrants tolerable to the white population, now a majority in California.

"Black Friday," the day the stock market fell in 1929, put a halt to this tolerance. As the economy unraveled, unemployment rose and people looked to the government for assistance. Politicians found a scapegoat for the state's economic woes: Mexicans were "taking jobs from Americans" and taking a share of scant state resources. A hue and cry was raised about the large "foreign" presence in the state. The deportation of Mexicans would free up jobs for Americans and simultaneously reduce the government's burden. This simplistic policy was put into practice on a large scale.

Thus, during the 1930s, Latinos lived in constant fear of deportation roundups. Those seeking employment assistance, food from a soup kitchen, or care from the county hospital ran the risk of being summarily deported. Worse, streets were closed off, trolley cars stopped and searched, and anyone who "looked Mexican" was liable to be forcibly deported (Balderrama and Rodríguez 1995, 55). The most egregious roundup took place in 1931 at La Placita, a popular public park at the end of Olvera Street in downtown Los Angeles. This site had particular importance as both the location of the founding of Los Angeles and then for more than a century and a half as a symbolic central meeting place for Latinos after Sunday mass. INS agents and sheriffs from cities as far away as San Francisco, San Diego, and Nogales surrounded La Placita, trapping as many as four hundred people. Those unable to show proof of residency immediately were detained (Balderrama and Rodríguez 1995, 57). Citizenship was no protection; many U.S. citizens, born in the United States, were deported. The mere fact of being identifiably "Mexican" was enough to place one under suspicion. The deportations were part of the familial memory of some of our respondents in 1998, who, although they were born after the 1930s, could still tell of the effects of massive deportations. "Because it happened in 1928 *[sic]*. They hauled all the Mexicans that were not citizens . . . to Mexico, all of them. And my father almost got kicked out of here" (CESLAC UW 1998, 1: U.S.-born Latinos, high school only, 77).

The deportation era's effects can be seen in Table 1. While there were 199,165 Mexican immigrants in the state in 1930, by 1940 that number had been reduced by nearly one half, to 111,900. One out of every two Mexican immigrants had been deported or otherwise disappeared; Latino population growth was virtually stagnant during that period, with the loss of immigrants offset by births of young Latinos. Robert McLean, a journalist of the times, noted the atmosphere of fear that prevailed during the 1930s: "It is very real . . . and that fear hovers over every Mexican colony in the Southwest is a fact that all who come in contact with them can readily attest. They fear examination by the Border Patrol when they travel; they fear arrest; they fear jail; they fear deportation" (Samora 1971, 41). The threat of forced deportation and the accompanying climate of intimidation lasted a decade, during which it was dangerous to seem "too Mexican." A whole generation of U.S.-born Latinos grew up learning that overt expression of Mexican culture—including such things as speaking Spanish, wearing a *rebozo* (a Mexican shawl), or reading a newspaper in Spanish—could endanger them. Deeply scarred by this experience, many of that generation vowed to protect their children by throwing a cloak over their culture and history.

In 1940, the Latinos remaining after the deportations were barely 5.4 percent of the state's population, numbering 374,000. These deportation-era Latinos fought in World War II and the Korean War, earning Medals of Honor far out of proportion to their small numbers in the armed forces (Ramos 2000, 33). After the fighting, they returned to their homes in the barrios, proud to have served their country, even if resentful over segregated military cemeteries and other tokens of official disdain. They started families, becoming swept up in the mighty demographic phenomenon called the baby boom.

Largely thanks to its high fertility rate, by 1950 the Latino population in the state numbered just over one million (see Table 1, 1,009,400; CA EDD

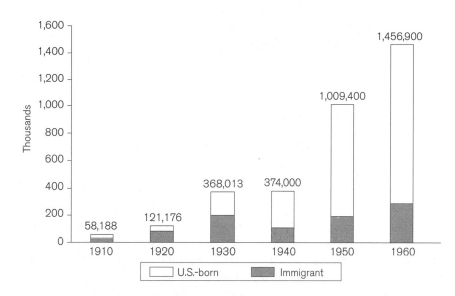

Figure 2. Latino Population in California, 1910–1960. Sources: Immigrant 1910–30 (U.S. Bureau of the Census 1952, table 24); 1910 total Latino (CESLAC estimate, 2003); 1920–30 total Latino (U.S. Bureau of the Census 1933a, 90, table 35); 1940–60 (CA EDD 1986, 10, table 2c).

1986, 9), and by 1960 nearly one and a half million (1,456,900) (see Figure 2). Latino children growing up in the postwar era had a vastly different cultural experience from that of their deportation-era parents, who almost always had Mexican-immigrant parents. Latinos of the postwar era were predominantly children of U.S.-born Latinos and grew up in Latino barrios populated almost completely by U.S.-born Latinos. Immigrants were very rare—more than four out of every five Latinos were U.S.-born: 81.2 percent in 1950, and 80.6 percent in 1960 (CA EDD 1986, 10).

Postwar Latinos—the Latino baby-boom generation—grew up heavily influenced by "mainstream" American culture. Even if they were raised in largely Latino barrios in Fresno, San José, San Francisco, or Los Angeles, the popular culture they absorbed from radio, television, and school was typical baby-boomer fare. Only rarely would this larger culture notice Latinos, except in caricatures such as Frito Bandito. There was the occasional breakthrough musician like Richie Valens (Ricardo Valenzuela), who had an identifiable Latino slant, but even the Chicano rock-and-roll bands of the era, for example, Thee Midniters, sang in English. Only a few subtle reminders—the burritos they would shamefully bring for lunch, the old romantic *trios* their grandparents would play on the 78-rpm record player, the large family gatherings to celebrate birthdays and anniversaries, a few familiar phrases in Spanish—held up a different cultural world. It was terra incognita, accessible only to those few who made extraordinary efforts to understand it. In those days, Latinos were an invisible group, seemingly on its way to either assimilation or extinction.

LATINOS DEFINED AS A RACE

Throughout the nineteenth and for a good part of the twentieth century non-Latino Californians routinely defined Latinos as belonging to a separate race and built their legal and public social behavior around that definition. Yet this racial definition has not fit Latinos very well, for Latinos are not a race, but a culture, which was itself shaped by centuries of racial mixture that produced today's mestizo Latino population.

Prior to 1492, an estimated 90 to 112 million people lived in the Americas (Sánchez-Albornoz 1974, 34), of whom an estimated 25.2 million lived in what is now Mexico (Cook and Borah 1971, viii). These peoples were not "Indians," a term applied to them only after the arrival of Europeans, but rather members of a variety of cultural groups. They were simply people living in a wide range of societies—large urban complexes of hundreds of thousands as well as farming villages and hamlets, tribes dedicated to the chase—speaking hundreds, if not thousands, of languages, worshipping hundreds of deities, engaged in a wide range of economic pursuits, from trade, construction, goldsmithing, and bookmaking to the healing arts. They waged war on one another, traded with one another, intermarried with one another. In Náhuatl-speaking Mesoamerica, they organized themselves into tribes *(calpulli)*, city-states *(altepetl)*, kingdoms, and empires, in an ever-shifting array of allegiances and betrayals. Some other regions organized themselves similarly.

On October 12, 1492, a Genoese in the employ of the newly united Spanish Crown, thinking he had just discovered India, designated as "Indians" the first residents he saw on the shores of Hispaniola (today's Dominican Republic). This misnomer remains to this day and has caused no end of confusion.

The European settlers who followed Columbus to the conquered territories interacted with the newly defined Indians politically, economically, spiritually, legally, maritally, sexually, and, most importantly, epidemiolog-

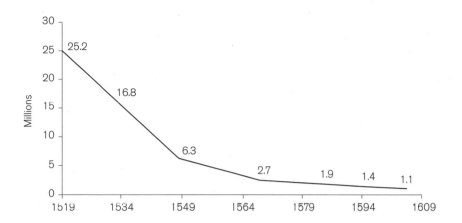

Figure 3. Population Curve, Mexico, 1519–1605. Source: Cook and Borah 1971, viii.

ically. Contrary to the "Black Legend"—that blood-thirsty Spaniards mercilessly slaughtered the Indians—the Spanish Crown wanted the Indians as subjects and treated them as productive, revenue-producing members of society. However, the peoples of the Americas lacked resistance to European diseases, especially smallpox, unwittingly carried by the colonizers, and the Crown's plans for steady revenues from a stable population were brought to ruin by the ravages of epidemics. In Mexico, the population dropped from an estimated 25.2 million to slightly more than 1 million within eighty years (see Figure 3; Cook and Borah 1971, viii), largely due to smallpox.[1] In the Caribbean islands, the mortality was close to 100 percent.

To make up for the population lost to disease, the European colonists imported slaves from Africa. Around the Caribbean basin, the slave trade grew to such an extent that Africans at times outnumbered Europeans or the remaining Indians. Slavery was not a perpetual condition; thus, a sizable African-origin population established itself in freedom, marrying and producing children.

Eventually, the Spanish and Portuguese reached India, China, Japan, the

1. Cook and Borah's estimates of the pre-Columbian population have been considered definitive for nearly forty years; however, some recent work suggests some variance and places the range from thirteen to twenty-five million (Whitmore 1992, 118–19). These estimates have created much controversy, so we are using those of Cook and Borah, realizing that ultimately their figures may prove to be somewhat high.

Philippines, and other parts of Asia. The Spanish treasure fleet sailed annually from Manila to Acapulco, and where trade went, settlement followed. Sailors and settlers from Asia—the Philippine Islands, China, India, Japan—also found their way to the Americas, establishing themselves in trades in Mexico City, Lima, Havana, and other communities large and small.

In a mere three centuries, the human species in the Americas changed from completely "Indian" to largely mestizo, in a biological union of Indian, European, African, and Asian peoples. From 1492 to 1821, these various populations married one another and created the peoples of the new world. The official registers of that period were not satisfied with simply designating a person as mestizo, however, and tried to pinpoint the exact combination of European, Indian, African, and Asian heritages a person might possess. These groups, called *castas,* illustrated the resultant *mestizaje:*

- *Mestizo:* offspring of Spanish and Indian
- *Castizo:* offspring of Spanish and mestizo
- *Mulato:* offspring of Spanish and African
- *Lobo:* offspring of African and Indian
- *Cambujo:* offspring of lobo and Indian

In total, there were as many as twenty-five different categories (García Sáiz 1989, 24–28). Such racial precision was, of course, an ideal not easily accomplished when baptism certificates were written from people's incomplete memory. We can imagine them asking themselves, "Was grandmother a cambuja or a loba?" Compounding the categorization process was the custom of "caste creep," whereby one's caste could change, usually in the direction of a lighter caste, on achievement of social standing. Mason (1998, 45–64) analyzed the California census of 1790 and discovered that the majority of Californios, who were originally Indian-African admixtures from northern Mexico, had exhibited "caste creep" between 1780 and 1790 and had become subsequently classified with categories used for persons of greater Iberian admixture, for example, mestizos or even "Spaniards."

At the spot commemorating the founding of Los Angeles in 1781, a bronze reproduction of the original roll call of the *pobladores* (settlers) tells us of the mestizaje present at the city's birth. Each family is listed by name, as are the husband's and wife's castas. A typical entry reads:

Lara

José Fernando   español

María Antonia   india

José Julián

María Faustina

María Juana

While the admixture category of the children was not noted, clearly the children of the Lara family would be mestizos. Interestingly, only two of the eleven heads of household were nominally Spanish—the rest were unmistakably Indian, African, or some combination, expressed as "mestizo" if the Indian lineage predominated or "mulato" if the African lineage predominated. The pairings included the following husband-wife combinations:

3 Indian-Indian couples

2 African-Mulato couples

2 Spanish-Indian couples

2 Mulato-Mulato couples

1 Indian-Mulato couple

1 Mestizo-Mulato couple

The children of these parents were, obviously, an extremely hybrid population racially—and on an ironic note, not too dissimilar from the racial and ethnic composition of the children of Los Angeles at the start of the twenty-first century (*Los Pobladores* 1981).

After the Mexican War of Independence (1810–21), the separate colonial laws for Indians and *gente de razón* (literally, "rational," Christian people) were done away with; the castas were abolished, and so was all official specification of racial background.[2] Henceforth, all residents of a country were Mexicans or Guatemalans, Peruvians or Chileans, and so on.

2. In the Americas, Europeans, who were supposed to be, ipso facto, Christians, were held accountable to European law; hence, they were called gente de razón. Unchristianized, unacculturated Indians were considered to be in a state of "diminished capacity" and were not ac-

After the Mexican American War of 1848, the United States acquired a huge territory that was carved up into the states of California, Arizona, Nevada, Utah, New Mexico, and Colorado. With a population that was decidedly not of British or other northern European stock, Texas had been acquired a decade earlier. As the United States took over administration of the new territory, its official bipolar racial understanding (that is, one was either white or black, but not both) was applied to a population that was irreversibly multiracial, and the modern problems involved in attempting to racially categorize Latinos began.

Some early U.S. visitors to the Southwest region had remarked on the "mongrel" nature of the population, an amalgamation of Indian, African, Asian, and Spanish. In 1835, Harvard student Richard Henry Dana took a leave of absence from his studies and sailed "around the Horn" to California as a common sailor (Dana 1986). He was intrigued by the racial composition of the Californios. There were lighter-skinned dons, wealthy ranchers who were termed "Spanish," whose daughters often intermarried with the incoming Americans. "Those who are of pure Spanish blood . . . have clear, brunette complexions, and sometimes, even as fair as those of English women" (Dana 1986, 126). He did note, however, that there were very few of these fair-skinned persons. Others were darker—suspiciously darker—hinting at a degree of miscegenation that was socially unacceptable back in his home country. Dana continued his description of mestizo Californios: "From this upper class, they go down by regular shades, growing more and more dark and muddy, until you come to the pure Indian, who runs about with nothing upon him but a small piece of cloth" (127).

Dana's book was a best seller in its day and provided an early description of California for Atlantic Americans. His portrait of the Californios included reflections on their character, which, to such a proper Bostonian, was none too savory. Warning his readers that California lay "at the ends of the earth, on a coast almost solitary; in a country where there is neither law nor gospel," he described Californios as "an idle, thriftless people" (143, 125), comprising a population "of hungry, drawling, lazy half-breeds" (235). The men, he wrote, were "thriftless, proud, and extravagant, and very much

---

countable to the laws applied to Europeans. At times, Indians had special legal protections because of this presumed diminished capacity, which amounted to a distinction much like the one made today between juveniles and adults.

given to gaming," while the women had "but little education, and a good deal of beauty, and their morality, of course, is none of the best" (236). Overall, Latinos in California appeared to him to be "a people on whom a curse had fallen, and stripped them of everything but their pride, their manners and their voices" (128).

The problem with California, Dana mused, was that it was populated by Californios, whose indolence kept them from realizing the full wealth of the states. "Such are the people who inhabit a country embracing four or five hundred miles of sea coast . . . blessed with a climate, than which there can be no better in the world . . . with a soil in which corn yields from seventy to eighty fold" (237). Dana was insistent that "nothing but the character of the people prevents Monterey from becoming a great town," and he finally declared, just a decade before the Atlantic American world rushed in to displace these character-challenged Latinos, "In the hands of an enterprising people, what a country this might be!" (237). If they had any picture at all, this was what many non-Hispanic whites imagined of Latinos when they came to California in 1849 in search of gold.

The 1848 Treaty of Guadalupe Hidalgo that ended the Mexican American War promised that Mexicans who had lived in the Southwest would be incorporated into the county with the "enjoyment of all the rights of citizens" (Menchaca 2001, 215). While this expansive promise satisfied the Mexican negotiators of the treaty, American racial law soon intruded on the assumption that all Mexico's former citizens would simply take up a new life in the newly annexed territories.

The bald fact was that full rights and citizenship in the United States at that time were restricted to white male persons, yet the Latinos of California were, in the main, a racial hodgepodge that defied simple U.S. racial categorizations. For the next century and more, the racial definition of Latinos was debated in the courts, as Latinos tried to exercise their rights to vote, hold property, marry, educate their children, and use public facilities as U.S. citizens in a country where nonwhites were not given these rights.

In spite of an international treaty that guaranteed full citizenship, within a year of its signing the federal government allowed states to determine the citizenship status of their Mexican residents (Menchaca 2001, 217). Mexicans who were considered "Indian" then became subject to applicable federal laws governing Indians, which often meant they were deemed ineligible to hold property, testify in court, or become naturalized citizens. If they were considered black, then the state laws sanctioned by the U.S. courts applied. For nearly a century California courts squirmed, trying to fit a bipolar racial category—white or nonwhite—onto a mestizo population.

Pablo de la Guerra was a descendant of a 1775 settler who had arrived in California in the service of the Spanish Crown. A member of the distinguished family for whom a major street in Santa Barbara is still named, he was a wealthy rancher who served California as a delegate to its first constitutional convention. For more than twenty years, he was a respected member of the newly admitted state of California and held many public offices. Then, in 1870, the state he had served so well turned on him and declared him no longer eligible to vote, hold office, testify in court against a white person, or own land. In short, the state declared that de la Guerra could exercise none of these privileges because he was not white. The state's attorneys argued that he could not be a U.S. citizen, in spite of the Treaty of Guadalupe Hidalgo, because citizenship was not available to Indians, and he did not appear to be at least three-quarters white. The Carrillo side of his family had originated in Baja California, of "dubious" racial background but quite possibly the beneficiaries of "caste creep" at the time of arrival in Alta California, and his appearance hinted at nonwhite ancestry (Menchaca 2001, 221; Mason 1998, 86).

Luckily for him, de la Guerra had the wealth to hire attorneys, who were able to establish that he was "white enough" to be classified a U.S. citizen. Nevertheless, the court's decision gave the state the right to exclude "nonwhite Mexicans" from citizenship (Menchaca 2001, 222). Much effort was spent subsequently trying to determine if any given Mexican should be considered "white" or "nonwhite."

The Homestead Act, which opened up the West to settlement, was limited to U.S. citizens, which meant that only persons classified as "white" could stake claims. This act not only effectively excluded "nonwhite" Mexicans from participation but also provided a legal basis for arguing that an "Indian" Mexican could not hold title to property. After three-quarters of a century of intermarriage between Mexican settlers, many of whom were themselves Indians and mestizos, and California Indian groups, the boundaries between "Indian" and "non-Indian" were quite blurry, even during Spanish and Mexican days. However, with the imposition of U.S. racial laws, Chumash, Diegueño, Gabrileño, and other Indians who had been raised speaking Spanish, who were practicing Catholics, and who worked as cowboys, were declared to be "Indians" and thereby unable to hold title to property. Even emancipated Indians, who had not lived under tribal law for decades, were placed under the jurisdiction of Indian laws. The job of the courts was to decide if a given Mexican was "too Indian" to be considered white.

Racial laws became even more important after the passage of the Fourteenth Amendment, which provided for citizenship for the former slave population. The narrow reading often used was that the new amendment applied only to African Americans, not to Indians, Asians, or other nonwhite peoples (Menchaca 2001, 278). Resident Latinos and those who arrived after 1848 who were obviously Indian were not allowed to become citizens. Their children, born on U.S. soil, were ineligible to become citizens under these interpretations of the Fourteenth Amendment. Only "white" immigrant Latinos and their children were eligible to become naturalized citizens.

As a result of being generally categorized racially as nonwhite, Latinos by and large suffered many petty racial injustices. In 1931, California Attorney General Ulysses S. Webb declared that Mexican children were basically Indian in origin and had to be treated in accordance with then-prevailing U.S. law on Indians, which included legal segregation for educational purposes. His opinion in the case of U.S.-born Latino children attempting to enter schools in Carpinteria, a town in Santa Barbara County, summarized the prevailing opinion: "It is well known that a great part of the population of Mexico is a mixture of Indian, and when these Indians immigrate to the United States, they need to obey the laws applicable to other Indians. . . . Children of Mexican origin are Indians, therefore, they should be sent to Indian schools" (González-Portillo 2001, 1B). A small technicality was that these laws did not apply to Latinos who were "white." Yet the burden of proof was on an individual Latino to go to the courts to prove "whiteness" in order to use public facilities. During Webb's forty years as attorney general, his views on race represented one school of opinion.

Many school districts had established separate "Mexican schools" for "unassimilable" Latino students (McWilliams 1949, 19–20; Moore 1970, 76–84), on the theory that Latinos were such slow learners that they would hold back non-Hispanic white student performance. Nine-year-old Sylvia Mendez was the first to challenge this century-old policy. In 1944, her parents moved to the then-largely non-Hispanic white community of Westminster in Orange County and tried unsuccessfully to enroll her in the neighborhood school. Whereas the local school was a brick-built source of neighborhood pride, the ramshackle Mexican school was next to an active dairy farm.

Teníamos que acostumbrarnos al olor del estiércol de las vacas. Comíamos entre el olor a estiércol. Teníamos que espantar los moscas cuando comíamos. La escuela de mexicanos era de madera vieja, y la de los blancos era de ladrillo y muy bonita. [We had to get used to the smell of cow manure. We ate with the smell of cow manure. We had to brush away the flies as we ate. The Mexican school was made out of old wood, and the white school was made of brick and very pretty.] (González-Portillo 2001, 1B)

Her father won the case, *Mendez v. Westminster*, on a loophole created by nearly a century of legal twists and turns about the race of Latinos. Webb's decision, and the federal *Plessy v. Ferguson* ruling, did not apply to Latinos because there was no federal law stipulating that all Mexicans were Indians. Sylvia's case later served as precedent for the more famous *Brown v. Board of Education* in 1954 (Menchaca 2001, 291).

From the late nineteenth century to the mid-1960s, real estate developments also were routinely segregated, usually in the form of a "restrictive covenant" attached to the property deed, stipulating to whom the property could, and could not, be sold. In Los Angeles, for example, in 1950 such a covenant stipulated, "No portion of the herein described property shall ever be sold, conveyed, leased, occupied by, or rented to any person of an Asiatic or African race . . . nor to any person of the Mexican race" (Camarillo 1984, 80).

While the courts battled over the fine line between a "white" Mexican and a "nonwhite" Mexican, daily life in California rarely bothered with such distinctions. From the first, it had been common to refer to all Latinos as a separate, nonwhite race. In 1886 eminent nineteenth-century UC Berkeley philosopher Josiah Royce summarized the prevailing opinion regarding Latinos in an only slightly overdrawn social portrait: "The native Californian or 'greaser' . . . had no business, as an alien, to come to the land God had given us. . . . We hated his whole degenerate, thieving, landowning, lazy and discontented race" (Royce 2002, 287). A good many of the attitudes collected by California labor economist Paul Taylor during a 1927–30 survey of agricultural labor conditions confirm that Latinos were considered a separate and inferior race. Taylor concluded that this persistent perception was hampering Latino progress in society. "Recognition of racial difference, and the attitudes which so commonly attach to color of skin, hamper free assimilation of the Mexicans . . . [and] is a factor, distinctly additional to those which characteristically have stirred hostility against new groups of European immigrants to the same area" (Forbes 1968, 85).

The courts may have rendered convoluted decisions to determine the race of individual Latinos, but the U.S. Bureau of the Census needed to define entire populations. The race question has bedeviled the bureau since the 1848 acquisition of the Mexican territories and the included resoundingly mestizo population. Over time, the bureau adopted various strategies to define the racially indefinable.

In 1930, for example, in an attempt to get around the legal fact that some Latinos were "white" while others were not, the category "Mexican" was designated as a separate race and was included along with the other racial categories: white, "colored," Indian, Chinese, Japanese. In its "Instructions to Enumerators," the 1930 census conceded that Latinos were generally a mestizo population, hence not easy to identify. Nonetheless, the "Instructions" enjoined the enumerators: "Practically all Mexican laborers are of a racial mixture difficult to classify, though usually well recognized in the localities where they are found. In order to obtain separate figures for this racial group, it has been decided that all persons born in Mexico, or having parents born in Mexico, who are not definitely white, Negro [sic], Indian, Chinese, or Japanese, should be returned as Mexican ('Mex')" (U.S. Bureau of the Census 1933b, 1399). Table 2 provides the heading of Table 29 in the census report (U.S. Bureau of the Census 1933a, 84), in which "Mexican" is grouped together with the other "minor races," including Indians, Chinese, and Japanese. The Bureau of the Census's definition of Latinos as a distinct "race" dovetailed with popular notions of a "Mexican race"; segregation based on race, common in parts of the country then, naturally isolated Latinos and affected their participation in society. Then, abruptly, their racial designation changed.

In an unexpected about-face in 1940, the Bureau of the Census recategorized Latinos as "white." This reversal of racial categorization followed implementation that year of the Nationality Act, which allowed indigenous immigrants from the Western Hemisphere and, later, immigrants from Asian countries to become citizens (Menchaca 2001, 285). It had been possible for the *children* of "nonwhite" immigrant parents to be declared U.S. citizens since the Supreme Court decided in 1898 that the Fourteenth Amendment was not restricted to blacks. With the Nationality Act, the "nonwhite" immigrant parents of U.S.-citizen children were suddenly eligible for citizenship. Indians, however, who were nonwhite but not immigrants, still could not be U.S. citizens (Menchaca 2001, 280–81). This

TABLE 2

"Mexican" as Separate Race, U.S. Census, 1930

Division and State	Total Population	White	Negro	Mexican	Indian	Chinese	Japanese	Filipino	All Other
United States	122,775,046	108,864,207	11,891,143	1,422,533	332,397	74,954	138,834	45,208	5,770
Geographic Divisions:									
New England	8,166,341	8,065,113	94,086	107	2,466	3,794	352	358	65
Middle Altantic	26,260,750	25,172,104	1,052,899	6,757	7,709	14,005	3,662	2,882	732
E. N. Central	25,297,185	24,277,663	930,450	58,317	19,817	6,340	1,022	3,027	549
W. N. Central	13,296,915	12,873,487	331,784	39,805	48,245	1,738	1,003	784	69
South Atlantic	15,793,589	11,349,284	4,421,388	691	19,060	1,869	393	861	43
E. S. Central	9,887,214	7,224,614	2,658,238	1,403	2,106	743	46	50	14
W. S. Central	12,176,830	9,099,981	2,281,951	695,996	95,670	1,582	687	839	124
Mountain	3,701,789	3,303,586	30,225	249,314	102,083	3,252	11,418	1,391	520
Pacific	8,194,433	7,498,375	90,122	370,143	35,241	41,631	120,251	35,016	3,654

SOURCE: U.S. Bureau of the Census 1933a, 84, table 29.

ruling added another layer to an already byzantine racial classification system in California. In some arenas, such as education, dark Latinos were still considered "nonwhite"; yet in others, such as naturalization, they were now treated legally as if they were white. The 1940 census took a Gordian knot approach to the racial designation of Latinos; Mexicans were no longer to be counted as a separate racial category but were to be enumerated racially as "white" (D. Hayes-Bautista and Chapa 1986, 64). The Bureau of the Census explained that Latinos were not to be considered "colored," as were the other major and minor races of the day. This method of color categorization was explained in the 1960 census: "The term 'color' refers to the division of the population into two groups, white and nonwhite. The color group designated as 'nonwhite' includes Negroes, American Indians, Japanese, Chinese, Filipinos, Koreans, Hawaiians, Asian Indians, Malayans, Eskimos, Aleuts, etc. Persons of Mexican birth or ancestry who are not definitely Indian or other nonwhite race were classified as white" (California Department of Industrial Relations 1964, 54). In many official records, however, Latinos went beyond white to transparent; they simply disappeared. For example, in the area of vital statistics, racial data were recorded for the categories of White, Negro, Indian, Chinese, Japanese, and "Other" but not for Latinos. As seen in Table 3, in a vital-statistics table for 1959 that records the number of deaths in each racial group, there is no column entry for "Mexican." Instead, at the foot of the table is the simple, cryptic note: "White includes Mexican" (California Economic Development Agency 1962, 58, table G-3). Official records, such as birth certificates, marriage certificates, and death certificates, now recorded Latinos as being of the white race. The census bureau continued to categorize Mexicans, and then other groups who appeared on the radar—such as Puerto Ricans and Cubans— as white for the 1950, 1960, and 1970 censuses.

Not surprisingly, many Latinos were themselves confused about the proper response when asked their race. Older Latinos remembered being told that Mexicans were a separate, distinct race. Yet Latinos who came of age from 1940 to 1970 were told that, officially at least, they were white. "Me and my mother have had an argument, because she says 'Mexican' is not a race. And I told her, 'But I'm not white, either.' And so we go back and forth" (CESLAC UW 1998, 3: U.S.-born Latinos, some college, 101). Any official mention of being Latino disappeared from public forms, leaving some Latinos to wonder if they existed as a group at all.

Yet, paradoxically, at the same time that Latinos did not exist in official documents, in daily life certain property was barred to members of the

TABLE 3
Latinos Included as Part of "White" Racial Category, 1959

Deaths,[a] by Sex, Race, and Age, California, 1959

Age Group	Total	White [b]	Negro	Indian	Chinese	Japanese	Other
Male Total	73,631	68,949	3,276	191	421	520	274
Female Total	54,577	51,444	2,599	129	120	227	58

SOURCE: California Economic Development Agency 1962, 58, table G-3.
[a]By place of residence; excludes fetal deaths.
[b]White includes Mexican.

"Mexican race"; Latinos were routinely shunted aside to "Mexican schools," and Latinos were not allowed into certain public facilities. "I was raised that I was Caucasian. . . . In the olden days, there was no Hispanic on there [any public document]. Except if you wanted to go in a public pool" (CESLAC UW 1998, 3: U.S.-born Latinos, some college, 101). How was it possible for Latinos to be considered a race for real estate, educational, and law-enforcement purposes, yet considered white for enumeration purposes? And, how could a population that emerged out of a continent-wide process of mestizaje be considered a single race?

LATINOS DEFINED BY RESEARCHERS

The general public had no doubt that Latinos were an identifiable group, even though after 1940 they disappeared from official records as such. In order to estimate the size of the Latino population, social scientists developed a series of surrogate measures that would approximate the count. Their first strategy involved counting Spanish surnames, for which the Bureau of the Census developed an initial official list of about seven thousand Spanish surnames (Word and Perkins 1996). Some were clearly Spanish, such as Garcia, Gonzalez, and Rodriguez. Other surnames, such as Silva, could be Spanish, Italian, Portuguese, or even French and therefore could not be counted directly; yet they could be apportioned, meaning that every sixth Silva would be counted as a Spanish surname, a surrogate for a Mexican. Of course, a small percentage of Mexicans, even in Mexico, do not have Spanish surnames, such as the artists Frida Kahlo and Juan O'Gorman, and such names would not have been counted at all. The Spanish surname method was not 100 percent accurate, but it did provide an approximation of the Latino population—and a new category, "White Persons with Spanish Surname."

Concerned that the Spanish-surname method might not capture Latinos as efficiently as desired, a question on Spanish-language home environment was added in the 1950 census. This was asked only in the five southwestern states. Those who responded positively to this question were then categorized as "Spanish-language white persons."

The general public often took this new statistical gambit to mean that only those who spoke Spanish were Latino. Thus, the speaking of Spanish was once again a measure of being Latino; a book on educating Latinos in the United States acknowledged the primacy of the language in its title, *Education of the Spanish-Speaking Urban Child* (Ogletree and Garcia 1975). In a slim book written for teacher training in the 1960s, Carey McWilliams concurred, "With most Mexicans, Spanish is the language of the home" (McWilliams 1968, 19).

While the Spanish language is often taken as a defining characteristic of Latinos, its presence in the Americas is relatively recent in human history. In the sixteenth and seventeenth centuries, only a minority in the Americas spoke Castilian, the language that we call Spanish today. In Mexico, literature was written and published in both Spanish and Náhuatl during the colonial period, up to 1821. Sor Juana Inés de la Cruz, the seventeenth-century protofeminist poet, playwright, and author, wrote in Spanish, Náhuatl, and Latin. Even at the end of Porfirio Díaz's rule in Mexico in 1910, about one-sixth of the population of Mexico did not speak Spanish (Moreno Toscano et al. 1983, 120). The Mexican census of 1995 found around 7 percent of Mexicans were monolingually functional in various Indian languages (*Anuario estadístico* 1998, 19, cuadro 2.4); contemporary Mexican bilingual-education programs teach in Spanish and Indian dialects. In Guatemala, about half the population is monolingually functional in various Maya dialects. Peru is officially a bilingual country (Quechua and Spanish), as is Paraguay (Guaraní and Spanish).

Even on the Iberian Peninsula, by the sixteenth century most inhabitants spoke Castilian, but a variety of languages and dialects were also spoken, including Basque, Galician, Portuguese, Asturian, and Catalan. In the centuries of colonization that followed, settlers from the far reaches of the Spanish Empire and its allies in Europe joined this polyglot population. Early documents indicate that Italians, Greeks, Germans, French, Dutch, and others lived in the Crown's lands.

In the New World, Spanish was declared the official language by the sixteenth century to forge a linguistic unity in the Western Hemisphere that was absent on the Iberian Peninsula (Cuevas 1914, 159). This official Spanish language, however, interacted with a bewildering variety of Indian languages and dialects, and a few African tongues as well, up and down Latin America, creating myriad variations on the Castilian tongue. In Mexico, for example, Spanish adopted a number of Náhuatl words already in use for centuries: *aguacate* (avocado), from *aguacatl; chocolate,* from *xocolotl; guajolote* (turkey), from *guajolotl;* and so on.

Over the past five centuries, Spanish has been absorbed gradually by most peoples of the Western Hemisphere; yet it was not until early in the twentieth century that one could safely say that Spanish was the majority language in most of the region. Many Latinos do speak Spanish. But like the possession, or absence, of a Spanish surname, language alone does not make one a Latino.

During the post–World War II era, social scientists began studying underdeveloped countries around the globe, discovering many cultures untouched by modern development and by the modern attitudes and behavior that sustain it. Researchers posited that there were two types of societies in the world: modern and traditional. Modern societies held the values necessary for development, such as showing up on time for work or taking orders from a boss, and traditional societies did not (Kahl 1974; Harrison 1985). Building on Max Weber's 1905 touchstone work, *The Protestant Ethic and the Spirit of Capitalism* (reprinted in 2001), which sought to demonstrate that Protestantism provided the very values capitalism required, researchers developed a typology of values held by both modern and traditional societies. Table 4, adapted from Talcott Parsons and Edward Shils, lists the "pattern variables" used to determine if a society was traditional or modern: it seemed clear that modern values had to be substituted for the dysfunctional traditional ones if a society were to develop modern, capitalistic structures. "Improving" traditional cultural traits became a policy imperative.

Meanwhile, a number of anthropologists and sociologists turned their attention to minority groups within the United States, using the same tools to assess them. These researchers have influenced the general public's view of Latino culture to the present day by placing it among the "traditional" societies. In this view, "mainstream" American society was a modern society, characterized by active orientation, future-time orientation, rationality, science, and an ability to defer gratification. By contrast, "traditional" Latino culture offered values diametrically opposed to the modern set: pas-

TABLE 4

Traditional versus Modern Values

Pattern Variables	
Traditional Society	Modern Society
Ascriptive	Achievement
Diffuse	Specific
Affective	Nonaffective
Particularistic	Universalistic
Collective	Individual

SOURCE: Perlman 1976, 109.

sivity, fatalism, present-time orientation, emotionality, superstition, and inability to defer gratification.

Study after study pointed out how dissimilar Latinos, and for that matter, African Americans, were to Anglos. Lyle Saunders observed, "A closely related trait of the Spanish-speaking people is their somewhat greater readiness toward acceptance and resignation than is characteristic of the Anglo. . . . Fate is somewhat inexorable, and there is nothing much to be gained by struggling against it" (Saunders 1954, 128–29). His findings were echoed a few years later by another anthropologist's description of the Latino's "fatalistic philosophy [which] produces an attitude of resignation which often convinces the Anglo that the Latin lacks drive and determination. What the Anglo tries to control, the Mexican American tries to accept. Misfortune is something the Anglo tries to overcome and the Latin views as fate" (Madsen 1964, 16). Once Latinos were defined as a traditional culture with values antithetical to individual progress, it seemed obvious that their unsatisfactory social position was a result of cultural character flaws. In the nineteenth century, Richard Henry Dana had ascribed many of the same traits to the Latino Californios. By the postwar period, Dana's crude observations had acquired the patina of science and research.

THE ZOOT-SUIT RIOTS

In 1942, the U.S. combat effort in World War II had not yet yielded many successes, and the American public was apprehensive about its ability to fight enemies on a number of fronts. They found an easy victory right at home. The Sleepy Lagoon trial and the subsequent "Zoot-Suit" Riots in Los Angeles seemed to prove that Richard Henry Dana was right about those lazy, fatalistic, present-oriented Latinos. The scandal tarnished the reputation of Latinos in California for twenty years.

A group of young Latinos not yet in the armed forces had taken up swimming in a reservoir called Sleepy Lagoon during the hot summer of America's first year of war. One morning after a party that ended in a fight, the body of one young Latino was found in the lagoon. Although it was not clear that a crime had been committed, the citizens of Los Angeles were outraged that such murderous goings-on should occur while a war was being waged. Hundreds of young men and women, mainly Latinos, were arrested. Twenty-two Latinos were tried on charges of murder (Mazón 1984, 20). The Los Angeles County sheriff, Captain E. Duran Ayres, testified that the murder was, no doubt, a result of the uniquely Latino racial character traits of the defendants: "The Mexican element . . . desire[s] to kill, or at least let blood. . . . When there is added to this inborn characteristic that has come down through the ages, the use of liquor, then we certainly have crimes of violence" (Daniels 1990, 316). The defendants were convicted of murder in early 1943, but this was not the end of the story. The press reported public worries about the unpatriotic appearance and behavior of Latinos wearing zoot suits—long-waisted, wide-lapelled coats paired with baggy, chest-high pants with narrow cuffs. Newspapers editorialized about menacing crowds of these outlandishly dressed young men who were described as unpatriotic. Finally, in June a number of servicemen descended on downtown and East Los Angeles and attacked zoot-suited Latinos, stripping them of their symbolically offensive clothing and beating them. A domestic enemy had been found and beaten.

For nearly a century prior to 1965, Atlantic America defined Latinos as a race, as a nonrace, as a language group, as a surname group, and as a dysfunctional, traditional folk culture. The language they could speak, the schools they could attend, the houses they could buy, the public facilities they could use: all were imposed externally, by a society only able to see in black and white. One focus group participant remembered how these externally imposed definitions had become internalized in her own family, to the extent that they defined the nature of the boys she could date. "All my life my mother has told me, 'If somebody asks what you are, you tell them you're white because you're taller. Don't tell anyone you're a Mexican. Don't like Mexican boys, because you're never gonna get ahead. Like a white boy.' Okay? I've had that drilled in me" (CESLAC UW 1998, 3: U.S.-born Latinos, some college, 33).

Cowed and scarred by the massive deportations of the 1930s and the Zoot-Suit Riots of the early 1940s, with virtually no political representation, no mass media, and no market clout, Latinos appeared to be on their way to extinction as an identifiable ethnic group, following the path supposedly taken by Irish, Italian, and Jewish immigrants earlier in the century (Gordon 1964). America had articulated its opinion of Latinos for more than a century and thought the matter was finished. But Latinos were about to find their own voice.

TWO

Latinos Reject America's Definition
1965–1975

> The thing that strikes me [as] funny is that . . . a lot of people who are
> my contemporaries . . . talk about "in the days of the Chicano
> movement" like it's past tense, like it happened and it's over. . . . To
> me, it's present and alive [in 1999]. . . . It's more like a glimpse of the
> future, if we understand it.
>
> *CESLAC CHM 1999, 5: Latino health administrator, 28–29*

DURING THE TEMPESTUOUS 1960s, various groups sought a more significant place in American policymaking than they had previously occupied:
the African American civil rights movement, the anti–Vietnam War movement, the women's movement, the first wave of the gay and lesbian movement, the American Indian movement, the disabled . . . the list of aggrieved groups seeking public redress seemed to go on and on. Among the
new currents of political activism of the time, Chicano Power, too, registered on the public consciousness albeit feebly. While this Latino movement was only one of many competing for attention in those heady days
when change was the only constant, it was powerful enough to change
Latino self-consciousness forever. "It was a time where there was a lot of political awareness, not just in the Chicano community, because it was during the Vietnam war; people were very active at the time. It was the flower
generation, peace generation, a lot of activism" (CESLAC CHM 1999, 8:
Latina pathologist, 2).

I was a participant-observer in the events of that era (1965–75), to the
point of changing my doctoral dissertation topic from a study of Latino patient behavior to a study of the socialization processes experienced by the
first generation of Latino medical, dental, nursing, and other health pro-

fessional students, so that I could better understand the social world we were creating with the formation of the National Chicano Health Organization (NCHO). Thirty years after those events, trying to understand the role that the Chicano generation continues to play in Latino daily life, I returned to many of those original informants of my doctoral study and reinterviewed them. I was curious: How had their participation in the Chicano movement marked them, their professional decisions, their family lives, their roles now as parents, providers, key economic nuclei in various communities, and high-impact political participants? Between 1997 and 2001 I interviewed forty-six of these *veteranos* (veterans of the Chicano movement), adding a few interviews of the older deportation-era generation who had interacted with these "young turks" during the sixties and seventies. The quotations in this chapter are from those interviews. "All of this activism had an interesting effect on the community and what I consider the mental health of the community. It gave us a purpose; it gave us a reason to be; it gave us a sense of community. And sometimes we felt like it was us against the world" (CESLAC CHM 1999, 7: Latina program administrator, 18).

NOT QUITE AMERICAN

By the late 1960s, the Latino population in California numbered nearly one and a half million, a tremendous upsurge from the one-third of a million just thirty years earlier. More importantly, more than half the Latino population was young, under twenty-four years of age, children of deportation-era parents. They had grown up during the increasing prosperity of the postwar era, but unlike their Anglo counterparts, Latino families did not fully share in the economic boom. For example, at the beginning of the 1950s, 60.6 percent of Latinos lived in poverty, compared to 25.5 percent of non-Hispanic whites (CA EDD 1986, 62, tables 24b, 24c). While non-Hispanic white Depression-era males were moving up the civil-service ladder or were opening up their own businesses, deportation-era Latinos largely worked for private-sector employers in agriculture, construction, and manufacturing, without the stability or benefits of civil service or the rewards of business ownership. "I was raised in what was then call *[sic]* Jingle-town, which was the barrio of Whittier; that's where the Mexicans lived. . . . It was a little barrio with dirt streets and no light, all that sort of stuff. It was very primitive" (CESLAC CHM 1999, 7: Latina program administrator, 18–19).

Having grown up in a more segregated California, the postwar-generation young Latinos were aware that, somehow, they were not quite accepted as "real" Americans. "I am very dark; I am very brown. I had more identity problems growing up as a teenager here in the U.S. I used to think that nobody was ever going to marry me because I was so dark. I was in a very white school" (CESLAC CHM 1999, 2: Latina health administrator, 14).

Particularly for those few who later went to college, schooling often took place outside of barrio schools, which only heightened their sense of being not quite American. "We went to that school until high school. So, for me, life was always being the oddball, the cute little Mexican kid among all these Anglos. My brother and I were the only Latinos, so it put us in a very difficult situation sometimes" (CESLAC CHM 1999, 7: Latina program administrator, 20).

Although they might speak English fluently and be able to recite all the favorite television shows, postwar Latinos were constantly reminded, in many subtle ways, that they were not quite American. "I was eight, ten [years old] at the time [1950s]. . . . I couldn't put my finger on it. . . . All I knew was, somehow, I was a lot different, and they [non-Hispanic white schoolmates] let me know I was really different. I mean, no question about it" (CESLAC CHM 1999, 6: Latino medical researcher, 23).

The population pressure supplied by the baby boomers had pushed the construction of new elementary and high schools in California, culminating in the formulation of the California Master Plan for Higher Education and a building boom at the community college, state college, and University of California levels. However, these new educational facilities were out of reach for Latinos. By 1960, fewer than one out of every four Latino adults had graduated from high school (24.2 percent), and very few had graduated from college (3.2 percent) (CA EDD 1986, 30, tables 12A, 12B). Yet, despite the lack of societal incentives, a small number of Latino high school students in the 1950s and 1960s caught the state's educational fever and were determined to go to college. "Well, I'm the first in my family to get a college education. . . . When I announced to my parents [in] my senior year in high school that I wanted to go to college, they were shocked. No one in their family had ever gone to college, and they were very proud and very supportive" (CESLAC CHM 1999, 8: Latina pathologist, 5).

When they arrived on the college campuses, the Latino students felt out of place. Even the campuses located in Latino barrios, such as California State University, Los Angeles, had very few Latino students. "[When] I got out of college early on in 1966 . . . at Cal State L.A. . . . you have to recall, at that point in time, Los Angeles had the biggest Latino population out-side of Mexico City, [and] you had forty-five Spanish surname students in a population of 24–25,000 students" (CESLAC CHM 1999, 12: Latino health law attorney, 1–2). In 1964, there were seventy Latino students at UCLA; this figure increased to three hundred by 1967. There were seventy-eight Latino students at UC Berkeley in 1966, and a total of two hundred Latinos enrolled at San José State University that same year (Ortego 1971, 130–31). The small number of Latinos in the graduate and professional schools was even more noticeable.

> The first month I was at USC medical school, I did get the alumni list—and USC med school has been there since 1885—and I could pick out about twenty Spanish-sounding surnames over the eighty-year pe-riod. [There was] some overlap—Portuguese, Italians, or could be Gon-zalez straight from Zaragoza, Spain, who ain't got nothing to do with the 'hood. So, for an eighty-year period, it was around twenty Latino possible [medical students]. (CESLAC CHM 1999, 9: Latino family physician, 8)

By the mid-1960s, a small number of soon-to-be highly influential Latinos made their way onto the state's college and university campuses, acutely aware that they were not quite American, with a gnawing outrage at the in-justices Latinos had endured for being "different."

> In the [19]64, 65, 66 period . . . I knew that there was a difference in the way the system functioned for Latino people and for non-Latino people. . . . One of the dynamics . . . molding me . . . was really anger and revenge. I felt that the Latino people were not getting their fair share, and I tried to turn those energies into positive energies, to work on issues that would enhance Latino power and give us a fair share of what our community was entitled to. (CESLAC CHM 1999, 12: Latino health law attorney, 1)

Although the Chicano movement had roots that ran generations deep, it was very much influenced by the spirit of the times. Early in his adminis-tration, the inspirational President John F. Kennedy had read Michael Har-rington's *The Other America* (1963), an indictment of poverty in prosper-ous America. President Lyndon B. Johnson picked up the assassinated president's banner and declared a "War on Poverty" as part of the civil rights agenda. For five successive years, urban America burned and witnessed riots and disturbances. Social change was in the air. "I would say my first overtly political experience was the Vietnam Summer, based on the Mississippi Summer when they registered black folks in Mississippi. The summer of 1967, I got involved in Vietnam Summer. I got trained; I focused on fund raising, media, and did a lot of draft counseling" (CESLAC CHM 1999, 9: Latino family physician, 3).

The Chicano movement would have happened without that context, but such an invigorating social environment certainly made the entree to social activism more acceptable than it had been for deportation-era Latinos.

> In the middle of my college career, coming home for the summer, I had to deal with the Chicano moratorium . . . and that helped kind of crystallize . . . this sense of the Chicano movement and what Chicanos were looking for, why they were protesting and why they felt certain injustices existed. And of course, the highlight of that whole experience was the unfortunate death of Ruben Salazar, the *[Los Angeles] Times* reporter. (CESLAC CHM 1999, 3: Latino surgeon, 5)[1]

THE CHICANO ZEITGEIST

Deportation-era Latinos had battled discrimination in their own way, suing to end segregated schools and military segregation, and organizing labor unions and community service organizations. The major generational difference was that Chicano-era Latinos insisted on asserting a cultural presence that had been conspicuously lacking during deportation-era efforts. This sudden insistence on being unmistakably Latino was, at first, upsetting and confusing for the deportation-era generation, as described by one interviewee in his eighth decade of life: "The younger generations of that particular time [1960–70] preferred to be called Chicanos, and my [1930s] generation preferred not to be called Chicanos. It's just a matter of choice between the two distinct elements, because we were completely distinct" (CESLAC CHM 1999, 11: Latino elected official, 9). The term "Chicano," used to assert that cultural identity, was indeed a shock for some members of the earlier generation. They had soft-pedaled their Mexican-

---

1. Ruben Salazar was a reporter for the *Los Angeles Times* who covered the Chicano moratorium. The moratorium itself ended in a police action, with tear gas used to disperse the crowd. Salazar was sitting inside a bar when a police agent on the sidewalk in front fired a projectile inside, which struck and killed Salazar.

ness, and for them "Chicano" was derogatory. It meant *pachuco;* it meant zoot-suiter; it meant juvenile delinquent.

> I remember, it must have been 1968, 1969. . . . My sister [and I] were having a discussion with my mother, and we used the term "Chicano" to describe ourselves, and my mother reacted like she got bit by a snake. "Don't call yourselves that! Don't use that word!" "Why not?" "That means pachuco, that means juvenile delinquent." "Aw, Mom, you're nuts." So it kind of egged her on, and at the time I guess part of the egging on for my little sister's and my part was a sense of anger at her . . . [for thinking] that the best thing they could do to us is not teach us Spanish, not teach us anything about this thing called Mexico; that would protect us. (CESLAC CHM 1999, 6: Latino medical researcher, 24)

Cultural self-determination—the right to express oneself in the terms one thinks fit—was a touchstone for Chicano-era Latinos. That cultural assertion was a key to rejecting the definitions imposed by mainstream American society. However, the cultural assertion was, at times, accompanied by a number of cultural contradictions. For instance, despite the emphasis on bilingual education, the stark reality was that very few Latinos of that era had developed a fluency in Spanish, because the vast majority—80.6 percent in 1960—had been born in the United States (CA EDD 1986, 10, table 2c). An elderly, deportation-era Latino physician offered his views on the Chicanos' Spanish-speaking ability: "The Californian Mexican American very seldom know [sic] Spanish [well] enough to communicate with [immigrant] people, so that is one of the deficits I see. . . . They say that 'I'm going to help my people,' so how can you help your people if you can't communicate with them? If they [immigrants] feel comfortable coming to talk to you in Spanish and you don't understand [it]?" (CESLAC CHM 1999, 4: Latino hematologist, 8).

Participants in this era invariably described their involvement as an emotionally involving, cathartic experience. The spirit of the times seemed to bind together those active in the movement. Many described feeling free to be "brown and proud"; it was a touching experience that few have forgotten. "These marches seemed to give [me] a means of expression, a means of pride. Because it is at this time, 1968 forward, that I became comfortable in my own skin, that I became proud to be identified as a Chicana" (CESLAC CHM 1999, 7: Latina program administrator, 18).

This catharsis was coupled with a pent-up resentment and anger at the many injustices suffered, both personally and collectively. The emotional release was described by respondents as being extremely intense. "And it felt like . . . this was the first time . . . that people were advocating for welfare rights, for health, for education, for real participation in a political arena. And I became, you know, very passionate, you know, very, *very*, VERY, *VERY* [increasing emphasis] passionate about these issues" (CESLAC CHM 1999, 7: Latina program administrator, 5).

But the down side of such passionate involvement in a movement that combined the cultural with the political was the emergence, at times, of a streak of intolerance for those who were not sufficiently "Chicano," whether culturally or politically. In the early 1970s, a medical student who had just had his Chicanoness questioned by another Chicano medical student confided that such remarks seemed to be a "game of *soy más chicano que tú*" [I'm more Chicano than you]. The personal became political: what one wore, what one ate, the friends one associated with, the music one listened to, all were symbols of being a good, or a bad, Chicano. Usually, an intense cultural nationalism was difficult to sustain beyond a few months or a couple of years. Even the most ardent nationalists during that time later relaxed their demanding standards to a more reasonable level. "I mean, I got fairly nationalist, you know, 1968, 1969, 1970 . . . you know, cultural nationalism, [as] in 'Latinos as the center of the universe.' . . . You go through a nationalist phase. Thankfully, I'm over it. I mean, I only lasted, in my view, a few years" (CESLAC CHM 1999, 9: Latino family physician, 43).

Of course, the political was political, too. Marxism and Marxist-inspired literature were on many reading lists, and even science students found themselves reading and pondering the many variations of Marxism. "At that time I was reading a lot of . . . Marxist philosophy and was interested in social justice and ideas of distributive justice. I wasn't really ever, you know, a hard-core Marxist. I was always a little nervous about some of the things that happened in some of the socialist countries and the communist countries. But as a philosophy, I was interested" (CESLAC CHM 1999, 10: Latino family physician, 20–21). College-campus-based leftist groups often splintered into factions, and each competing brand of Marxism declared the others invalid. Thus, a Trotskyite Chicano could be declared not sufficiently Chicano by a Maoist Chicano.

Often, Chicano-era groups used the imagery of Latino revolutionary figures—Emiliano Zapata, Pancho Villa, Ché Guevara—as a way of asserting presence in the face of huge institutions, such as university campuses. At times, this inspirational imagery was misinterpreted by non-Latinos unaware of the emotions the images touched.

> I should tell you a side story. Our [student group] emblem at that time—
> remember, we are going through the sixties and the Vietnam War and all of
> that stuff—was the face of Ché Guevara with his beret and his star in the
> middle. Some of our faculty, who were ex-military, became alarmed . . .
> [and] informed me that the FBI was investigating the organization because
> it could be subversive. Of course, nothing was farther from the truth. I
> think we just wanted an equal opportunity. (CESLAC CHM 1999, 1:
> Latino dentist, 6)

Even thirty years later, the reinterviewed Chicano-era Latinos still felt a sense of pride at that rebellious period in their lives. The rebellion was not that of a lonely "rebel without a cause"; rather, it made individuals feel they were part of a larger, dynamic social movement that provided concrete meaning to their lives, then and thirty years later. "I am very comfortable with the term 'Chicano,' but I recognize that it's a loaded word in some people's minds. They don't like it, but for me it was a political word that had political significance during my days as an undergraduate student" (CESLAC CHM 1999, 13: Latino ophthalmologist, 22).

STRUCTURING THE REJECTION

The decade 1965–75 was the heyday of the early Chicano movement: César Chávez and the United Farmworkers; Corky Gonzalez's Crusade for Justice; the new Raza Unida Party that promised to bring the boys home from Vietnam; the high school "blowouts" in East Los Angeles; the student strikes at various college and university campuses around the state to agitate for courses in Chicano studies; the Chicano moratorium in San Francisco and Los Angeles; the Brown Beret occupation of Catalina Island.

Rejecting the expectations social analysts had of Italian, Irish, or Jewish immigrants of earlier generations, Latinos of the Chicano generation did not slip quietly into the American mainstream, culturally speaking. Researchers of European immigrant groups, such as Gordon (1964), had expected that the grandchildren of these immigrants would be, in nearly all things, "American," with a mild "third-generation return" resulting in a thin residuum of St. Patrick's Day parades and other pro forma ethnic festivals once a year. Chicano-generation U.S.-born Latinos overtly and publicly rejected this expectation as the only possible outcome. Instead, they burst out on the state's cultural and political scene with the energy of waters that had long been pent up behind a dam athwart a natural riverbed. "It was one of those, I guess, youth rebellion things, where people would tell you not to do [something] is more of the reason why you would do it. And on top of that, we didn't . . . know what we couldn't do. And so we said, 'Let's try it' " (CESLAC CHM 1999, 5: Latino health administrator, 5).

Like flood waters overrunning the cement channels of the Los Angeles River, the energies of the Chicano generation flowed around attitudes and institutions that had been built regarding the Latino presence in the state. The Chicano activists scoured the surface of more than 150 years of smug, exclusionary definitions.

> There were several arenas. One was the whole area of police and police brutality, concerns about how the police were beating Chicanos. There was a whole lot of work done on welfare rights. . . . And there was a whole other arena that was concerned about the role of the [Catholic] church and its inclusion of Latinos in its work. And out of that were concerns about the quality of education. (CESLAC CHM 1999, 7: Latina program administrator, 6)

Angered by the high percentage of Latino high school dropouts, Chicano activists applied pressure on schools for better educational outcomes. They insisted that this new educational environment include bilingual and bicultural education. Thirsty to learn the Mexican and Latin American history their schools had not taught them, they pushed schools, colleges, and universities to offer courses, then to establish centers and departments of Chicano studies. "My commitment . . . goes back to the student movement, as I mentioned, in Santa Barbara. And we had what was called a Plan de Santa Bárbara . . . which is really about higher education" (CESLAC CHM 1999, 5: Latino health administrator, 6). Fed up with years of petty insults and segregation, they established civil rights organizations, such as the Mexican American Legal Defense and Education Fund (MALDEF), the Southwest Council of La Raza, and California Rural Legal Assistance, which doggedly defended Latino civil and cultural rights whenever they were attacked.

> We did form our Brown Beret chapter; I was the minister of health. [For me] it was a health problem if the goddamn cops take a Mexican out at 3:00 in the morning, take him behind the K-Mart, and beat the shit out

of him and dump him into a canister [dumpster]. . . . A bunch of Mexicans were pissed off about having the cops beat the shit out of them. (CESLAC CHM 1999, 9: Latino family physician, 6)

And outraged by years of neglect by basic public institutions—schools, highways, parks, streets and lighting, health care services—they established hundreds of alternative community health centers, bilingual libraries, job-training centers, mental health programs, community-development centers, and the like. "I think the zeitgeist, the spirit of the times, was that all of us were aware of our roles and responsibilities in issues of social justice in general. Everybody . . . did their own personal things, but that was one sort of uniting feature that was part of the culture of the times" (CESLAC CHM 1999, 10: Latino family physician, 14).

Given the overtly political nature of many Chicano-era organizations, culture and politics were intertwined. The muralist movement, for example, saw itself as both aesthetic and political. Murals were meant to move Latinos emotionally, to motivate them to become involved. Like wildfire, mural artistry spread: soon murals covered walls up and down the state. While I was taking a weekend course on silk-screen poster printing at a community site in the early 1970s, the instructor, a muralist, was so tightly attached to the political nature of his work that he vowed to the class never to create "private art," smaller works that could be bought and collected privately, away from public view.

The radio waves were another medium for organizing, and a small Chicano public radio movement began. In rural areas of California, such as Santa Rosa and Fresno, small FM stations started up, whose target audiences were rural agricultural workers. In urban areas, public radio stations introduced Chicano programming for an hour or two per week: a lowrider program with a political message in Berkeley, a Saturday-night soulful oldies show in Pasadena, a day of salsa music on a Jesuit college station.

Some Chicano-era Latinos threw themselves, body and soul, into *"la causa."* The needs were so great that they could consume their every waking hour. Rather than being daunted at the enormity of the task ahead of them, however, some Chicano-era Latinos recalled that, in those days, they took to the task with relish. Their very involvement was invigorating, refreshing, and all-consuming.

It felt good. It was a lot of fun, to be honest with you. . . . When you do something that had never been done [before] and other people don't think you can do it, you've got to generate this enthusiasm, and . . . and then, you know, something happens. It kind of has a momentum of its own. And everybody that was involved, I mean, they weren't involved with it to serve themselves. I mean, basically, we were tied together by a common ethic about what we wanted to do. And we still had a lot of other things that we did, studies and work. And [we] had fun, you know. We had good parties, all that. So it was really pretty exciting. (CESLAC CHM 1999, 5: Latino health administrator, 10)

Thanks to such enthusiasm, a tremendous amount of social infrastructure was created. But this high level of involvement could not be sustained forever.

NOT QUITE MEXICAN

When they were younger, this generation had been told in many subtle ways that they were not truly American. Now they embraced the Mexican portions of themselves that they had once felt compelled to hide. They enrolled in courses in Chicano studies and in Latin American studies provided by the newly instituted programs in Chicano studies.

For some, this included traveling to Mexico, the motherland, expecting to be welcomed as lost relatives. They were quickly disabused of the notion that Mexicans would consider them fellow Mexicans. Often, when Chicanos traveled to Mexico for the first time, relatives, friends, and even hotel-room maids would be quick to let them know that they did not speak Spanish properly; that they dressed like Americans; that their values, attitudes, and opinions were not "really Mexican." They were *pochos* (U.S.-born), from the other side.

> I remember in about '71, a group of students from UCSF, Chicanos who had never been to Mexico, climbed in a Volkswagen bus, drove to Tijuana to go visit the "motherland." They told me about it afterwards. . . . Literally, the minute they got across the border, they stopped and got off and kissed the ground. "Motherland, we're here." And they got robbed, and they got cheated and stolen; their van was picked clean. . . . They got treated miserably. . . . The motherland rejected them. (CESLAC CHM 1999, 6: Latino medical researcher, 32)

Thus, many Chicanos were caught in a quandary: too Mexican to be American, too American to be Mexican. They were somewhere between two worlds.

By and large, Chicano activism came from the state's college and university campuses, but there were very few Latinos in higher education during the 1960s and early 1970s. "We were this passionate little rag-tag group of activists, and yet the majority of these people [Chicano activists] have gone on to become very productive professional leaders in their own areas . . . doctors, writers, professors, lawyers, movie producers. I mean, they're artists; they've become everything" (CESLAC CHM 1999, 7: Latina program administrator, 18). Deportation-era adults were not eager to join in, and the U.S.-born blue-collar segment was rarely active. Even including demonstrations such as the 1969 Chicano moratorium in Los Angeles and San Francisco, it might not be an exaggeration to estimate that fewer than thirty thousand Latinos participated in the movement, out of a Latino population of close to two million. The vast majority of Latinos at that time did not even wish to call themselves Chicano.

The assertion of cultural presence was an attempt to awaken their deportation-era Latino parents, who, some Chicanos felt, had sold out their cultural heritage in an attempt to blend in. "I'd be at these demonstrations. I had long braids, and I'd wear what my mother called funny clothes, and she said, 'Lucia, you look like an *india* [Indian].' I said, 'But, Mother, we are Indians.' And my mother would just go, 'Absolutely, this one is hopeless'" (CESLAC CHM 1999, 7: Latina program administrator, 20).

Some respondents described how their initial resentment at their parents' lack of support mellowed over the years, as they came to understand that their parents, too, had their own issues to deal with during the deportation era that the Chicano era, in its zeal, had overlooked. "So, for me, it was a romantic notion. Here's César Chávez trying to improve the lot of the farmworker. And for my mother, it was a painful memory . . . because I had forgotten, in my own zeal, that my mother had to work the migrant [farmworker] streams too, as she was a child. She never graduated . . . because she'd be taken out of school [to work]" (CESLAC CHM 1999, 7: Latina program administrator, 20–21). As the militant, more confrontational Chicano activity gradually mellowed, even the older deportation-era generation grudgingly allowed that some important things had been accomplished—even the word that once meant "juvenile delinquent" had become a part of the Latino lexicon. "You didn't want to be called a Chicano in my day [deportation era]. There would be a fight if you called me a Chicano, but today [1999] it is acceptable" (CESLAC CHM 1999, 11: Latino elected official, 9).

In the spring of 1971, about twenty Latino medical and dental students met in the Millberry Student Union at the University of California Medical Center, San Francisco. While the student conference rooms in the building enjoyed a panoramic view of the Golden Gate Bridge and the rolling Marin County headlands, none of the young Latinos looked out the window once. Their attention was riveted to the business at hand, a peace conference of sorts.

They had come from medical and dental schools in the Southwest—Texas, Colorado, New Mexico, Arizona, and California. Only two years earlier, there had been a total of three Latino medical students in all nine of California's medical schools, and similar small numbers in the other states. In 1969, under pressure from the American Association of Medical Colleges, health professional schools in the country began to admit significant numbers of Latino applicants.

Once they had entered the medical and dental schools, they organized themselves into affinity groups, with names like Chicanos for Health and Education (CHE) at UCMCSF, Chicanos for Creative Medicine (CCM) at UCLA and USC, Mexican American Students for Health (MASH) in Arizona, and the Texas Association of Mexican American Medical Students. The organizations differed slightly, but they had arrived at the same conclusion: there was a need to pressure health professional schools for ongoing Latino recruitment, admissions, retention, and financial aid.

The meeting in San Francisco was an attempt to create a new organization out of these separate groups, to be called the National Chicano Health Organization (NCHO). At times, the gathering became tense: the groups had been unconsciously engaging in a quiet tug-of-war over which organization was the "most Chicano." At stake was the moral authority to organize this new national organization. A state's Chicano political activism was taken as the surrogate measure of its moral worth. Those from Colorado invoked the organizing ability of the boxer Corky Gonzalez; those from Texas extolled the political power base of the Raza Unida Party established by José Angel Gutiérrez to take the mayorship in Crystal City; those from New Mexico reveled in the armed rebellion of Reies Tijerina to reestablish the old Spanish land grants; and those from California pointed with pride to the achievements of César Chávez and the farmworkers. Those who were able to do so sprinkled their English with Spanish phrases.

Late in the tense, nonstop day without a meal break, one of the San Francisco host students suggested the group grab a burger and some fries down at the corner stand, then get back to battling over ideological turf. Eyes flashing with fury, a pony-tailed medical student from southern California, wearing an embroidered Mexican peasant shirt and huarache sandals, stood up and said, "That's what I would expect from a bunch of *vendidos* [sellouts]—going out for a hamburger. Eating a hamburger is committing cultural genocide. We eat tacos, or we eat nothing." A debate ensued, and meeting participants voted to find a Mexican restaurant, a show of solidarity with the Latino community and a reinforcement of their cultural heritage. A real Chicano, it was decided, would never eat a hamburger.

Participants left the meeting that day filled with agonizing questions. Am I really Chicano? After all, I don't speak Spanish. My parents were not farmworkers; in fact, they were middle class. I didn't go to high school in a barrio. I don't own a lowrider, and no one in my family is a *vato loco* (gang member) or a *pinto* (former prisoner). I studied science while my classmates were boycotting grapes. What does a "real" Chicano act like? Was I admitted to medical school under false pretenses?

The National Chicano Health Organization was finally founded in the summer of 1971 as an umbrella organization aiming to satisfy the needs and demands of medical and dental students from San Francisco to Houston. A governing board of representatives from each of the states met often to set policy, develop programs, and provide guidance to each group of incoming medical students. As with many organizations, the more important policies were never written down but were passed orally from one class of students to the next. Each year, this lore became increasingly succinct, providing an informal model of what a "real" Chicano physician should be like:

Use the Chinese "barefoot doctor" as a community service model.

Swear never to set up a private practice, because that is capitalist medicine.

Swear to avoid the specialties, because the Latino community needs primary-care physicians and few Latinos can afford specialty care.

Be an employee physician, ideally with a farmworkers' clinic. If that is not possible, at least be a salaried employee of a community clinic.

Never, ever be caught dead talking to a member of the California Hispanic American Medical Association. They are the enemy. After all, they aren't even Chicano—they're *Hispanic.*

DEMOGRAPHICS OF CULTURAL CHANGE: THE NEW IMMIGRANTS

Two policy changes at the national level had an impact on the Latino community as profound as the energies of the Chicano generation had: the ending of the bracero program and the elimination of national-origin quotas for immigration. Curiously, like the Chicano movement, these policy initiatives contributed to emerging Latino self-confidence, but in a different way. The Chicano movement—angry young people with rhetoric, theory, and plans—took the path of confrontation. The federal decisions initiated changes in a quieter, less self-conscious, but very basic way: the way of the immigrant Latino.

The bracero program began in 1942, the result of an agreement between the United States and Mexico to provide emergency labor for designated employers, usually in agriculture, suffering from World War II's drain on the labor force. Braceros were not immigrants; they were temporary guest workers, with none of the rights of immigrants. They were under contract for a limited period, and their movements were heavily restricted; they could not leave farm labor camps without permission, they could not rent or buy property, they could not bring their families with them, and they could not marry a resident of California. Nevertheless, they were the first tendrils of later, more voluminous, immigration. As seasonal guest workers, braceros were often not captured in public enumerations such as the census.

Thus, the 1950 census showed that fewer than two out of every ten (18.8 percent) of the 1,009,400 resident Latino population were of immigrant origin. But this total did not include the shadow population of braceros (CA EDD 1986, 10, table 2c). During the late 1950s, an average of 430,000 braceros per year came into the United States, most destined for employers in agribusiness-dominated California (Grebler, Moore, and Guzman 1973, 68), representing nearly half-again the total number of Latinos enumerated in the census. These braceros had needs that were tended to by the small but growing Latino business base.

Agricultural interests profited from this cheap, docile labor force, which was essentially bound labor, contracted to one specific employer. For twenty-two years, prospective employers sent recruiters to Mexico; for twenty-two years, repeated journeys between specific villages in Mexico and specific employers in California gradually hardwired these routes, and a tremendous annual seasonal immigration took shape. An entire generation of Mexican workers grew up dreaming of work opportunities *en el norte* (up north).

The end of the bracero program in 1964 did not mean that the need for Mexican labor had expired. Rather, coupled with the 1965 changes in immigration law that finally allowed immigration from Mexico and the Western Hemisphere, it meant that former braceros returned to their old jobs, but increasingly as immigrants rather than guest workers. For nearly the first time since the late 1920s, immigrant Latinos returned in force to familiar haunts in East Los Angeles, East San José, the Mission District of San Francisco, and scores of other neighborhoods around the state where settlers from Mexico had established themselves ever since 1769. At first, they came timidly, by themselves, establishing post-bracero links with the old employers, with whom some had relations stretching back twenty-two years. Once jobs were secure, they brought their wives and older children. Slowly they began to settle down and raise their families. Even though many had learned English, they spoke Spanish when they wanted to relax with family and friends.

Unlike U.S.-born Chicanos, who were acutely aware of their cultural choices, immigrants rarely thought about what a "real" Latino would do; they simply were parents, workers, neighbors, godparents, cousins, and parishioners. Immigrant Latinos did not feel that they committed cultural genocide by eating a hamburger. They did not feel the need to wear huaraches or peasant clothes to feel Mexican. By and large, they did not see themselves consciously as "Latino," much less as a group with a political agenda. Daily life was consumed by making a living, and their aspirations rarely reached beyond the four walls of their houses. They were gratified, however, to have a couple of radio stations play some music they remembered, a television station that showed programs they had seen in Mexico, and an occasional market where they could find tortillas and *pan dulce*.

Among the trickle of immigrant Latinos beginning to arrive in California in the post–World War II era were physicians trained in medical schools in Mexico, Argentina, Peru, the Dominican Republic, and other Latin American countries. During that period, immigrant Latino International Medical Graduate (IMG) physicians entering the state comprised close to 90 percent of all Latino physicians, as all the state's medical schools combined managed to graduate only one or two Latino physicians each year until the mid-1970s. Fluent in Spanish and comfortable with a Latino clientele, they established thriving practices in East San José, Fresno, East Los Angeles, the Mission District of San Francisco, and other barrios densely populated by a quietly increasing number of Latinos. "If you went to the east side [of Los Angeles] in the late fifties and sixties, you found out that health care was provided by foreign-trained [Latino] physicians, not American-trained [Latino] physicians" (CESLAC CHM 1999, 4: Latino hematologist, 10).

A number of these immigrant Latino IMGs wound up practicing at Monterey Park Hospital, east of Los Angeles. They commiserated with one another over the issues all Latino immigrants, even highly educated immigrant physicians, faced in California: the travails of forming a family and buying a house, the limited Spanish-language television or radio programming, the paucity of Spanish-language newspapers, the challenges of raising children in a state that was largely non-Hispanic white, the difficulty of finding the types of food products they really enjoyed, the difficulty of having their children speak Spanish, the subtle indignities of living in a state that still practiced widespread but informal segregation.

Their most common ground, however, was in the professional world. Their medical education in Mexico and other parts of Latin America, they felt, was as good as the training offered in California, yet they were told, in many different ways, that they were really just second-class doctors. They continued to have difficulty gaining privileges at other hospitals. Not sure they were welcome, very few had joined their local medical associations or the state-level California Medical Association. In the early 1970s they formed their own professional group, the California Hispanic American Medical Association (CHAMA), whose official business language was Spanish. "CHAMA was founded in 1975 . . . by a group of Latin American doctors who had received their medical education in either Mexico, Argentina, Peru, in Latin America, who trained outside of the United States and then immigrated . . . and were called at that time Foreign Medical Graduate" (CESLAC CHM 1999, 13: Latino ophthalmologist, 6).

Beginning in the early 1970s, the informal group affiliated with the Monterey Park Hospital had the idea of organizing a small social get-together for the immigrant physicians and their spouses, as a way of combating the loneliness they felt. Various pharmaceutical companies offered to help sponsor the event. Before long, the informal social gathering had grown in size to a full-fledged dinner and dance. It was a dressy affair that soon became a biannual black-tie event held at various top hotels in southern California. While there were few Latino bands available in the early 1970s that played the type of music the party-goers had grown up with, they managed to find one, by asking among their patients, to play danceable music they remembered from their student years in Latin America: rumbas, cha-chas, tangos, merengue. A trio would wander through, playing old favorites written by Agustín Lara or Los Panchos. Friendships would be rekindled, conversations about the latest novels from Mexico or Argentina flowed spontaneously, young children would scamper around, and for an evening the difficulty of establishing a medical practice in California could be put aside. In a rare event for the times, a U.S.-born Latino medical student was invited to a CHAMA dinner to receive a CHAMA scholarship, and he reported being impressed at a group whose existence he had not suspected. "I was able to go to a big [CHAMA] banquet [in the late 1970s] at the Los Angeles Athletic Club, downtown. And it was a real eye-opener for me to see doctors out there [who were Latino], but they weren't U.S.-born like I was. They were Latin American, like my parents, but they were educated, not laborers" (CESLAC CHM 1999, 13: Latino ophthalmologist, 7).

Interested in building up their professional skills, CHAMA members soon established a Continuing Medical Education (CME) component in their social events and were able to pay top fees for speakers who could present the latest research to them. All the doctors were fluent in English, but they preferred to conduct CHAMA business in Spanish. As a result, their greatest difficulty was finding speakers who could present in Spanish. It was not that they needed to have a Spanish presentation; it was just that they preferred it, as it made them feel welcome, for once.

With the next generation in mind, CHAMA established a scholarship fund for future medical students. Members who had children hoped that their offspring would want to follow in their footsteps and study medicine. They had heard vaguely about the Chicano movement but did not personally participate in it. Indeed, it appeared the Chicanos were hot-headed political radicals, probably not too different from members of the various leftist militant movements that had been part of the context of their education in Mexico or elsewhere in Latin America.

In the late sixties and early seventies, U.S.-born Latinos and newly arriving Latino immigrants tended to live in different worlds. Those involved in the Chicano movement fought daily for the right of "cultural self-determination," but the world they lived in was predominately English speaking. Chicanos generally did not watch the first imported Spanish-language television shows or the six o'clock Spanish news that reported events in Mexico and, increasingly, Central America; nor did they listen to Spanish-language radio. Meanwhile, in the period from 1970 to 1975, 69.5 percent of Latino population growth was due to immigration rather than births (CA DOF 1999). Immigrants not only significantly increased overall Latino population numbers; they also had far higher fertility rates than did U.S.-born Latinos. Once immigrants started to give birth, their children would quickly outnumber the children of U.S.-born Latinos. Somewhere down the road, the children of the Chicano generation and those of the new immigrants were bound to meet.

MARIACHIS OR BEETHOVEN?

In 1970, Alec Velasquez was an unusual participant in the Chicano movement at UC Berkeley. He was an immigrant, born to an upper-middle-class family in Mexico City. He had been educated there in private schools and through his university-educated parents was familiar with the capital's rich cultural offerings: the Mexico City Philharmonic, the Teatro de Bellas Artes (the Fine Arts Theater), museums, art galleries, and bookstores. As a child, Alec had joined a junior *charro* (Mexican cowboy) association and learned the traditional art of horsemanship, occasionally performing dressed in the charro's glittering outfit. Then, at age thirteen, a family dispute sent him to live with a grandmother in San Francisco. To finish high school there, he became fluent in English in a matter of months. Thanks to his intellectual drive, he became one of the few Latino undergraduates at UC Berkeley in the late 1960s, where I met him in a biology class.

Familiar with student politics in Mexico City, he joined the Chicano movement at Berkeley and was an active leader. Yet he was an unusual member of *el movimiento* (the movement). For one thing, he dressed in sport coats, while other militants preferred the paramilitary Ché Guevara look. He smoked a pipe, rather than hand-rolled, lumpy cigarettes, and was comfortable with a wine list, yet he did not hesitate to volunteer for extra duties *por la causa* (for the cause).

One spring morning, he heard that the Mexican conductor Carlos Chávez was to be a guest conductor for a local performance of Beethoven's Third Symphony. He invited me to accompany him. We spent an enjoyable afternoon, and Alec reminisced about the last time he had heard the conductor; years earlier, he had joined his parents for a preconcert cocktail beneath a Diego Rivera mural in the lobby-bar of the Hotel Prendes, had heard the concert, then had had a typical late-night dinner in a sophisticated Zona Rosa restaurant.

A week after our outing, Alec hosted a breakfast meeting of the local Chicano student group leadership at his apartment. As he and I waited for the others to arrive, he shared with me a treasure he had just found in a used record bin on Telegraph Avenue in Berkeley: a recording of the same symphony, conducted by the celebrated German conductor Wilhelm Furtwengler. He put it on, and we discussed the differences in conducting style between the Mexican and German conductors. An incredulous U.S.-born Chicano wandered into the room, mouth agape, and watched us, lost in our appreciation of classical music. Unable to contain himself any longer, the young Chicano blurted out, "Hey, you can't do that. Chicanos can't listen to classical music!" "What do you mean, 'Chicanos can't listen to classical music'?" Alec replied. "I mean, classical music isn't Chicano. Chicanos can only listen to mariachi music. That's what I was told, that a real Chicano does not listen to white man's music." Alec then launched into an impromptu lecture on Mexican classical music composers, starting with the baroque music of Gutiérrez de Padilla written in 1652 and winding up with Silvestre Revueltas. Chastened, the young Chicano slunk away, still muttering that real Chicanos should not listen to Beethoven.

If the 1960s were an exciting time for the country as a whole, they were a decisive time for Latinos in California. On the one hand, U.S.-born Latinos consciously rejected mainstream definitions of themselves that had molded their self-awareness for generations and through the fiery energy of the Chicano movement, they had created an infrastructure of institutions, programs, and policy and legal decisions that provided a tochold for Latinos in U.S. society. On the other hand, immigration flow began to dramatically increase after nearly forty years of stagnation. These newly arrived Latinos went about the business of life guided by their own internal cultural compasses and in so doing unconsciously also rejected America's definitions of the Latino.

Still too small to register on corporate America's radar screen, at best considered "America's second-largest minority," and at times referred to as a "sleeping giant," Latinos of the 1965–75 period existed in the public consciousness as simply another political group pushing for its civil rights. Yet all the growth dynamics for the remainder of the twentieth century were in place, beginning their work. Latinos and non-Latinos alike were blithely unaware of what was about to happen. Demographic and cultural changes were about to propel California into the multicultural twenty-first century.

THREE

Washington Defines a Minority
1965–1975

Those discussing the underclass are usually referring to people who are concentrated in urban neighborhoods and who are predominately black or Hispanic.

US GAO 1990, 1

DURING THE PERIOD OF THE "LONG HOT SUMMERS" from 1966 to 1969, every major American city—from the South Bronx to Newark, from Southside Chicago to Philadelphia—seemed ready to explode, just as the Watts area of Los Angeles had two years before. Leather-jacketed advocates of Black Power strode through the charred inner cities, denouncing America's treatment of African Americans and demanding that something be done. In guilty response to the anger, programs flooded out of Washington to quench the burning urban cores. A minority group had found its voice, and the federal government had responded. Other groups—women, gays and lesbians, the disabled, Asian Americans, and American Indians—likewise sought to make their private grievances public. To most policymakers, it appeared as if Latinos, too, numbered among the aggrieved minorities seeking notice. But among the Latino community something much more fundamental was at work than the identity politics of an aggrieved minority.

Nearly two hundred years ago, the Federalist Papers had imagined minorities in a strictly political sense, as holders of unpopular political opinions, whose voices needed to be protected from the tyranny of the political majority. In the mid-twentieth-century civil rights era, the word "minority" came to refer to numerically small racial or ethnic groups, whose rights needed to be defended. Today, "minority" has come to suggest a host of negative images—poverty, unemployment, welfare dependency, broken homes, crime, poor health—which, taken together, paint a picture of community dysfunction, an impaired ability to engage in the patterns of behavior commonly expected by society.

Although many Latino leaders initially accepted the designation of "minority," many have come to repudiate it. A significant body of knowledge now suggests that Latinos do not conform to the "minority dysfunction" model described above. Moreover, in California, as of 2001, Latinos are no longer a numerical minority among the babies born in the state. As these babies grow into adulthood, Latinos will gradually become the majority in the older age groups. At the same time, however, most non-Latino policymakers in Washington DC and Sacramento still see Latinos as merely one more minority group, engaged in the politics of identity, and they assume that Latinos exhibit typical minority characteristics, attitudes, and behavior.

POVERTY, MINORITIES, AND PUBLIC POLICY

Anthropologist Oscar Lewis, studying poor families in Mexico (Lewis 1959) and Puerto Rico (Lewis 1965) from the 1940s to the 1960s, introduced the notion of a "culture of poverty." In his 1965 book *La Vida*, Lewis provided conceptual detail for this idea that had been implicit in his earlier work. The culture of poverty, he claimed, is "an adaptation to a set of objective conditions of larger society"; in other words, the existence of poverty creates a culture of poverty.

> Once it [the culture of poverty] comes into existence, it tends to perpetuate itself from generation to generation because of its effects on the children. By the time slum children are six or seven, they have usually absorbed the basic values and attitudes of their subculture, and are not psychologically geared to take full advantage of changing conditions or increased opportunities which may occur in their lifetime. (Lewis 1965, xlv)

Key features of this culture of poverty include lack of impulse control, present-time orientation, inability to defer gratification, and inability to plan for the future. Psychological consequences include senses of failure, resignation, fatalism, marginality, helplessness, dependence, and inferiority (Lewis 1965, xlvii–xlviii).

While the culture of poverty identified some of the same features used by "traditional society" theorists (see chapter 1), there was one important difference: the culture of poverty was not confined to underdeveloped countries. Even in a modern society, even in the United States, Lewis could find groups who had all the characteristics of the culture of poverty. This cultural maladaptation was universal and worldwide: "[In] the United States . . . [the] culture of poverty . . . would consist of very low-income Negroes, Mexicans, Puerto Ricans, American Indians and Southern poor whites" (Lewis 1965, li).

Another seminal text in the evolution of the "culture of poverty" construct was Michael Harrington's 1962 classic, *The Other America: Poverty in the United States*. Harrington asserted that there were more than fifty million poor people in the world's richest economy, living a life the better-off could not understand: "Poverty in the United States is a culture, an institution, a way of life. . . . There is, in short, a language of the poor, a psychology of the poor, a worldview of the poor. To be impoverished is to be an internal alien, to grow up in a culture that is radically different from the one that dominates society" (Harrington 1993, 16–17). The physical manifestations of this subterranean culture are unstable families, female-headed households, teen pregnancies, inadequate medial care, more and longer illnesses, lost wages, lost jobs, and poor housing, all of it perpetuated through generations. It was a dire portrait.

Harrington's description of the poor living invisibly in newly affluent America was a revelation to a country and to a charismatic young president, both of whom had believed the rising economic tide was lifting all boats. President John F. Kennedy committed himself to eliminating poverty, but it was President Lyndon B. Johnson, after Kennedy's assassination, who built on the passage of the civil rights initiative by providing for economic progress for those left out. As American cities exploded in violence and flames, attention focused on the most visible minority, African Americans.

In the late 1960s, Daniel Patrick Moynihan, then working in the Department of Labor, prepared an analysis of poverty in urban communities, which focused on the "tangle of pathology" present in "the Negro family in urban ghettos." In the crumbling African American family, he found high divorce rates, a high percentage of unwed mothers, and a high percentage of female-headed households. Trapped in segregated housing, such communities spawned socially costly behaviors: failure of youth to perform in school, juvenile delinquency, crime, unemployment, drug addiction, isolation, and alienation (Rainwater and Yancey 1967, 39–132). Nothing short of a massive national program could ever hope to address this tangle of pathology.

Against the backdrop of shattering glass, wailing sirens, and mobs chanting "Burn, baby, burn," President Johnson declared a "War on Poverty" and enlisted the nation to help him fight it. During this era, the phenomenon of "minority politics" was born, and rivers of federal largesse were routed to those involved in bettering the "minority condition."

President Kennedy had focused much of his attention on poor whites living in Appalachia, but events of the 1960s focused the public's attention on African Americans and "other minorities." Harrington had shown that by sheer numbers far more white people than African Americans were poor, yet he also noted that the concentration of poverty was greater among the latter. As policymakers in Washington responded to the chaos threatening to engulf America's inner cities, geographic terms like "urban" (for example, the National Urban Coalition) and "inner city" become code words for African American. Gradually, the discourse on poverty became racialized, so that discussion of poverty meant discussion of minorities, and discussion of minorities focused on poverty. Numerous newly established organizations (such as the Race and Poverty Institute at the University of Wisconsin) embodied this racialization of poverty.

Two decades after the long hot summers had passed, William Julius Wilson's powerful book, *The Truly Disadvantaged: The Inner City, the Underclass and Public Policy* (1987), further linked African Americans and life-shattering poverty and continued to define the inner-city ghetto as a community "increasingly isolated from mainstream patterns and norms of behavior" (Wilson 1987, 8). Guardedly, he used Moynihan's twenty-year-old phrase, the "tangle of pathology in the inner city," to highlight how economic restructuring had, once again, crippled the black family. Lack of job skills or long-term unemployment, out-of-wedlock births, female-headed families, crime and aberrant behavior, persistent poverty, and welfare dependency yielded what he termed "the underclass." The inner city, its pathological poverty, and black Americans were firmly linked in the American imagination.

For more than a century, many Latino communities also had chafed under conditions of segregation, discrimination, poverty, low educational achievement, and low income similar to those of the African American community.

Census statistics and other studies show the Mexican Americans in the Southwest to be worse off in every respect than the non-whites (Negroes, Indians, Orientals). . . . They are poorer, their housing is more crowded and more dilapidated, their unemployment rate is higher, their average educational level is lower. . . . In California, Mexican Americans outnumber Negroes by almost two to one, but probably not one Californian in ten thousand knows that simple fact. (Rowan 1970, 295)

Activists of the Chicano era saw that if the scope of "minority" were enlarged to include Latinos, federal resources could be put to use in Latino barrios. Their intense lobbying spurred President Johnson to send representatives of his administration to El Paso, Texas, in 1967, where they held the first-ever cabinet hearings on Mexican American affairs. A number of federal agency directors and cabinet members listened to speaker after speaker discuss major problem areas for Latinos: health, education, welfare, labor, agriculture, housing, and economic development (Rendon 1970, 307). For the first time, Washington officials were made aware that Latinos could be legitimately considered another minority. The purpose of these and other hearings, goaded by many peaceful demonstrations, was to enroll Latinos in the African American–oriented minority policy agenda: increased War on Poverty funding (Rowan 1970, 295), more federal job hiring, greater participation in the Manpower Development Training programs (Rendon 1970, 318), and more hiring by federally financed contractors. One immediate result of the hearings was the establishment of the Southwest Council for Mexican Americans, whose purpose was to pressure various federal programs to include Latinos in their minority-oriented initiatives (Rendon 1970, 315). "Across the board the barrios of Aztlan are victimized by increasing poverty, unemployment, inadequate education, scarcity of affordable housing, crime, gang violence, drug and alcohol abuse. These social problems threaten to relegate Chicanos to a permanent underclass status" (Navarro 1995, 243).[1]

1. The term "Aztlán" became popularized during the Chicano movement. The historical term refers to the quasi-mythical home of the Aztecs before they journeyed to Tenochtitlan, present-day Mexico City, to found their empire. Activists used the term to refer to the modern-day, heavily Latino region of the U.S. Southwest, to a spiritual "homeland." Some Chicano activists place Aztlán near the Four Corners region of the United States, where Arizona, Utah, New Mexico, and Colorado meet; most recent scholarship places the historical Aztlan closer to today's Mazatlan, on the Pacific coast of Mexico.

Measuring Minority Status

President Richard Nixon once again changed the course of Latino data history when, in 1973, after thirty years of Latino invisibility in official records, he mandated that all federal records begin to include an identifier for "Hispanic." The new definition sidestepped the earlier concerns about the "race" of a largely mestizo Latino population by defining it out of the way, as "a person of Mexican, Puerto Rican, Cuban, Central or South Americana or other Spanish culture or origin, regardless of race" (D. Hayes-Bautista and Chapa 1986, 64). Latinos, finally, had been designated a recognizable group that was not a racial group. Slowly and sketchily at first, federal, state, and local offices began to revise their records systems to include the "Hispanic" entry. Once the data were available that identified Latinos, analysts could see if Latinos exhibited the same kind of social-dysfunction risk factors characteristic of the typical "minority" community.

There is no question that Latinos have been poorly served by the nation's educational structures. In general, the percentage of adults who graduate from high school is a good general indicator of educational status. Low Latino educational attainment can be expressed in a number of other ways as well: average years of schooling, percentage going to college, percentage graduating from college, and so on. But, however it is expressed, there is no denying one basic characteristic: Latino adults have the lowest educational levels of any group of Americans. Figure 4 shows that during the sixty-year period from 1940 to 2000, a consistently lower percentage of Latino adults has graduated from high school than any other group. While African American adults once had a low percentage of high school graduates, by 2000 they had nearly caught up with non-Hispanic whites. Asians, similarly, once had a low percentage of graduates but by 2000 had nearly reached non-Hispanic white levels of high school graduation.

Low income, coupled with high poverty, is another major risk factor mentioned in "minority policy" analyses. Figure 5 shows the percentage of California's population living in poverty from 1960 to 2000. During that period, Latinos consistently had far higher poverty levels than non-Hispanic whites or Asian/Pacific Islanders. Since the mid-1980s, Latinos have had a higher percentage living in poverty than African Americans. Whether measured in percentages living in poverty, household income, or per-capita income, there is no question that Latinos have accessed the smallest portion of the state's economic pie.

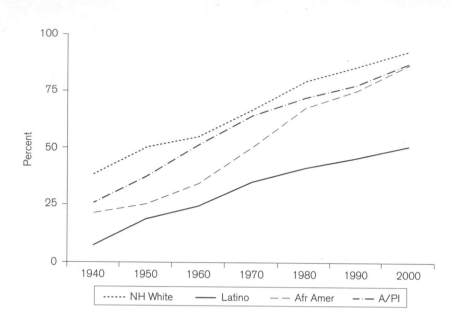

Figure 4. Adults 25+ Graduated from High School, California, 1940–2000. Sources: 1940–80 (CA EDD 1986, 30, tables 12a and 12b); 1990 (D. Hayes-Bautista 1996, 36); 2000 (U.S. Bureau of the Census 2000a).

As Latino-specific information gradually became available after President Nixon mandated "Hispanic" data, it appeared that the Latino population matched the African American population in low educational and income levels. Policy analysts assumed that since the Latino population so closely matched African Americans in the risk factors of low income, poor education, and high poverty, it was logical that Latinos also would match African Americans in terms of other "minority characteristics." This may have been a logical assumption to make, given the nearly complete lack of data on Latinos at the time and the growing conviction that minority problems were largely the result of poverty and low educational levels. By the early 1990s, the General Accounting Office stated unequivocally that Latinos constituted a large portion of the urban underclass.

Minority Health Disparity

Just as the national discourse on poverty in the 1965–75 period tended toward a racialization of poverty, the discourse in health care likewise veered toward racialization of a policy area, although it took longer to develop. The

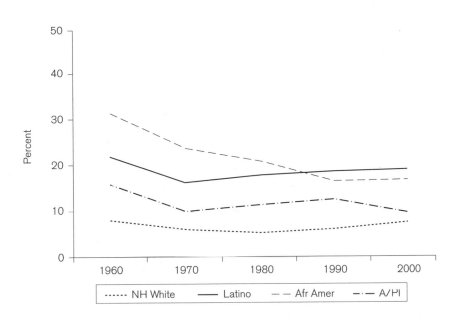

Figure 5. Percentage of Adults Below Poverty Level, California, 1960–2000.
Sources: 1960–80 (CA EDD 1986, 62, tables 24B–24E); 1990 (D. Hayes-Bautista 1996, 30); 2000 (U.S. Bureau of the Census 2000b).

seminal report *Health Status of Minorities and Low-Income Groups* (US DHEW 1979) was an initial attempt to pull together what had been learned about the effects on health status of low income and of being a racial or ethnic minority in the United States. Because Latinos had been eliminated from data collection efforts since 1940, there was almost no information available about Latino health profiles. Tiptoeing around the lack of Latino data, a series of categories were presented in the report that were supposed to include Latinos: "Minority," "Black-and-Other," "Non-White," "Black and Minority," "Racial Minority," "Persons of Color."

No matter how the other-than-white category was denominated, the conclusion was the same: that group suffered from higher mortality rates than whites for nearly all conditions, including heart disease, cancer, stroke, accidents, influenza and pneumonia, diabetes, cirrhosis, and infant mortality. Of the top-ten causes of death listed in that report, in nine categories "minorities" had a higher death rate than whites. Only for suicides was the "minority" rate lower than the white one. "Nonwhites . . . continued to experience an excess mortality, relative to whites, of 39 percent in 1975" (US DHEW 1979, 33).

The report of the Office of Health Resources Opportunity, within the Health Resources Administration, grappled with which was more important—low income or minority status—in determining the poor health status observed in urban, inner-city areas. "We really would like to . . . factor out whether it is membership in the racial/ethnic minority or being poor that determines differential health status" (US DHEW 1979, 23). After much anguish, the report writers came to the following conclusions: (1) members of racial and ethnic minorities tended to live in metropolitan areas, which had poorer health status; (2) members of racial and ethnic minorities tended to have lower incomes than the general population; and (3) members of racial and ethnic minorities tended to have less education than the general population. Gradually, the office began to accept the idea that since minorities were more likely to be disadvantaged, their health was more likely to suffer.

In 1984, Margaret Heckler, secretary of the Department of Health and Human Services, appointed the Task Force on Black and Minority Health, which provided data and information on the health of African Americans and other minority populations living in urban America. The task force also introduced the concept of "excess deaths," those additional deaths in a minority group beyond the number observed in a white population of similar size and age.

Most data available for analysis in the early 1980s only identified whites and African Americans; hence, most of the policy recommendations were based on the white-black comparison. However, other "minorities" were added, on the assumption that low income and low education would have similar effects on their health. In African American populations, nearly half of all deaths in the 1979–81 period were excess deaths, which would not have occurred if this population had fit the white mortality profile. Secretary Heckler extended the African American death profile to other minority groups and expressed her concern that "there was a continuing disparity in the burden of death and illness experienced by Blacks *and other minority Americans* as compared with our nation's population as a whole" (US DHHS 1985a, ix; emphasis added). Her policy response was to establish the Office of Minority Health, charged with removing the disparities in health status between blacks and other minorities and the general population.

The prevailing health model used by the Office of Minority Health in preparing its publications has been the "race/ethnic health disparity model," in which a number of health problems appear to be related to race and ethnicity alone. In 1998, the Office of Minority Health, in its report titled *Eliminating Racial and Ethnic Disparities in Health*, noted, "Compelling evidence that race and ethnicity correlate with persistent, and often increasing, health disparities among U.S. populations" (US DHHS 1998). Continuing in this vein, a recent press release (April 14, 2000) baldly announced: "African American, American Indian/Alaska Native, Asian and Pacific Islander, and Hispanic citizens suffer poorer health and higher rates of premature death than the majority population" (NIH 2000). Since the late 1960s, social policy analysts have concluded that Latinos are a minority group and exhibit all the dysfunctional behavior attributed to minority groups. But this conclusion is wrong.

Minority Fatigue: Seeds of Backlash

When Harrington described the plight of the poor in the early 1960s, America responded with compassion, as well as with practical solutions. While the public watched America's cities burn in the mid-1960s, few dissented openly about the need for policy aimed at minority issues—to save America's cities, if nothing else. Even a Republican president, Richard Nixon (1968–74), embraced the minority policy agenda. In fact, Nixon actually implemented many of Johnson's "Great Society" programs. Affirmative Action, for example, was a major program of the Nixon administration, starting with the Philadelphia Plan that mandated minority participation in unions and construction.

The election of President Ronald Reagan in 1980 signaled a change in social policy direction. Charles Murray's seminal book, *Losing Ground: American Social Policy, 1950–1980* (1984), posed a simple question: Why, after the expenditure of billions of dollars on social welfare programs, were conditions getting worse for minorities? More people were living in poverty, more were on the welfare rolls, families were crumbling, crime was rising, and cities were less safe. He answered that question in a way compatible with the new Republican president's political philosophy: programs such as public assistance were making the situation worse, not better, by subsidizing, possibly even rewarding, dysfunctional behavior. "It was wrong to take from the most industrious, most respectable poor . . . so that we could cater to the least industrious, least responsible poor. . . . [S]tatus was withdrawn from behaviors that engender escape from poverty. . . . [F]or the first time in American history, it became socially acceptable within poor communities to be unemployed" (Murray 1984, 219, 179, 185). A new policy position began to solidify, which emphasized that poor minorities' own behavior contributed to their plight. Drug addiction was not a maladaptive response to alienation caused by poverty; it was a personal choice, which, by driving out decent folk, destabilized neighborhoods. Teenage, unwed pregnancy was not a maladaptive response to poverty but a personal choice that created poverty. In the rising economy of the 1980s—now referred to as the "me decade" or the "greed decade"—unemployment was cast as a personal choice. "The greatest cause of today's poverty may simply be that the attempts in recent decades to equalize opportunity have *failed to persuade many Blacks and Hispanics that it is worth working*" (Mead 1991, 7; emphasis added).

Murray argued that easy access to a wide variety of welfare and medical benefits discouraged people from working and, over time, actually robbed them of initiative. Programs designed to eliminate poverty, the argument went, were creating it. "Underclass poverty stems less from the absence of opportunity than from the *inability or reluctance to take advantage of opportunity*" (Mead 1991, 5; emphasis added). After fifteen to twenty years of policy efforts, the situation did indeed seem worse. Minority need seemed to be a bottomless pit. Worse, rising crime rates and incidents of public disorder—panhandling, urban gangs, graffiti, drug dealing, and so on—were interpreted as the acts of an ungrateful population biting the hand that had fed it. "Minority fatigue" began to set in.

By the presidential elections of 1980, 1984, and 1988, the term "minority" had become a code word for dysfunction. As War on Poverty veterans fought a rearguard action to keep the flame of 1960s compassion alive, their increasingly dire descriptions of the poor and minorities were taken by the Reagan administration as reason to abandon the efforts. For example, there was Lisbeth Schorr's description of minority families in poverty: "These families are so devoid of structure, or organization, they can disorganize *you!* When you leave after a visit, *you* have a headache" (Schorr 1988, 149; original emphasis). Schorr's words were meant to elicit empathy, but they also engendered antipathy and opposition.

Policymakers began to polarize into two camps: the Great Society holdovers, who painted an increasingly negative picture of minority dysfunction in order to argue for more programs, and the Reagan reactives, who used those same portraits to inveigh against lax morals and the erosion of societal standards: "The solution [to poverty] is within the reach of most people. Marriage and family prevent poverty. Schooling prevents poverty. Working at almost any job prevents poverty" (Weidenbaum 1990, D2).

As if to prove the point, an exceptional subcategory of minorities emerged during this period: Asians, the "model minority." The argument held that Asians had suffered terrible discrimination. Chinese had been expelled from California, the Asian Exclusion Act halted Chinese immigration, the Gentleman's Agreement had limited Japanese immigration, and Asians had also been, at times, the target of restrictive covenants. Yet, in spite of discrimination, Asians were succeeding in school, were not involved in public disorder, and did not seem to exhibit the social pathology commonly associated with minority populations. Why couldn't all minorities be more like the Asians? Why did minorities have to have so many problems?

REFRAMING LATINOS

As an undergraduate in the social sciences at UC Berkeley in the 1960s, and later as a graduate student in medical sociology at the UC Medical Center at San Francisco during the early 1970s, I had been taught the prevailing wisdom about minorities and dysfunction. I started my academic career firmly convinced that the models of minority dysfunction were appropriate for understanding Latino patterns of behavior. The low income and poor education so often observed in Latino populations would lead to maladaptive behavior, including low labor-force participation, welfare dependency, disintegrating families, health-harming behavior, greater burden of death, increased infant mortality, greater drug use, and the like. It was only years later, as data for Latinos gradually became available, that I was able to see that this model of minority behavior, which continues even today to undergird most federal-level social policy, is completely inappropriate for most Latino populations.

In 1977, when I was a young assistant professor in the School of Public Health at UC Berkeley, I received a letter from the president of the university, David Saxon, warning of difficult times ahead. The University of California system had been built up during the 1960s, in the expectation that the post–World War II baby boom would continue indefinitely. Yet the much celebrated baby boom ended in 1964; for the first time in nearly twenty years, fewer babies were born that year than in the preceding year. Five years later, fewer children enrolled in kindergarten. By the mid-1970s, the declining enrollments due to the "baby bust" began to be seen in high school enrollments. The drastic drop in high school enrollment was expected, by the fall of 1982, to translate into declining enrollments in the prestigious University of California system. President Saxon promised to do his best to maintain a "steady state" system that would, at least, not shrink. However, he warned, enrollment drops might be so drastic that the university would be forced to contemplate the unthinkable: the closure of one or more of the recently built campuses.

The following year, I was appointed a member of the UC Systemwide Health Sciences Committee, which supervises all health professional education in the UC system (medicine, dentistry, pharmacy, nursing, optometry, and public health). When I attended my first meeting in January 1978, I was struck by how many of the committee members had taken President Saxon's message to heart and had come to the informal consensus—fortunately, never put to a vote—that at least one medical school would have to be closed. As the top-ranked medical schools at UCLA and UC San Francisco could not be touched, the recurring question during the year I was a member of the committee was this: Should we close the medical school at UC Davis, at UC Irvine, or at UC San Diego?

I offered a contrary opinion: the university should not close any schools, because there was likely to be significant school-age population growth in the future. The catch was that the growth would not be in the non-Hispanic white population, but rather in the Latino population. I had difficulty convincing others of my opinion because data on Latinos were still very sparse in the late 1970s. President Nixon had only recently mandated the inclusion of a "Hispanic" identifier on federal forms, and that mandate's implementation was still fledgling. All other population-based data sources indicated that fertility rates among the entire population were falling and that immigration was a thing of the past. I was often asked on what I based my opinion.

From 1970 to 1974, I had been the founding executive director of La Clínica de la Raza, a small, grassroots community clinic founded, in the heat of the Chicano movement, in the Fruitvale District of Oakland, California. The clinic still operates today as a major provider of health services in the East Oakland area. Although reliable data on the health of Latinos—and even census data on them—were virtually nonexistent, I knew firsthand that female patients at La Clínica were giving birth to a great number of babies and seemed to have a much higher fertility rate than non-Hispanic whites. In addition, it was clear that many of La Clínica's patients were recent immigrants. Administrators of other community clinics around the state were reporting a similar pattern of high fertility and significant immigration.

I roughed out a demographic model with sketchy 1970 census data and spotty subsequent birth data, supplemented by my observations on immigration patterns, and saw a disturbing pattern. The non-Hispanic white baby boomers, a huge population numbering some eighty-five million Americans, would start to retire by 2010. The younger working-age population that would have to support their retirement through public (for example, Social Security) or private (pensions, investments, and so on) means likely would be increasingly comprised of Latinos. California seemed to be headed for a future population highly stratified by age and ethnicity; the older, graying population would be largely non-Hispanic white, and the younger population, whose earnings would support the future elderly via either public or private means, would be largely Latino.

When I first announced this pattern publicly, in a paper I gave at a meeting of the American Public Health Association in Los Angeles in the fall of 1978 (D. Hayes-Bautista 1978), I was greeted with disbelief. I was given many reasons why this projected growth was not likely to occur. The data were wrong; immigration had ceased long ago; if there were immigration in 1978, it would soon be stopped; Latino fertility could not *possibly* be as high as I assumed; if it were, it could not possibly continue for more than a year or two. And so on.

As soon as the 1980 census data—the first comprehensive data set to systematically use a Hispanic identifier—were available in 1982, I began to refine those earlier roughed-out demographic projection models. Working with Werner Schink, then of the Employment Development Department, and Jorge Chapa, then a doctoral student at UC Berkeley, I created a set of more precise projections that pointed to one inescapable conclusion: there would be significant growth in the state, largely in the Latino population. In *The Burden of Support: Young Latinos in an Aging Society* (D. Hayes-Bautista, Schink, and Chapa 1988), we provided Latino demographic projections to the year 2030 in California and presented two possible scenarios for a state with a population that by then would be about half Latino. One was a scary, *Blade Runner*-like "Worst-Case Scenario," in which the state would be economically bankrupt, riven by ethnic rivalry, and at the point of civil insurrection. The other was a somewhat Pollyannaish "Best-Case Scenario," in which everything wound up serene and productive, but we did not specify how such a happy state of affairs was to be achieved.

I was unprepared for the negative commentary the book elicited. Criticism was not directed at the methodology; the projections were sound, defensible, and virtually irrefutable. Rather, the criticism was directed at the *fact* of Latino growth. If the state were to become half Latino, so the criticism went, it would be the end of California. Such a poorly educated, poverty-stricken minority population had little to offer the state. The public imagined that Latinos were largely gang members, welfare mothers, high school dropouts, and drug users; some thus feared a significant erosion of non-Latino quality of life. In essence, the criticism ran, if a small "minority" population was bad enough, a state with a "majority-minority" population would be a disaster.

I had to admit that I had not thought about the social effects of Latino population growth. My effort had been limited to creating a set of fairly simple demographic projections. By the time the book was released, I had left UC Berkeley and the East Bay, where Latinos were an extremely small minority population, to take up an appointment at UCLA's School of Medicine and residence in Los Angeles, where 2.9 million Latinos (as of 1986) comprised more than one-third of the county's population (CA DOF 1999). As I watched the English-language eleven o'clock news in the "Southland" every night, I noticed that whenever a Latino was in the news, it was in the usual "dysfunctional minority" context: school dropouts, drug dealers, welfare moms, and the like. Curious about the effects of so many Latinos on society, I embarked on a survey with two colleagues, Aida Hurtado from UC Santa Cruz and Robert Valdez, then at the School of Public Health at UCLA, to see what, if anything, Latinos had to contribute to society.

As we developed a survey—questionnaire items, sampling methods, a data analysis plan—I began to worry about the policy implications of what we might find. What if the public stereotypes of Latinos were actually borne out by the data? What if most Latinos, in fact, were antisocial miscreants? Would our research fuel every anti-Latino group in the state? My professional side was in conflict with my personal convictions. Yet, as a researcher, I wanted to see this project to the end. Even if my research proved the hate groups correct, I had no alternative but to practice the best science possible.

At that time, my wife, María, as part of her work at UCLA's School of Nursing, was engaged in a project concerning drug-exposed infants born in Los Angeles County. One morning, before I began collecting field data, I made my way to her office, planning to join her for lunch. As I waited for her to return from the Academic Computing Center with a run of data, I glanced at her desk, curious about how her project was turning out. There I saw a report, just issued by the Los Angeles County Department of Health Services (1989), on mortality patterns in the county for the year 1985. That report was one of the first to use data that separated Latinos from non-Hispanic whites and African Americans.

My attention was caught by a seemingly anomalous finding: Latino infant mortality was *lower* than that of non-Hispanic whites, and *far lower* than that of African Americans. This favorable statistic contravened all the minority health models I had been taught. I remember thinking, "Well, even if we Latinos turn out to be social misfits, at least we can bear healthy children." Curious, I turned to the section on causes of death and mortality rates. My attention was suddenly and completely riveted by the pattern that emerged from the data. Compared to non-Hispanic whites and African Americans, Latinos had far lower death rates for heart disease, cancer, stroke, and, indeed, nearly every other cause of death (while these data were for 1985, data for 1990 to 2001 are given in Figures 9 to 13 later in this chapter). This highly unexpected result ran counter to the prevailing wisdom about the poor health of minorities.

Puzzled by finding data in an official report that flew in the face of conventional thinking, I dug around María's desk until I found her raw data on drug-exposed infants. A baby born to a drug-using mother is a reportable incident (that is, the attending physician must submit the information to health authorities), and María had collected the birth certificate data of every drug-exposed baby born in the county the previous year. During the late 1980s, much of the public viewed Latino immigrants as drug runners and heavy drug users. What pattern would we see in the drug-exposed infants?

I arrayed her data by ethnicity; then, using the population estimates provided by the LA County Health Department report, I quickly created a comparative cross tabulation. I saw a similar, puzzling pattern: Latina mothers gave birth to drug-exposed infants at only one-third the rate of non-Hispanic white mothers and at about one-tenth the rate of African American mothers. I could not argue with the data. With such a low rate of drug-exposed infants, Latina mothers had to have an equally low rate of drug use.

Lower infant mortality. Fewer heart disease deaths, fewer cancer deaths, and fewer stroke deaths. Lower rates of drug-using mothers. The health profile did not seem to be that of a dysfunctional minority group. Yet Latinos did exhibit the minority pattern of high rates of poverty and poor education. Something did not compute.

Suddenly, I remembered a data source that could provide some additional insight. Although Latinos had been classified as "white" in the 1940 through 1970 censuses, their surnames were recorded, although they had not been much used for analysis. But in 1986 the Bureau of the Census had released a post-coded set of Public Use Microdata Samples (PUMS) from 1940 to 1980, in which Spanish-surnamed individuals were separated out from non-Hispanic whites (CA EDD 1986). I had a copy of that data set at my office and in fact had used it a little to develop the methodology for the survey on which I was about to embark. I rushed to my office—to this day, I still owe María that lunch date—opened up the data set, and saw a pattern that completely changed my thinking about Latinos and their contributions to California society.

LATINO SOCIAL BEHAVIORAL PARADOX

Chronic unemployment; labor-force desertion; loss of a work ethic; welfare dependency; failing families: these key features of the minority urban underclass were reflected in the general media image of Latinos. Would forty years of Latino-coded data prove them true?

A key feature of the urban underclass population is male nonparticipation in the labor force. According to received theory, lacking skills, ambition, and proper attitude, the urban underclass male becomes a "discouraged worker," unemployed for so long that he ceases seeking employment and begins to depend either on welfare programs or on illicit economic behavior, such as drug dealing or crime. At this point, the underclass male has become structurally unemployable.

Labor-force participation was measured by the census for males over sixteen years of age, both those who were employed and those seeking work. In the forty-year period from 1940 to 1980, Latino males consistently had the highest labor-force participation rate of any group, higher than Asian/Pacific Islanders, African Americans, and even non-Hispanic whites. In Figure 6, I have continued the trend line by adding in data from the 1990 census and the 2000 Current Population Survey, to create a sixty-year figure. For nearly three generations, Latino males have been the most active element in the state's labor force.

An indication of attachment to the labor force also can be seen in the measurement of hours worked per week, with the census's top indicator being thirty-five or more hours worked per week. While we lack data for the period 1940 to 1980, in 1990 and 2000, Latino males have been the most likely to work thirty-five or more hours per week.

Employment in the private sector generates wealth, while employment

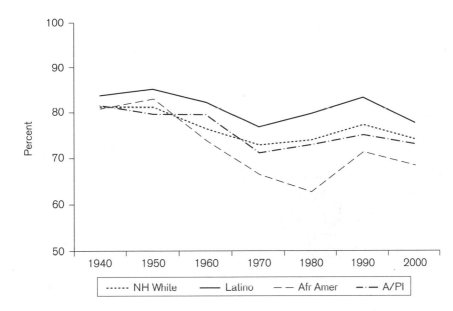

Figure 6. Labor-Force Participation, Male 16+, California, 1940–2000. Sources: 1940–80 (CA EDD 1986, 33–35, tables 13-L, N, P, R); 1990 (UCLA Institute for Social Science Research Data Archives 1996); 2000 (U.S. Bureau of the Census 2000a).

in the public sector basically redistributes wealth. From 1940 to 2000, Latino males counted in the census have been far more likely to be employed in the private sector than non-Hispanic whites, Asian/Pacific Islanders, or African Americans. Again, for nearly three generations, Latino males have been the most active element in the workforce participating in the wealth-generating private sector.

Another key feature of the urban underclass is a heavy welfare (that is, public assistance) dependency. The census provides data about sources of income, including cash income from public assistance. As public assistance is means-tested—that is, one must live in poverty to receive welfare—the welfare usage figure shown in Figure 7 shows those receiving public assistance as a percentage of those living in poverty. In 1990, Latinos had the lowest welfare use of any group; Latinos receiving public assistance represented just 29 percent of all Latinos in poverty. By contrast, in other groups, those receiving public assistance formed a much higher percentage, ranging from 61 percent for non-Hispanic whites to 75 percent for African

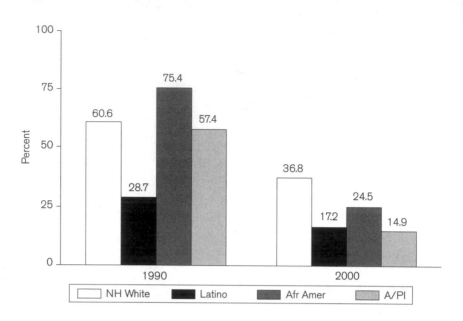

Figure 7. Public Assistance as Percentage of Poverty Population, California, 1990 and 2000. Sources: 1990 (D. Hayes-Bautista 1996, 34); 2000 (U.S. Bureau of the Census 2000b).

Americans. Thanks to welfare reform in the late 1990s, by 2000 the welfare use rates for all groups had dropped. Still, continuing the 1990 picture, a far lower percent of Latinos in poverty received public assistance in 2000 than non-Hispanic whites or African Americans.

The deterioration of the nuclear family in inner cities is another classic feature of the urban underclass. In another surprising reversal of expectations, Latinos in California have the highest percentage of households composed of couples with children. This pattern has held true from 1940 to 2000. In this sixty-year period, Latino households were far more likely than non-Hispanic white, African American, or Asian/Pacific Islander households to be composed of couples with children. It should be noted that there are overall secular trends in household composition, which suggests that, regardless of ethnic variations, larger societal forces are at work. In 1940, just as the United States was leaving the Great Depression, a relatively low percentage of all households was so composed. In the postwar period, the percentage rose for all groups. In the 1950s, for example, nearly half of all African American households were composed of couples with children.

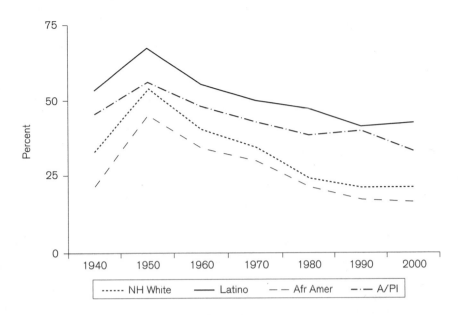

Figure 8. Percentage of Households Composed of Couple with Children, California, 1940–2000. Sources: 1940–80 (CA EDD 1986, 18–20, tables 7B–7F); 1990 (D. Hayes-Bautista 1996, 20); 2000 (U.S. Bureau of the Census 2000b).

Beginning in the 1960s, the percentage fell for all groups, including Latinos. By 2000, the couple-with-children household was a minority in all groups but was more common in Latino and Asian/Pacific Islander households than in either non-Hispanic white or African American households (see Figure 8).

According to current social policy, a vigorous work ethic should prevent poverty among a population. "Poverty is common among non-workers, but is rare among workers" (Mead 1991, 4). Latinos in California contradict the "dysfunctional minority" policy model used by both Republicans and Democrats for the last forty years. Since 1940, Latino males in California have demonstrated the highest labor-force participation, the longest work week, the greatest involvement in the wealth-generating private sector, the lowest use of public assistance, and the greatest propensity to form intact families. In fact, they demonstrate the same social behavior that Murray and other conservative analysts decried as being missing from poor communities.

Yet what has been their reward for such hard work? The highest poverty level of any segment of American society. Latino poverty is not the result of any rejection of societal values regarding work and family. Incongruously, it is the community's reward for their vigorous involvement in an economy that, in the throes of globalization, offers them low wages and few, if any, benefits such as health insurance. While Latino poverty is very much a reality, its cause is not dysfunctional minority underclass behavior.

As a result of these surprising data about California's Latino community, my attitude about the findings in our forthcoming survey began to change. While still concerned about low income and poor education, factors worrisome to all policymakers, I began to consider that perhaps Latinos, as a population, had things to contribute to the state: a strengthening of the work ethic, an independence from welfare, a new injection of family values. I was anxious to see if the pattern continued. Were the trends observed from 1940 to 1980 merely some sort of aberration? Would Latino behavior suddenly change from 1980 to 1990? And if our survey data continued the trends, would they be corroborated by the 1990 census data when the latter were finally released?

In brief, the survey data did show the same demographic trends continuing through 1990 (D. Hayes-Bautista, Hurtado et al. 1992; Hurtado et al. 1992). When the 1990 census data finally became available in 1992 and 1993, they, too, verified the trends. Since then, I have tracked these data in the annual current population surveys, and year after year they continue to hold. In terms of social behavior, Latinos are far from being the antisocial miscreants still shown nightly on the television news.

LATINO EPIDEMIOLOGICAL PARADOX

After an analysis of the 1940 through 2000 census data, a social behavior paradox became obdurate. While all policy models concluded that a low-income, poorly educated population must be socially dysfunctional, the expected dysfunctions were not observed in Latino populations. The health data, however, were not so immediately clear. Health data on Latinos (identified as such) in California had only been collected since the 1980s and were just being reported in the 1990s. Were the Los Angeles County data I had seen on my wife's desk, which contradicted the minority dysfunction model, some sort of local aberration?

Ironically, I had looked at the answer years earlier but had not seen it. When we were preparing the demographic projections for *The Burden of*

Support, we had to develop age-specific death rates in order to make our projections of Latino population growth. We had access to the earliest death certificate data that had identified Latinos, which was from 1980, and we had observed an anomaly that we could not explain. "One particular intriguing pattern is suggested. . . . In 1980 the Latinos had lower death rates, at all ages, than Anglos—in fact they had the lowest of any ethnic group in the state" (D. Hayes-Bautista, Schink, and Chapa 1988, 101). We were not sure these data were accurate, and we suggested that the finding might result from underreporting Latino ethnicity on death certificates or from a large number of Mexicans returning to Mexico to die. We could not explain the seemingly anomalous finding, but neither could we explain it away. We did note that colleagues had seen a similar pattern of low Latino mortality in Texas (Fonner 1975).

Perplexed by the Los Angeles County data, I hunted through state-level health data. Drawing on data files with Hispanic identifiers, I saw the same pattern. In a state with, at that point, 7.6 million Latinos reporting (US DOC 1990, 1), I had a very robust population platform for these patterns. I have continued to track these trends for more than a decade now, and they have remained stable.

Every year, nearly one-quarter of a million persons in California die. Yet, not all groups have had the same mortality rate, which is the number who die in a given year out of every 100,000 persons. There is great variation in the mortality rate, depending on the ethnicity of the group. Figure 9 shows the comparative mortality rates for the eight-year period 1990–98 for Latinos, non-Hispanic whites, and African Americans. Figure 10 shows the rates for 1999–2001. These mortality rates have been adjusted for age, so that the youth of the Latino population and the aging of the non-Hispanic white population have been controlled for. In 2001, the Latino age-adjusted mortality rate for all causes of death was 551.0 deaths per every 100,000 Latinos in the state. The non-Hispanic white age-adjusted rate for all causes was 796.3 deaths per 100,000 individuals, and the African American age-adjusted death rate was 1,092.4 deaths per 100,000. While the "Minority Health Disparity" model would predict Latino age-adjusted rates much higher than those of non-Hispanic whites, and possibly even higher than those of African Americans, because of Latinos' lower income and education, the bald fact is that the Latino age-adjusted death rate is 30.8 percent lower than the non-Hispanic white rate, and 49.6 percent lower than the African American one. In this respect, California is not an unusual state. In fact, in nearly every state with a sizeable Latino population—Arizona,

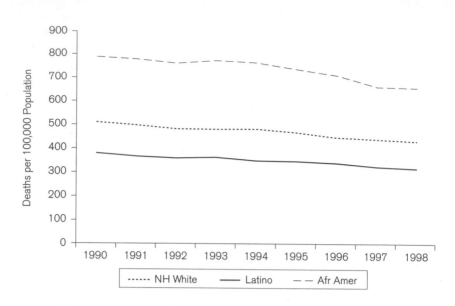

Figure 9. Age-Adjusted Death Rates for All Causes, California, 1990–1998. Source: CA DHS 2003. Age-adjusted using the 1940 U.S. Standard Million.

Texas, Florida, New York, and Illinois—Latinos have a lower death rate than do non-Hispanic whites and African Americans. The only two states where this is not seen are New Mexico and Colorado (D. Hayes-Bautista 2002, 228).

The top-ten causes of death for the year 2000, and the number of deaths due to each cause, are shown in Figure 11. The number-one cause of death in that year was heart disease; more people (68,533) died from some form of heart disease than from any other cause. Cancer (that is, malignant neoplasms) caused the deaths of 53,005 Californians. Strokes (that is, cerebrovascular disease) accounted for 18,090 deaths. These three causes—heart disease, cancer, and stroke—accounted for 61.2 percent of all deaths in the state. The remaining top-ten causes of death, in descending order, were: chronic lower respiratory diseases, accidents, influenza and pneumonia, diabetes, Alzheimer's disease, liver disease, and self-harm. The Latino age-adjusted mortality rates for the top three causes of death are substantially lower than the rates for non-Hispanic whites or African Americans.

For heart disease, the Latino age-adjusted rate of 154.9 deaths for every 100,000 Latinos is 37.6 percent lower than the non-Hispanic white rate of 248.1 and 55.9 percent lower than the African American rate of 351.1 (see

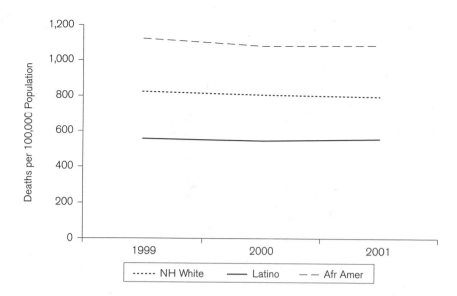

Figure 10. Age-Adjusted Death Rates for All Causes, California, 1999–2001. Source: California Center for Health Statistics 2002. Age-adjusted using the 2000 U.S. Standard Million.

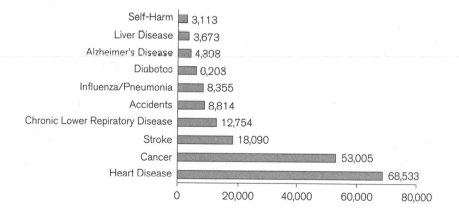

Figure 11. Total Deaths for Top-Ten Causes of Death, California, 2000. Source: CA DHS 2000d.

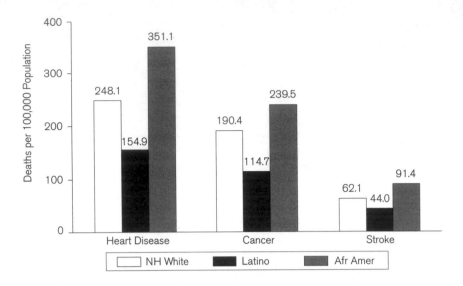

Figure 12. Comparative Age-Adjusted Death Rates for Heart Disease, Cancer, and Stroke, California, 2000. Sources: CA DHS 2000d; CA DOF 1999.

Figure 12). The Latino age-adjusted cancer death rate of 114.7 deaths for every 100,000 Latinos is 39.8 percent lower than the non-Hispanic white rate of 190.4 and 52.1 percent lower than the African American rate of 239.5 (see Figure 12). The Latino age-adjusted death rate of 44.0 deaths from stroke per 100,000 Latinos is 29.1 percent lower than the non-Hispanic white rate of 62.1 and 51.9 percent lower than the African American rate of 91.4 (see Figure 12).

Table 5 compares mortality rates for the top-ten causes of death among non-Hispanic whites, Latinos, and African Americans. The Latino mortality rates are lower than the non-Hispanic white rates for nine of the ten causes and lower than African American rates for all of the top-ten causes of death. With the exception of New Mexico and Colorado, a Latino population anywhere in the United States will have about 25 percent lower age-adjusted death rates than non-Hispanic whites, and about 50 percent lower than African Americans (D. Hayes-Bautista 2002, 228).

I had missed a second chance to make the conceptual break from the Minority Health Disparity model mold about five years before that illuminating morning in my wife's office. In the mid-1980s, I attended an annual meeting of health officers and providers from the border states of Califor-

TABLE 5
Age-Adjusted Rates of Death, California, 2000

	Non-Hispanic White	Latino	African American
Heart disease	248.1	154.9	351.1
Cancer	190.4	114.7	239.5
Stroke	62.1	44.0	91.4
Chronic lower respiratory disease	51.6	16.0	39.8
Accidents	28.2	24.8	29.9
Influenza/pneumonia	30.3	19.6	33.2
Diabetes	17.0	31.1	46.5
Alzheimer's disease	17.8	7.1	15.1
Liver disease	10.9	18.3	11.2
Self-harm	12.2	5.0	6.5

SOURCE: CA DI IS 2000d.

NOTE: Beginning with 2000, the California Department of Health Services shifted from the *International Classification of Diseases,* 9th Edition (ICD-9) to the *International Classification of Diseases,* 10th Edition (ICD-10), so direct comparisons with categories used in earlier years is not possible. In addition, the age-adjusted rates are now calculated using the 2000 Standard Million, instead of the 1970 Standard Million or the 1940 Standard Million, so that direct comparison of rates with earlier years is not possible. The relative differences, however, between Latinos, non-Hispanic whites, and African Americans remain constant, irrespective of disease classification or standard population used.

nia, Arizona, New Mexico, and Texas on the U.S. side, and from Baja California Norte, Sonora, Chihuahua, Coahuila, and Tamaulipas on the Mexico side. Ron Williams, the head of the Maternal and Child Health Research Unit at the University of California, Santa Barbara, had been analyzing the first run of birth certificates using Hispanic identifiers. He presented data that defied the conventional wisdom on minority infant mortality; his study was among the first to demonstrate that Latinas, in spite of high risk factors—low income, poor education, less access to care—had far better infant mortality rates than did African Americans, even better than those of non-Hispanic whites (Williams, Binkins, and Clingman 1986).

Fortune, as we know, favors the prepared mind. Back then, my mind was not prepared. I saw his data, I even asked some questions about them, but in the early 1980s, my mind was unprepared to reframe Latino health. The stranglehold of the Minority Health Disparity model was so strong that I did not see the pattern underneath Williams's data. Five years later, as I looked at the Los Angeles County health data report, I finally understood what he had presented.

Compounding low income and poor education, access to health care has long been considered another risk factor for birth outcomes. The Task Force on Black and Minority Health concluded, "Risk factors associated with poor perinatal outcome among minorities that appear to be related to low socioeconomic status include: low income; limited maternal education; and inadequate health insurance that often reduce access to appropriate medical care" (US DHHS 1985b, 174). That same year, the Health Resources and Services Administration summarized the role of prenatal care in birth outcomes. "It is clear that mothers who seek care early, who have an appropriate number of visits . . . have better outcomes than others" (US DHHS 1985a, 54). Data from the California Department of Health Services show that from 1990 to 1998 Latina mothers in California have been among the most likely to receive late prenatal care, either in the last trimester of pregnancy or not at all (CA DHS 2001b, table 2–11). According to the model of minority health disparities, this should result in very high Latino infant mortality.

Yet the data from California definitely show otherwise. Nearly thirty years of infant mortality data, from 1970 to 2000, show that Latino infant mortality in California is virtually identical to that of non-Hispanic whites. In any given year, the two are very close, with Latino infant mortality lower in some years, and non-Hispanic white lower in others. Non-Hispanic white mothers have the highest education and the highest income, yet Latinas, with the lowest income and least education, have virtually identical infant mortality rates. African American infant mortality is nearly twice as high as either Latino or non-Hispanic white rates (see Figure 13).

In March 2000, the American College of Physicians released a report on minority health, focusing more closely on Latino health. Titled *No Health Insurance? It's Enough to Make You Sick—Latino Community at Great Risk* (American College of Physicians 2000), the report demonstrated that Latinos were far more likely to be without health insurance than non-Latinos. The report went on to extrapolate from this underinsurance that Latinos must necessarily be in poorer health, must suffer from more crippling illness, and must die younger in life. "Because Latinos are more likely to be uninsured, they are at far greater risk than other population groups of . . . poorer health outcomes, increased suffering, and even premature death" (American College of Physicians 2000, 5).

No one can argue against the finding that Latinos are the most likely to

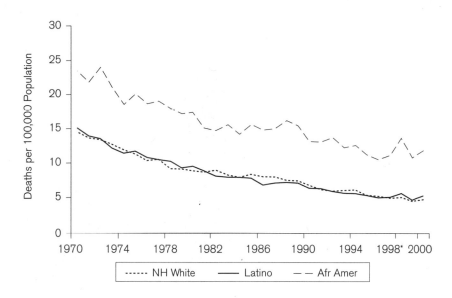

Figure 13. Infant Mortality, California, 1970–2000. Sources: 1970–84 (CA DHS 1989, 130, table 4–3); 1985–92 (CA DHS 1996, 144, table 4–3); 1993–97, 1999 (CA DHS 2000a, table 4–6); 1998 (CA DHS 2002a) (*1998 was calculated using the birth and death records, not the linked birth cohort file); 2000 (CA DHS 2000b).

be without health insurance. Data from birth certificates, the Behavioral Risk Factor Surveillance Survey, and the census's Current Population Survey, as well as numerous private surveys (Brown et al. 2002; Hurtado et al. 1992), all point to the same conclusion: Latinos are the group most likely to be without health insurance.

Yet this lack of health insurance does not necessarily translate into shorter lives for Latinos. In California, a non-Hispanic white baby born in 1995–97 had a life expectancy of—that is, could reasonably expect to live— 77.3 years. An African American baby born in the same period had a shorter life expectancy of 71.1 years, fitting the American College of Physicians' conclusion that urban populations will "live sicker and die younger" (American College of Physicians 2000). Yet Latinos, who now make up the majority of the inner-city population in Los Angeles County, offer a sharply different picture. With a life expectancy of 82.5 years, a Latino baby born in the same period can expect to live more than five years longer than the non-Hispanic white baby and about eleven and a half years longer than the African American baby (see Figure 14).

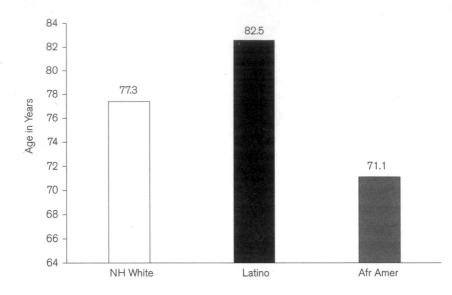

Figure 14. Life Expectancy at Birth, California, 1995–1997. Source: California Center for Health Statistics 1999.

LATINOS AND THE FUTURE OF PUBLIC POLICY

After becoming thoroughly familiar with the health and behavioral data, rather than seeing California's Latinos as a helpless, incapable, fragile, "endangered" species, I realized that Latinos were a robust, dynamic, vigorous population, soon to be a majority, whose basic values and behavior could contribute greatly to strengthening the civic society of California. This view, however was not shared by most researchers and policy analysts.

In the early 1990s, I was the principal investigator on a project funded by the National Institutes of Health (NIH). My project officer was a brainy Latina MD-PhD, a scientist, with an unwavering devotion to the health of minority populations in this country. My research center at UCLA, the Center for the Study of Latino Heath and Culture, had just finished a report on Latino health, with an extensive section on the Latino Infant Mortality Paradox. I thought my colleague might appreciate the data, so I briefed her on them. I thought her reaction as a scientist might help me understand this seemingly paradoxical Latino health profile.

Her first reaction, literally, was to cover the sheets with her arms and to implore me not to show the data to anyone else at NIH. A little shocked, I asked why not. She explained that she had built her career advocating increased funding for prenatal care to underserved populations, and these data would undermine her efforts, which were based on the conviction that lack of prenatal care led to adverse consequences for Latinas and their babies. I replied that it was certainly not my intention to undermine services and that I well knew how underserved Latino communities were (and still are). However, I continued, as scientists involved in policy, did it not make sense to have our policy informed by research? No, she shook her head, these data were not useful and possibly, she hinted, might be faulty. Was I completely sure Latinas had infant mortality as low as that of non-Hispanic white women?

An early criticism of the infant mortality data posited that Latinas did not inform health authorities of a newborn's death but instead took the small bodies back to Mexico in shoeboxes for burial. While this may occur on a very limited basis in border towns, lower Latino infant mortality also occurs in areas far away from the border, such as Los Angeles, Sacramento, Chicago, and New York, from which return to Mexico for a "shoebox" burial would not be feasible. Another early criticism posited that Latinas gave birth at home and hence did not register infant deaths. Again, this may be true in small southern Texas border towns, but nearly all Latinas in large urban settings give birth in hospitals, and home births are extremely rare overall.

Another body of criticism aimed at the general mortality data is that Latinos are misclassified as non-Hispanic whites, so the reported number of Latino deaths is artificially lower than it should be, had they been reported correctly. A close examination of death certificates registered with the National Center for Health and Vital Statistics showed that, at most, there is a statistically insignificant misclassification of Latinos on death certificates (Sorlie et al. 1993; Rosenberg et al. 1999).

The health data are quite obdurate, long-term, and stable. Latino health profiles cannot be described by the Minority Health Disparity model. Yet Washington continues to define Latinos as a minority and to treat them as dysfunctional.

—

As a result of War on Poverty policy efforts, minority populations have been targeted for special federal-level attention, and for forty years their perceived failure to thrive has powered this policy. Whether the dysfunction is the result of external oppression or internal moral failure, dysfunctionality has been assumed for nearly all "minority" populations, with the exception of the "model minority" Asian American populations.

As data have become increasingly available on Latino behavior and health, it has become abundantly clear to me that, while Latinos suffer from poor education and low income, most Latino populations nonetheless exhibit very middle-class behaviors in terms of work, welfare, and the family. In addition, they exhibit extraordinary health behaviors and outcomes. A small body of scholars have recently come to the conclusion that the urban underclass model does not fit the Latino populations found almost everywhere in the United States (Moore and Pinderhughes 1993).

Half the babies born in California now are Latino and will be raised in a Latino family. It should be a priority to understand how those babies' parents, with little education, low income, and miserable access to health care, are able to achieve such consistently outstanding health outcomes. The accomplishments of these Latino babies—how they survive infancy, how well they perform in school, the types of jobs they seek, the businesses they create, the strength of the families they establish, their voting patterns, their support for the arts—eventually will become the statistical "norm" for the state. Understanding Latino social dynamics—health, family, employment, business development, education—is the key to understanding the future of California. Yet they cannot be understood through the minority-dysfunction policy lens. Even though Washington continues to define Latinos as a "minority" group, their actual behaviors and health status do not fit the model of a "minority."

FOUR

Latinos Define Latinos

1975–1990

We [the bank] understand there is an incredibly important group of
people in Los Angeles, New York. We have to become much smarter
about talking to these people. . . . We know that [these] consumers
are different. We have to market differently. . . . We are no longer in
denial.

CESLAC MAGA 1995, 4: Latino executive, banking, 2–3

FROM 1940 TO 1965, Atlantic America defined nearly every aspect of Latino
existence, from race classification, to language usage and access to residential areas, educational opportunities, and career options. From 1965 to
1975, activist Latinos of the Chicano generation rejected those definitions,
but institutional America paid little heed. In fact, from its Washington DC
headquarters, official America stamped Latinos anew, this time as an underclass minority, a definition still used in the early twenty-first century.
But between 1975 and 1990, a new sort of definition began to take shape:
Latinos began to define Latinos. The return of immigrant Latinos provided a new point of departure for defining Latino culture—not, as in the
Chicano era, in relation to white or mainstream culture, but simply in relation to itself.

In the United States, demographic changes, and cultural changes of any
sort, can be tracked by reference to the media giants that so dramatically
shape our perceptions. By the early 1990s, it had become commonplace to
see television advertising aimed at Latinos—confirmation, of a sort, that
Latinos had become a force in American society. By the early 1990s, the
number-one television news program in southern California was in Spanish, and the number-one radio station likewise was broadcast in Spanish.

Latinos had redefined the market in California. And in so doing, they have redefined the nature of being Latino.

LATINOS DEFINE THE FOOD INDUSTRY

Steve Soto, president of the Mexican American Grocers Association for nearly twenty years, grew up in the grocery business. His uncle, Joe Sanchez, opened up a cannery remainders store, La Quebradita, in East Los Angeles in the 1950s. Steve's father, Cal Soto, used his brother-in-law's purchases to stock the shelves of his own mom-and-pop grocery, which opened at the same time. Steve swept the store's floors, stocked shelves, unloaded trucks, and ran the cash register from the time he was ten.

Even in the 1950s, the days of the mom-and-pop store were numbered, as the industry favored larger, more efficient supermarkets and regional chains of supermarkets over small, independently owned, two-or-three store chains. The Sanchez-Soto family expanded from a corner store to a small supermarket, then they acquired a second and a third store, to create a small chain. Yet, as quickly as they evolved, the industry always seemed to be one or two steps ahead. However, contrary to national trends, a specialized niche emerged in South Central Los Angeles. After the Watts riots of 1965, many big chains closed their stores in this and other inner-city areas; from 1965 to 1985, small independent grocers became the only grocery sources for these areas. Nevertheless, although they had a near monopoly in the urban areas, the Sanchez-Soto family, like other Mexican American grocers, were at an increasing financial disadvantage. Because they ordered in relatively small volume, their suppliers demanded cash payment, whereas credit was extended to the larger chains. The Sanchez-Soto stores also often did not receive their stock shipments in time to participate in the industry's weekly specials. The small independents serving largely Latino areas of southern California were frequently not even notified of special promotions, much less invited to participate.

All these practices meant that the independents had to charge higher prices than the large chains, which had in any case abandoned the urban core. The increasingly Latino population of inner-city southern California was paying more money and they had fewer product and store choices. The independent grocers sought to change these policies and provide better conditions for the Latino consumer and grocer alike. The Mexican American Grocers Association (MAGA) brought together the small, independent grocers serving the barrios of southern California to push, prod, and threaten to sue the large distributors and chains until they offered the same facilities to the independents serving Latino communities as they did to the larger chains serving non-Hispanic white areas. As the first MAGA president and CEO, Steve Soto quickly formed a large coalition of stores, based not on ownership—some of the most successful independent chains were not run by Latinos—but on clientele. The Latino consumer had to be as well served as the non-Latino consumer. And, in any event, a funny thing happened on the way to civil rights and equal opportunity: the Latino market exploded in size.

A firm believer in the market economy, Soto expanded MAGA's objective from advocating equal access to credit and shipments, to applying marketing principles to the Latino market. The MAGA member stores rode the growing wave of Latino grocery purchases to an unprecedented level of sales; the food product preferences of the increasingly immigrant Latino families became the basis of profitability for these stores (CESLAC MAGA 2003: Steve Soto, 2). Latino food consumers contradict classic consumer models. Although Latino consumers on average earn 24 percent less than non-Hispanics and have far lower education levels (40 percent lower), they spend 18 percent more than non-Hispanics in the checkout line (US BLS 2002).

But Latino food purchases are not 18 percent greater for all items; there is tremendous specificity, with some items more likely to be purchased by Latino consumers, and other items far less likely. Figure 15 provides an overview of Latino food purchase patterns. Latino consumers are from 42 to 50 percent more likely than non-Hispanics to purchase fresh food items: fresh meats, fresh fruits, and fresh vegetables. A very different pattern is seen regarding processed foods, such as canned and frozen products. Latino consumers are far less likely than non-Hispanics to purchase these (see Figure 15). Latino disposable income in the United States grew during the 1975–90 period, to reach $207.5 billion in 1990 (Humphreys 2000, 14), nearly three-fourths of the entire Gross Domestic Product of Mexico of $266 billion during that same period (Wilkie, Alemán, and Ortega 2001, 1005, table 3404). In fact, by 2001, the U.S. Latino buying power of $452.4 billion had become nearly as large as the entire GDP of Mexico. It was something of a shock to the Food Marketing Institute to discover, in 1993, that salsa now outsold catsup and that tortillas outsold white bread, in dollar value amounts, in the United States (Davila 2001).

The changing consumer base was taken seriously by Von's, a large supermarket chain in southern California. That company's president and

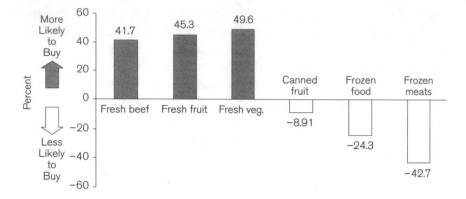

Figure 15. Latino Food Purchase Preference Compared to Non-Latino, United States, 2000. Source: US BLS 2002, table 1701, unpublished data estimates.

CEO, Bill Davila, prided himself for being in touch with customers; indeed, he personally invited customers into his stores in English-language radio ads that ran in the 1980s. Being Latino doubtless sensitized him to the rapid changes in the chain's customer base. In 1986, according to Steve Soto, Davila surprised the industry by featuring his own voice in a Spanish radio commercial. But Davila did more. He visited supermarkets in Mexico, visited the small independent chains in California, invested in research, and, in 1988, opened a subchain, Tianguis, a fifteen-store group located in heavily Latino areas, which emphasized Latino products and services. The very name reflected an insider's knowledge of Latino shopping habits: *tianguis,* a word of Náhuatl origin, denotes the small, weekly, open-air farmers' markets of Mexico.

The aroma of freshly made tortillas and *bolillos* (small bread rolls) filled the air. A large, colorful selection of vegetables such as *nopales* (a type of edible cactus) and *jícama* (a root vegetable) and fruits such as *chirimoya* and *membrillo,* uncommon in the big chain supermarkets, spilled out of the bins. Meat was cut in ways rarely found in non-Latino areas. Imported products from Mexico and Central America—soap, soup stocks, preserves, candies—were available in great quantity. On Friday and Saturday evenings, strolling mariachi bands and trios played. Tianguis elevated the shopping experience to a new level for the previously ignored Latino customer, and its success blew the small independents out of the water.

A competing chain, Fiesta, opened its own specialty supermarkets, seeking a competitive advantage in the growing Latino market. The battle between these two giants took its toll on the independents. Unable to compete in the areas of volume, prices, and amenities, some independents moved to underserved areas; others simply went out of business. Steve Soto wryly comments that all MAGA's efforts to bring corporate America to the barrios had succeeded beyond his wildest dreams and Mrs. Gomez now had access to low prices and special promotions—but his own independent grocery stores had paid the price (CESLAC MAGA 2003: Steve Soto, 5).

DEMOGRAPHICS OF SELF-DEFINITION

The demographics of fifteen years, from 1975 to 1990, changed the course of California social history, and did so in such a quiet way that the transition was not even noticeable at first: it all came down to the fact that mothers giving birth in the delivery rooms and their newborn babies in the state's bassinets were increasingly Latino. At the beginning of this period, the Latino population was still considered a small minority. At 3.5 million in 1975, it was barely 16 percent of the state's total population. In just fifteen years, by 1990, it had exploded in size, growing to over 7.8 million, more than 25 percent of the state's population (CA DOF 1999). Everything else followed from that.

The Latino immigration boom of the 1970s and 1980s did not come from out of nowhere. Most immigrants were formerly involved in the bracero program, which from 1942 to 1964 had brought hundreds of thousands of Latinos to work in agribusiness to provide the essential labor for the industry that has consistently generated more state income than all of Hollywood's pictures. As they changed status from bracero to immigrant, these farmworkers were able to bring their wives and children. Central Americans fleeing civil strife augmented immigrant numbers. For the first time since 1930, Latino barrios in East Los Angeles, East San José, Fresno, and Oakland saw immigrant Latinos establishing households in areas initially settled, in some cases, as long ago as 1769.

An immediate effect of the immigrant Latino-driven growth was that the Latino population became, overall, more "immigrant" in its composition. After the massive deportations of the 1930s, immigrants had become a small part of the Latino population. As recently as 1960, only 19.4 percent of the state's Latinos were immigrants (CA EDD 1986, 10). However, the arrival of hundreds of thousands, then millions, of Latino immigrants caused a shift in the community's composition. Figure 16 shows that, in 1970, nearly

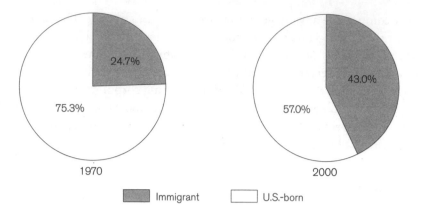

Figure 16. Immigrant and U.S.-born Portions of Latino Population, California, 1970 and 2000. Sources: 1970 (CA EDD 1986, 10, table 2C); 2000 (U.S. Bureau of the Census 2000a).

one out of every four Latinos was an immigrant. By 1990, the percentage of immigrants in the Latino population peaked at 44.7 percent (D. Hayes-Bautista 1996, 40), dropping by 2000 to 43 percent of all Latinos (U.S. Bureau of the Census 2000a).

Latino immigration can be characterized by two features that make its presence loom larger than mere numbers would indicate. First, immigrant Latinos are nearly always young adults, between fifteen and thirty years of age; few children, few middle-aged, and almost no elderly Latinos immigrate. This is a very important age in social dynamics; it is when young people begin to form families and create households.

Second, immigrant Latinas have very high fertility rates. Among the U.S.-born Latina population, fertility had dropped to replacement level (that is, the number of births equaled the number of deaths), and little net growth (natural increase) occurred. Immigrant Latinas have a fertility level far above replacement (that is, many more births than deaths, a high natural increase), so that there has been net population growth.

In 1975, there were 83,638 Latino babies born, constituting just 26.5 percent of all babies born in the state. By 1990, 229,244 Latino babies—more than 38.6 percent of all births—were born. Figure 17 shows the changes in the racial and ethnic composition of babies born in California, year by year, from the beginning of that period to the end. In 1975, non-Hispanic white births predominated; nearly two-thirds (61.3 percent) of all babies were in

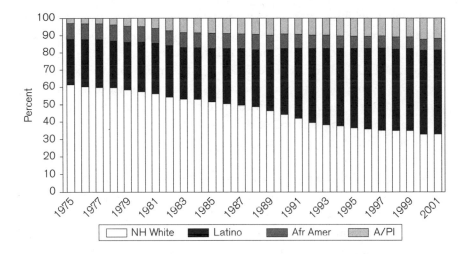

Figure 17. Composition of Births, by Year, California, 1975–2001. Sources: 1975–89 (CA DOF 1999); 1990–99 (CA DOF [2001b]); 2000–2001 (California Center for Health Statistics 2002).

this group. By 1990, they accounted for only 43.7 percent of all babies born, just slightly more than the Latino representation of 38.6 percent. The African American percentage remained nearly constant, dropping slightly from 8.9 to 8.1 percent, while the Asian/Pacific Islander percent grew from 3.0 to 9.1 percent (CA DOF 1999). Continuing the trend after 1990, by late 2001, Latino births were over half (50.6 percent) of all births in the state, while non-Hispanic white births were under one-third (30.4 percent) (Hayes-Bautista et al. 2003). In twenty-five years, Latino births had gone from being a minority to becoming over half of all births; non-Hispanic white births dropped from a nearly two-thirds majority to a minority, around one-third of all births.

IMMIGRANT LATINO BEHAVIORS

The growing immigrant Latino population changed the community by creating a cultural environment woven from more "typically Latino" behaviors and attitudes. If Latinos overall presented a paradox to the "minority model" of behavior, immigrant Latinos heightened and emphasized the paradox. With lower levels of education and income, the immigrants nevertheless exhibited even higher rates of labor-force participation and family formation, and lower rates of welfare usage, than U.S.-born Latinos. In the following section, the marked differences between U.S.-born and immigrant Latino patterns of behavior will be shown for two years, 1990 and 2000. While the latter year will be discussed in greater detail in chapters 6 and 7, the data are provided here to demonstrate how stable the differences are in the patterns of behavior. The year 1990 was not an unusual one. Rather, it typified the differences between U.S.-born and immigrant Latinos.

A key tenet of the urban underclass model is that low educational levels and low income lead, almost inevitably, to socially undesirable behaviors. While Latinos have consistently had both low income and low education, they do not demonstrate "typical" dysfunctional behavior.

Immigrant Latinos had, and continue to have, far lower educational levels than U.S.-born Latinos. At the beginning and the end of the 1990s, immigrant Latinos were about half as likely as U.S.-born Latinos to have graduated from high school (see Figure 18). In 1990, about two-thirds of U.S.-born Latino adults had graduated from high school, and by 2000, nearly three-fourths had done so. By contrast, in 1990, less than one-third of immigrant Latino adults had graduated from high school, and by 2000 only slightly more than one-third had done so.

In a similar fashion, a far lower percentage of immigrant Latinos graduated from college than U.S.-born Latinos (for a preview, see Figure 36, on page 222). However educational attainment is measured, immigrant Latinos show far less education than the U.S-born. Yet this lower educational level did not translate into socially undesirable behaviors.

Another key tenet of the urban underclass model is that poverty leads to dysfunctional behavior. Overall, Latinos have had higher poverty levels than any other group. And immigrant Latinos have had even higher poverty levels than U.S.-born Latinos. In 1990 and in 2000, immigrant Latino households were nearly two times as likely as U.S.-born Latino households to have incomes below poverty levels (see Figure 19). Conclusively, immigrant Latino households can be described as having far less income and education than U.S.-born Latino households. Yet these greater risk factors do not translate into urban underclass behaviors: in fact, immigrant Latinos show far stronger behaviors than U.S.-born Latinos with higher educations and higher incomes. The Latino Social Paradox is heightened by immigrant Latino behaviors.

Despite their high poverty and low education levels, Latino males have

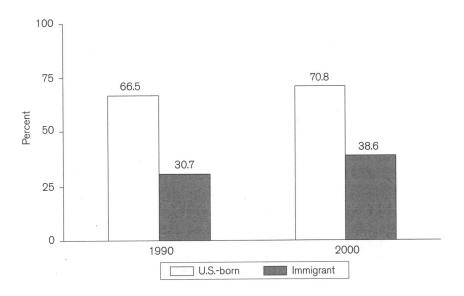

Figure 18. Latino High School Graduates, Adults 25+, U.S.-born and Immigrant, California, 1990 and 2000. Sources: 1990 (D. Hayes-Bautista 1997, 31); 2000 (U.S. Bureau of the Census 2000a).

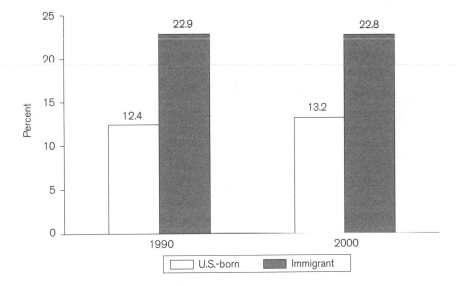

Figure 19. Percentage of Latino Adults Below Poverty Level, U.S.-born and Immigrant, California, 1990 and 2000. Sources: 1990 (D. Hayes-Bautista 1997, 33); 2000 (U.S. Bureau of the Census 2000b).

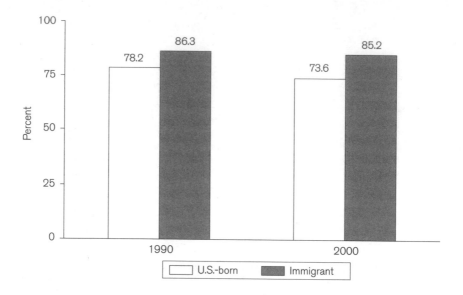

Figure 20. Labor-Force Participation, Latino Male 16+, U.S.-born and Immigrant, California, 1990 and 2000. Sources: 1990 (UCLA Institute for Social Science Research Data Archives 1996); 2000 (U.S. Bureau of the Census 2000a).

consistently had a higher labor-force participation than the non-Hispanic white, African American, and Asian/Pacific Islander males, for the sixty-year period from 1940 to 2000 (refer to Figure 6 on page 75). Immigrant Latino males have had an even higher rate of labor-force participation than U.S.-born Latino males. In both 1990 and 2000, while U.S.-born Latino males had a respectable labor-force participation rate, immigrant Latino males had an even higher rate (see Figure 20). They are even more likely than their U.S.-born counterparts to work in the private sector and more likely to work thirty-five or more hours per week (U.S. Bureau of the Census 2000a).

If one approaches immigrant Latino labor-force characteristics from the perspective of the urban underclass, this evidence of a greater work ethic seems surprising, given the low educational and income levels. However, from the perspective of employers in California for the last few decades, this work ethic is considered by many employers a normal character of immigrant Latino males; and, as the U.S. ambassador to Mexico, Jeffrey Davidow, pronounced in an economic summit held in Michoacán in 2000, it

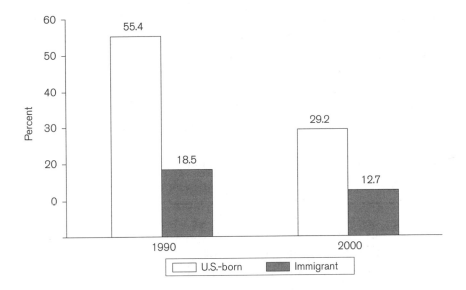

Figure 21. Public Assistance as Percentage of Poverty Population, U.S.-born and Immigrant Latino, California, 1990 and 2000. Sources: 1990 (D. Hayes-Bautista 1997, 36); 2000 (U.S. Bureau of the Census 2000b).

undergirds key segments of the California economy, especially agriculture (Gutiérrez 2000, 1).

In general, Latinos do not exhibit the greater use of welfare predicted in the urban underclass model by their low educational and income levels. And immigrant Latinos, with lower education and income than U.S.-born Latinos, demonstrate even lower levels of welfare usage. Welfare is "means tested"—that is, one must demonstrate low income in order to be eligible—so its use can be measured as a percent of all those who live in poverty. Using this metric, immigrant Latinos in 1990 and 2000 showed a welfare use rate that is less than half that of U.S.-born Latinos (see Figure 21).

In spite of lower income and education, Latinos overall showed the highest rate of households composed of the classic married couple with children. Immigrant Latino households were nearly twice as likely as U.S.-born Latino households to be composed of the classic nuclear family in 1990 and 2000 (D. Hayes-Bautista 1997, 35; US BLS 2002; U.S. Bureau of the Census 2000a, 2000b).

Nor do the higher risk factors for the Latino population lead to disastrous health outcomes. Instead, Latinos in California exhibit the "Latino Epidemiological Paradox," in which their health is actually far better than that of non-Hispanic whites, even though the latter have far better income, education, and access to health care services. Continuing the trend seen in the work ethic and family formation, immigrant Latinos, even though faced with greater risk factors—lower income and education—than U.S.-born Latinos, show even better health. Infant mortality rates provide one indicator of this unexpected differential. During the thirty-year period from 1970 to 2000, Latinos had an infant mortality rate virtually identical to that of non-Hispanic whites, and far lower than that of African Americans (refer to Figure 13 on page 85). Immigrant Latinas, with far lower education and less access to prenatal care than U.S.-born Latinas, fared even better. In 2000, immigrant Latinas had a lower infant mortality rate (4.8 deaths per 1,000 live births) than U.S.-born Latinas (5.8 deaths), one equal to that of non-Hispanic whites (4.8 deaths per 1,000 live births) (see Figure 22).

Not only were immigrants a growing portion of the Latino adult population in the 1975–90 period, but also they strengthened patterns of behavior that were already typical of Latino populations and that were in contradiction of those predicted by the urban underclass model:

highest levels of labor-force participation

lowest levels of welfare use

highest levels of family formation

healthiest babies

In short, immigrant Latinos reemphasized the very paradoxical Latino patterns of behavior described in chapter 3.

Older U.S.-born Latinos remember when public use of Spanish was actively discouraged and bilingualism was considered a liability. Few U.S.-born Latinos of that generation were able to speak Spanish fluently. Spanish appeared to be headed toward the same fate that other American immigrant languages—such as Italian, Greek, Swedish, and German—had suffered. The loss of Spanish among Latinos in the postwar period was so high that, in 1988, Barrera noted that "the 'struggle of cultural survival' . . . is rapidly being lost" (1990, 5), and he suggested the establishment of politically distinct "ethnic autonomous regions" where young Latinos could pursue their distinctive "music, art, literature, food [and] styles of dress" (Barrera 1990, 158).

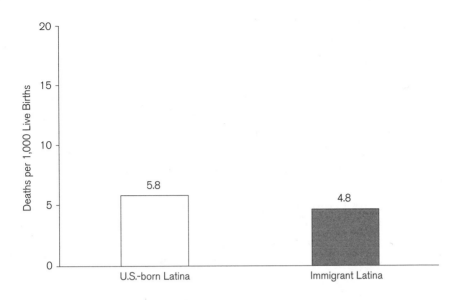

Figure 22. Infant Mortality, U.S.-born Latina and Immigrant Latina, California, 2000. Source: CA DHS 2000b.

The immigration of 1965–90 changed that dynamic, perhaps permanently. As the immigrant presence increased from less than one out of every five Latinos in 1960 (CA EDD 1986, 10) to nearly one out of every two in 1990 (D. Hayes-Bautista 1997, 28), Spanish became the preferred language of half the Latino population. Among immigrant Latinos aged forty to forty-nine years, 76.6 percent spoke primarily Spanish. By comparison, U.S.-born Latinos of the same age were nearly completely English-dominant; only 12.8 percent spoke Spanish to any extent.

Immigrant Latinos, by 1990, usually had completed elementary school (UCLA Institute for Social Science Research Data Archives 1996) prior to immigrating, exposing them to years of formal education in their country of origin, which was primarily Mexico, but also the Central American countries. There they had been exposed to narrative, poetry, theater, music, art, and history. As a result, they reintroduced contemporary Latin American culture to California. Comfortable with their culture, immigrant Latinos did not exhibit the anguish of the Chicano generation about what a "real" Latino would do. Eating a hamburger was not seen as an act of cultural genocide. Speaking Spanish was not an act of cultural defiance. Listening to music in Spanish was not a political choice.

Because of their age and fertility, immigrant Latinos increasingly became the population that created families and underwent the nesting process. Increasingly, immigrant Latinos were the ones who bought or rented houses and fixed them up, furnished them, purchased food regularly, clothed their children, gave them toys, saw them off to school, dealt with the problems of teenagers. Their focus was intensely domestic. Their hopes, dreams, and fears for their families became the norm for young families in the area. As one United Way focus-group participant expressed her perspective, *"Queremos superarnos, queremos tener una casa, queremos tener un buen trabajo, queremos que nuestros hijos vayan a la universidad"* [We want to get ahead, we want to have a house, we want to have a good job, we want our children to go to college] (CESLAC UW 1998, 5: Immigrant Latinos, 6). They pursued their dreams, often dreaming in Spanish and using Mexican and Latin American cultural references to make those dreams come true.

BUSINESS AND THE LATINO MARKET

As with the grocery industry, other businesses that catered to the needs of these young immigrant families began to see their bottom lines improved by Latino purchasing decisions. By 1990, most industries in the state were at least thinking about marketing products and services to Latinos. As businesses moved to accept the Latino market, they often had to modify their products and services to better suit the Latino market's tastes, desires, and demands.

By 1990, the annual Mexican American Grocers Association conference had attracted a following among Latinos working in large food and beverage corporations. Corporations in various aspects of the food and beverage industry—soft drinks, fresh produce, processed meats, snack foods, breakfast cereals, soups, and detergents—and others sent their Latino executives to the conference, held each winter in sunny Palm Springs. Many of these Latino executives shared frustrations about their corporations' indifference to growing Latino markets. By 1992, these informal "gripe sessions" had tipped Steve Soto to the fact that all was not well with Latino executives in corporate America. At the behest of MAGA, he asked the staff at CESLAC to undertake a research project that would help them understand how American corporations approached the burgeoning Latino market. This is what we learned from Latino executives of these firms during our research.

Latino Market Denial

Although the study was not quantitative, nearly all the participating Latino executives had, at least once in their careers, chafed under the situation we came to label "Latino market denial," which is the collective conclusion by other, usually non-Latino, executives in their corporations that a viable Latino market simply does not exist. As one participant in the study observed, "Twenty percent of corporations are not going to do anything [in the Latino market], no matter what statistics we present. They've already made their minds up. . . . Presentations are exciting [but] often fall on deaf ear [sic]" (CESLAC MAGA 1995, 2: Latino executive, processed meats, 1–2). Therefore, these executives told us, corporations suffering from Latino market denial would not engage in the market research necessary to understand this new market. In a vicious cycle, the lack of investments would keep the company from developing the understanding it would need to approach these potential customers. "My company does not have an ethnic marketing department or even anyone focused on that piece" (CESLAC MAGA 1995, 3: Latino executive, soaps and detergents, 6).

The most virulent form of Latino market denial was physical rejection; when faced with the prospect of a growing Latino customer base, in a few instances corporations would take steps to keep Latinos away from their stores, out of fear of driving away the "good" customers. "When people don't know the first thing about the Hispanic market, they believe if we advertise in Spanish, we're advertising to a group of illegal people, and they have to consider, 'What do other people think of us? What impression does this make on other people who don't like illegals?'" (CESLAC MAGA 1995, 7: Latino executive, food and beverage, 5). When the Latino population began to move out of the barrios of East Los Angeles into areas previously closed to them, some grocery chains preferred to close their stores in the areas that had just "turned" Latino rather than meet the needs of the new customer base. "My company simply bought its first store [in the Los Angeles area], and the one they bought just happened to be in a Latino marketplace. They didn't realize what they were in" (CESLCA MAGA 1995, 6: Latino executive, food industry, 2).

The rejection sometimes was psychological. Some corporate executives feared the Latino customer base, succumbing to the media-driven stereotypes of Latinos. "You're trying to convince people who come to L.A., stay in Bel Air, and don't dare get east of downtown [to the Latino neighborhoods].

They're afraid for their lives. They think, 'If I go out there, I'm going to get shot; people will carjack me'" (CESLAC MAGA 1995, 7: Latino executive, food and beverage, 18). Of course, some store owners did not have the option of moving out of newly Latino neighborhoods, but the rejection still could be heard in their comments. I recall that in a workshop we facilitated for MAGA, one advertising salesperson told of a small-business owner who refused even to consider placing an ad in Spanish-language media, for fear that the Latino customers it attracted would shoplift him out of business.

Many of our interviewees' non-Latino colleagues had grown up with the typical stereotypes of Latinos, presented over decades on nightly news programs. Convinced that the urban underclass model of social dysfunction applied to Latinos, they based business decisions involving billions of dollars on these stereotypes. "It's extremely difficult to get the top ten to twenty VPs to accept that this is a vital, growing segment, it has money, they're not all welfare-living, drug-taking, baby-having heathens. But that's really what some think of us" (CESLAC MAGA 1995, 7: Latino executive, food and beverage, 18–19).

A less intense form of Latino market denial involves minimizing, in which a business does not believe that the Latino market is important to the company's bottom line. "Business is emotional, to a certain extent. . . . A business decision may be made on the assumption that a Hispanic consumer is on welfare, and it may not ever be pulled out [and examined rationally]" (CESLAC MAGA 1995, 1: Latina executive, food and beverage, 4, 7). Believing that the Latino market was not important, these companies would continue the practice of not giving priority to Latino market research, thereby stunting the growth of the knowledge base needed to engage that customer base. "[Hispanic marketing] takes a back seat to regular product development, regular product marketing, a new-item introduction. All those things come before you get to Hispanic marketing as a focus. So, in terms of focus, it's a very low priority" (CESLAC MAGA 1995, 3: Latino executive, soaps and detergents, 16).

Latino Market Confusion

Some Latino executives saw that their companies had moved out of Latino market denial but had not yet been able to move proactively to engage this population. They described confusion, dithering, vacillation. "Many companies jumped on the wagon and said, 'I don't know what we're going to do, but we've got to do something. And fast'" (CESLAC MAGA 1995, 1:

Latina executive, food and beverage, 8). These corporations could see that the Latino market had potential but did not know how to engage it. Ignorance of Latino habits was often cited as a reason for the confusion. "They know it [the Latino market] is viable, but they don't have the internal expertise to make anything happen" (CESLAC MAGA 1995, 3: Latino executive, soaps and detergents, 6).

As the Latino market took off in the 1980s, a few "gazelle" corporations—that is, those who spring quickly to the head of a herd—became quite profitable by successfully engaging it. Those in the confusion stage would hear of such success stories but could not figure out how to achieve similar results. At times, companies would spend money on a few research projects but without any strategic planning. Some jumped into ill-advised activities that burned cash but produced few tangible results. Some Latino executives felt that the public failure of some noted Latino marketing attempts poisoned the well for their own efforts. "A lot of companies are looking to make a buck. What they find is that the investment can be extensive, and the return is long-term, not short-term. The difficulty is to get people to continuously make the effort. Those who have deeper pockets reap it. Others, who do it [Latino marketing] haphazardly, have created problems in the marketplace" (CESLAC MAGA 1995, 2: Latino executive, processed meats, 1). Latino executives estimated that perhaps the majority of companies in California were in the confusion stage.

Companies transitioning from the confusion stage entered the contemplation phase; although they saw the Latino market as viable, they realized that they were woefully unprepared to engage it. At the contemplation phase, Latino executives felt that it was their job to shepherd their colleagues through to full acceptance. They could best do this, they reported, by providing the information their colleagues needed to make decisions. Despite being rational businessmen working in large, rational corporations, they described a surprising amount of emotional "hand-holding," helping their colleagues overcome stereotypes and fears.

[The ones] who run these businesses are people . . . [who] get their experience on Latinos from the media. . . . Our job is really hard, to break down the stereotypes and biases. . . . Not only does this guy "know" that, he feels in his heart that these people are bad news. . . . You need to feed in [Latino market] numbers on one side, and on the other are the emotional things you have to work on. (CESLAC MAGA 1995, 7: Latino executive, food and beverage, 18, 10)

Latino executives in contemplation-stage companies, however, did feel confident that they could move their organizations to acceptance.

Latino Market Acceptance

Finally, an increasing number of Latino executives claimed that their companies had come to accept the Latino market; these organizations realized that they must be competitive in that segment to survive in the new California. The sheer growth in population numbers and purchasing power had won some companies over. At the initial stages of acceptance, companies aimed just to get their fair share of the Latino market. "[The Latino market] is growing [in] population and in income, and we are taking [an] aggressive approach toward that market. . . . We know we have to do something, and we are taking those steps to address it" (CESLAC MAGA 1995, 1: Latina executive, food and beverage, 2–3).

Once the increased sales showed on the bottom line, however, many wanted to go after more. Once budgets had been committed to it, the decision to pursue the Latino market was serious. "Embracing is when a company says, 'Okay, I see it, I believe in it. I'm going to go for it, and spend what it takes to get that business'" (CESLAC MAGA 1995, 7: Latino executive, food and beverage, 15).

In most Latino-committed businesses, at least one senior executive, or one business unit—usually the sales unit, initially—led the way. "[The] CEO worked in . . . Latin America . . . [and] always had an appreciation for the Latino culture. He knew what he wanted. . . . [It's not just] a matter of information. It's a matter of *attitude in key positions,* [executives] who have lived it and understand it" (CESLAC MAGA 1995, 4: Latino executive, banking, 10, 21; emphasis added).

A small number of Latino executives worked for companies that had decided to be the dominant presence in their industry in Latino markets. Such a position requires a significant investment, and these Latino executives described their companies as enthusiastically making such commitments, not only in marketing—finding Latino ad agencies, cultivating Latino product endorsers, buying time on Spanish-language television and radio—but also in product-line development; Latino markets are simply not receptive to some products (for example, sauerkraut). "Everyone else, of course, thinks the same thing, so you have to differentiate yourself from the competitors. . . . Other companies are spending more just to catch up with us. As the pie gets bigger, if we don't spend more, our slice of pie gets smaller. If we want to outdistance the competitors, then we have to spend faster than the pie is growing" (CESLAC MAGA 1995, 7: Latino executive, food and beverage, 7–8). While companies in the denial or confusion stages might shrink from redefining their core business, companies in the acceptance stage made full investments in redefining their product and service lines.

The extreme form of acceptance is affiliation with the Latino market; a company sees that its future is tied to the Latino market. No longer a foreign, unknown "them," the Latino market was seen as, and more importantly felt to be, part of the larger community in which the company functioned. In the cases recounted to date, affiliation was achieved when top-level executives felt comfortable with the Latino market. The top executive did not necessarily have to be Latino but did have to have significant experience with Latino markets; in international corporations, a Latin American posting often provided that connection. Such executives usually hired Latino vice presidents in order to give decision-making to those who had a "feel" for the market and its tastes. "[The] top cookie [in this bank] grew up in Mexico, grew up in [a banking corporation], always knew that South America was [the bank president's] favorite place. A lot of Latinos in the bank [are] doing extremely well" (CESLAC MAGA 1995, 4: interpolation by non-Hispanic white female executive, banking, 12). The Latino executive respondents were nearly unanimous in estimating that only a small proportion of corporations had moved to the full acceptance and competitive stages.

As the young adult demographic in the state became increasingly Latino from 1975 to 1990, the musical tastes of young adults increasingly came to reflect the tastes of immigrant Latinos. Perhaps it was inevitable that a growing consumer base with an ever-increasing discretionary income would support the local musical industry. A new musical genre that developed in California swept the Southwest and had a "blowback" effect in Mexico.

Although Latino consumers had a wide array of musical options available to them—classic mariachi, *norteña* music (from northern Mexico), and standard Latin American pop music—many rural immigrants were partial to a danceable style of music played by brass bands in the village squares back home. The city of Zacatecas in Mexico takes credit for developing this style, which features a lively polka beat and a bouncing tuba bass line, called *banda*. Bands in California took that basic style, updated it with electronic instruments, and called it *techno-banda*.

In 1992, few FM stations played Latino music. Heftel Music had just acquired an FM signal and wanted to carve out a niche. On a hunch by the musical programmer, who once had been an undocumented Latino immigrant himself, the station was the first to pick up the new techno-banda format and play it, along with more traditional banda songs, round the clock. KLAX tapped a consumer vein that had been ignored until then, and in a matter of months, it became the number-one station in Los Angeles (Puig 1993).

Banda music was itself quite a social phenomenon, an indigenously developed alternative to the *cholo* "gangbanger" ethos of baggy pants and lowriders. Banda youth did not glamorize violence and did not get involved in spiraling rounds of gang killings and paybacks that characterized the cholo life. As banda clubs sprang up all over the state, Latino youths embraced the traditional culture that inspired their music. They danced *la quebradita,* a Latino-style updating of Country Western-style dancing. Even banda clothes reflected the style's Mexican country origins; both men and women wore tight Levis and Mexican cowboy boots, hats, and belt buckles. The men also wore a vestigial riding crop. It being California, there was also a characteristic vehicle: a pickup truck, with a coiled lasso hung over the rearview mirror.

In January 1993, when the Arbitron ratings showed that KLAX, a station playing a type of music unknown to most non-Latinos, had leapt to the top spot, it created a stir in the radio industry. Some felt that it was a fluke, perhaps caused by a glitch in the way ratings were calculated. New York "shock jock" Howard Stern, self-proclaimed "king of all media," was outraged that his program, and the station identified with it, was not crowned number one. He even claimed that Latino consumers had confused the upstart station's call letters (KLAX) for his (KLSX). But KLAX and its quirky format remained in the number-one position during the next quarter. In fact, it increased its lead. For the third quarter, KLAX continued in the number-one position, and the radio industry understood that its ranking reflected the growing market power of the Latino consumer.

Other radio stations in southern California were not long in noticing the banda bandwagon, and before long three other FM stations had changed to a banda playlist. After twelve consecutive quarters as the number-one station, KLAX finally lost its top ranking, becoming merely one of the top five stations. The new number-one station was KLVE (pronounced K-love), a Spanish-language station playing Latin American pop music. The radio industry learned its lesson; by the early 1990s, 110 radio stations had focused their programming on the ten million Latinos in the state (Whisler and Nuiry 1996).

Latino cultural dynamics influenced the television industry as well. The two major Spanish-language chains, Univision and Telemundo, saw their ratings increase quarterly in this period. By the early 1990s, the growth in immigrant Latino viewership had catapulted Univision's six o'clock news program into the lead, and fifteen television stations were transmitting in Spanish throughout California (Whisler and Nuiry 1996).

Likewise, print media were affected by the increase in Spanish-language readership. The number of new newspapers, magazines, journals, and other publications grew threefold in this fourteen-year period. Between 1975 and 1979, Latino publishers in the state started a total of twenty-one publications. Between 1980 and 1984, this number grew by 50 percent, to thirty-four new publications. In the next five years, the number of new publications doubled, to fifty-eight new print publications (Whisler and Nuiry 1996). Even the stately *Los Angeles Times* mulled over the idea of printing a Spanish-language edition of its daily coverage. After conducting a number of focus groups with Latino leaders (in which I participated), the *Times* opted to buy a 50 percent interest in *La Opinion,* a Spanish-language daily published since 1926.

Latinos were not merely the consumers but also increasingly the manufacturers, distributors, and sellers of the products California needed. Initially, Latino-owned businesses in California were few in number, barely 28,166 in 1972. They tended to be small in size, too; only 24 percent had employees, and their average gross receipts were $46,230 (US DOC 1975, 84). Facing common problems of access to capital and business know-how, Latino businesses shared contacts and knowledge in Hispanic Chambers of Commerce.

The Latin Business Association (LBA), established in Los Angeles in 1974 with only seven members, mainly in the printing business, and no budget (Lopez-Williams 2002), has become the largest Latino business interest group in the state. Like the Mexican American Grocers Association in the food industry, its original focus was on civil rights. The LBA helped its members become officially designated Minority-Owned Businesses, so they could qualify for set-aside contracting. The LBA also lobbied city, county, and state governmental entities to contract with Latino businesses.

The explosion of interest in the growing Latino market added new dimensions to the LBA agenda: to assist its members in better serving the needs of the expanding Latino consumer base and to assist non-Latino corporations in their pursuit of Latino market share. LBA's annual conference grew to a have a large marketing focus. Figure 23 shows the growth in

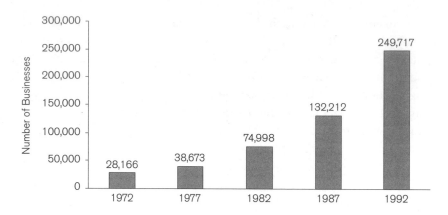

Figure 23. Latino-Owned Businesses, California, 1972–1992. Sources: 1972 (US DOC 1975, 84, table 2); 1977 (US DOC 1980, 61, table 2); 1982 (US DOC 1986, 43, table 2); 1987 (US DOC 1991, 20, table 4); 1992 (US DOC 1996, 21, table 4).

Latino businesses from 28,166 in 1972 to 249,717 by 1992. While the Latino population tripled between 1970 and 1990, Latino-owned businesses grew even more rapidly, becoming nine times as numerous between 1972 and 1992.

By 2002, LBA had 42,000 members in southern California, with average annual sales and receipts of around one million dollars. Nearly one out of every five LBA members had average annual sales and receipts more than five million dollars. The LBA itself grew tremendously and by 2002 had achieved an annual budget of over three million dollars, with twelve full-time employees (Lopez-Williams 2002).

U.S.-BORN LATINOS RESPOND TO IMMIGRANTS

Immigrant Latinos made the speaking of Spanish more commonplace. Billboards began to advertise food, beverages, and consumer items in Spanish. The buses that crisscrossed southern California started carrying ads in Spanish. Both construction workers in East Los Angeles and movie stars in Beverly Hills could be stuck in traffic behind ads for diapers, long-distance service, and legal representation, in Spanish.

Immigrant Latinos created new nodes of civil society. Still enthralled by the soccer they had played at home, they created youth soccer leagues for their children. Nostalgic for home, they formed hometown associations: *clubes jaliscences, clubes zacatecanos, clubes michoacanos*. The clubs often sponsored youth sports leagues in soccer, baseball, and basketball. Annual dinners, increasingly held at the better hotels in southern California, awarded scholarships to college students and crowned "Miss Zacatecas" or "Miss Jalisco."

These immigrant Latinos did not see themselves as creating anything new or different; they were only trying to establish themselves and their families. They saw themselves primarily as homemakers and breadwinners, doing what they felt was needed and appropriate for their young families. But in so doing, they changed the face of the state. They had arrived in such great numbers that their presence affected nearly every facet of California's life. One portion of the state's population in particular that they changed first was the U.S.-born Latino.

Retro-assimilators

One group of U.S.-born Latinos, referred to as "retro-assimilators" (Strategy Research Corporation 1994, 59), felt comfortable in the new cultural conditions. Although these Latinos had been born and raised in the United States and were quite familiar with Atlantic American cultural cues, they nonetheless felt that they were part of this cultural revolution.

U.S.-born Latinos are, almost by definition, English-dominant speakers. Typically, a U.S.-born child of immigrant Latino parents will learn to speak some Spanish in the home before starting the formal educational process. Once in kindergarten, however, by and large his or her formal education after that point is conducted in English. Even if the child retains some Spanish, its acquisition usually does not advance along with that of English. Only in a few cases do bilingual programs strong enough to create true bilingualism exist.

High school-level Spanish then typically presents the first opportunity for many U.S.-born Latinos to study the language formally; but while they are learning to say a simple sentence such as "Hola, me llamo José," in Spanish, they are learning physics, calculus, and chemistry in English.

In earlier decades, when Spanish-language radio and television did not exist and few people they interacted with as adults spoke Spanish, there was no reinforcement for growing in the language. However, the growth of Spanish-language media detailed above and of the Spanish-speaking adult population has provided reinforcement for speaking the language; during this period, 1975 to 1990, many U.S.-born Latino young adults engaged in "retro-assimilation," that is, they became increasingly engaged in the Spanish-speaking world, as opposed to leaving it. Whereas the ability to speak Spanish had been discouraged in earlier generations, with the growth in a Spanish-language environment it acquired a certain cachet.

CESLAC focus groups conducted among English-dominant U.S.-born Latinos brought some of these feelings to the surface. A number of participants, English-dominant Latinos who retro-assimilated as college students, remarked:

> Things have much, like, more meaning in Spanish.
>
> Yeah. Most things sound so much prettier.
>
> It's more of a passionate language. (CESLAC Health Definitions 1999, 9: U.S.-born Latino college students, 30)

The use of Spanish language was also described as adding emphasis to a spoken comment.

> I always want to tell her [girlfriend] something [in Spanish], just because I know it will be stronger, what I'm trying to get across, in Spanish.
>
> Yeah, [things sound] so much meaner, like when they yell at you. (CESLAC Health Definitions 1999, 9: U.S.-born Latino college students, 30–31)

A cultural retro-assimilation linked itself to this language reacquisition. Part of this occurred by cultural osmosis; in listening to Spanish-language radio, one picked up knowledge about the artists and musical genres, as well as news of Latino California and Latin America. Watching Spanish-language television, one learned about events in Mexico and Latin America and was presented with different media treatment of Latinos. While English-language media tended to concentrate on stereotypical depictions of Latinos as illegal immigrants, gangbangers, or welfare mothers, Spanish-language news media treated Latinos as a larger, whole community with school bands, soccer leagues, musical artists visiting town, human-interest stories, Latino businesses, and politics.

Formal knowledge constituted another part of this cultural retro-assimilation. While the Chicano studies programs established a generation earlier had been treated by campus administrators as politicized, marginal activities, U.S.-born Latino students increased their enrollment, eager to spend time learning Latino history, literature, music, theater, and Latino-focused social sciences. One focus-group participant reminisced, "My dad was born and raised here in the U.S. . . . . I lost the ability to speak Spanish from fourth grade to high school. [In college] I learned what being Chicano meant, and Mexican American culture and the mariachi and banda [music]" (CESLAC Health Definitions 1999, 9: U.S.-born Latino college students, 31).

Retro-assimilated U.S.-born Latinos, with their ability in Spanish and knowledge of Latino California, served as a bridge between California institutions and organizations and the burgeoning Latino adult population. Leading-edge private businesses hired these young adults, who could tell them about the tastes and desires of this growing market. "I was . . . born in the U.S. . . . Once, [in college], I discovered that, I just fell in love with the fact that, wow! I could speak Spanish, so there was a connection there [with other Latinos]" (CESLAC Health Definitions 1999, 9: U.S.-born Latino college students, 31).

Proud, but Confused

Not all Latinos experienced retro-assimilation. CESLAC also held focus groups with U.S.-born Latinos who did not speak Spanish to any functional degree, to probe their reactions to the growing influence of the immigrant Latino population. They described a more confused picture.

Older U.S.-born Latinos described growing up not being able to speak Spanish. Prior to 1975, when the vast majority of Latinos were U.S.-born and English-dominant, and immigrant Latinos were comparatively rare, this was nothing remarkable. The 1975–90 growth of the Spanish-language environment created language confusion for them because of an assumption made by many immigrant Latinos that a person who "looks Latino" should be able to speak Spanish. One focus-group participant complained, "Now I have somebody who comes [into the store] and speaks Spanish to me and makes me feel, 'Oh, you can't even speak your own language.' But that wasn't my language. My language was English" (CESLAC UW 1998, 3: U.S.-born Latinos, some college, 36). She went on to describe an exchange she found herself engaging in more and more, as the store's clientele became increasingly immigrant Latino-based. "They'll say, 'Well, how come you don't speak Spanish? You're a Mexican, aren't you?' And I just tell them, 'But I was born here'" (CESLAC UW 1998, 3: U.S.-born Latinos, some college, 30).

The growth in the Spanish-language environment also leads some non-Hispanic whites to assume that someone who "looks" Latino must be able to speak Spanish. "When I go to Mexico, they [Mexicans] speak to me in

English. When I'm here, they [non-Hispanic whites] speak to me in Spanish" (CESLAC UW 1998, 3: U.S.-born Latinos, some college, 38).

When a Latino is not able to engage in the Spanish-language environment, this informal cultural osmosis does not occur. Latinos who do not continue their education to college are limited to what they learned about Latinos in high school, which is still a very small part of the state's high school curriculum. "Out here in the LAUSD [Los Angeles Unified School District], they don't teach you about Hispanic heritage at all. It's mostly all American heritage" (CESLAC UW 1998, 1: U.S.-born Latinos, high school only, 55). Those who are not comfortable in Spanish miss out on the constant flow of information about musical events, theater, health tips, and corporate Latino initiatives expressed as ads in Spanish prepared by Macy's, Nordstrom's, Sears, J.C. Penney, and other large national chains; on night club openings, elections in Mexico, municipal strife in El Salvador, the latest gossip of Mexican singer-turned-accused-panderer Gloria Trevi, and the growth of rock en español.

Instead, they have been limited to Atlantic American presentations of Latinos in English-language programming, which have not changed fundamentally from the images of 1940: Latinos as gang members, undocumented immigrants, and welfare mothers. "Well, we have mixed images. Like when you . . . [watch TV the] first thing on the news, *cholos,* you know, or killings. That's negative. . . . And then we have that [Latino elected official] doing drugs, and then, first thing, they put him in the news" (CESLAC UW 1998, 1: U.S.-born Latinos, high school only, 60–61). Non-Spanish-fluent Latinos, in short, had become accustomed to Atlantic American definitions of Latinos. When faced with the sudden presence of Latino-derived definitions, they were confused. Which image was the "real Latino"?

U.S.-born Latinos in these focus groups described, with a twinge of envy, observing immigrant Latinos moving into their communities with high levels of energy, dedication, and self-esteem. "Immigrant . . . students who come here are so eager to learn. . . . They're so outgoing . . . so self-oriented; you know their initiative is there. . . . They're doing better than the second- and third-generation Mexican American" (CESLAC UW 1998, 7: Latino civic leaders, 39). Poorly educated second- and third-generation respondents described themselves as having lost some of their initiative, in a sense internalizing the discouragement they found in their schools. "The Chicanos are the ones that are saying, 'Oh, it's not good to go to college. Who are they, and why are they [immigrants] trying to be better than me?'" (CESLAC UW 1998, 7: Latino civic leaders, 40).

U.S.-born Latinos, especially in the focus groups with less-educated participants, described feelings of frustration, that somehow they were no longer sufficiently Latino. "[Immigrant Latinos], well, they're making me feel like, you know, I'm not a Mexican" (CESLAC UW 1998, 3: U.S.-born Latinos, some college, 36).

Their confusion was compounded because, during the 1940–65 era, they had been told in numerous ways that they were not completely "American," either. "In high school I didn't look like all the other Mexican girls, and I hated that 'cause I wanted to be able to identify with . . . the other Mexican girls . . . but I couldn't identify with white girls either" (CESLAC UW 1998, 3: U.S.-born Latinos, some college, 38).

The major difference is that, by the end of the 1990s, Latinos did not have to use the Atlantic American definition as the only standard; they could also use the immigrant-driven definitions. Retro-assimilators could do this easily. The confused U.S.- born, those who did not speak Spanish and did not know the formal and informal worlds of culture, felt caught in a state of limbo: not able to retro-assimilate, not accepted by the Atlantic American world, and feeling vaguely caught up by Latino-derived cultural forces they could not understand.

The key to their uneasiness was precisely the transformation in Latino identity dynamics. Atlantic Americans no longer were the sole suppliers of images and definitions. Increasingly, Latinos, especially immigrant Latinos, were supplying alternative definitions and images, in very unconscious, apolitical ways.

Immigrant Latinos in our focus groups described their understanding of why U.S.- born Latinos would show ignorance about the Spanish language, about Latin American history, or about their feelings of identity. "These [Mexican American] folks that they are complaining about us [immigrant Latinos] now were some of the very ones that were punished for speaking Spanish, or their parents were punished for speaking Spanish. . . . When I used to travel here [to the United States] as a young kid . . . being Mexican was a bad thing" (CESLAC UW 1998, 7: Latino civic leaders, 35). Although they had not lived through the 1940–65 period when Atlantic American definitions predominated, they were sensitive to the fact that those older U.S.-born Latinos had undergone a different experience. "The American-born Latino lived a different reality than we would like to live, than I would like to live. The reality was that being Latino mean[t] you had to hide the Latino aspects of your life" (CESLAC UW 1998, 7: Latino civic leaders, 35).

The conversion of braceros to permanent immigrants, just at the moment when the non-Hispanic white "baby bust" began, created the conditions both for a tremendous Latino population growth and for an unexpected reinforcement of Latino cultural choices. The market choices of millions of Spanish-dominant immigrants and their Spanish-familiar children created a new language and cultural environment that offered new personal opportunities and challenges to U.S.-born Latinos.

Far from disappearing as a "dead language," Spanish became the language of choice in radio and television media for a majority of Latinos. Far from dwindling into numerical insignificance, Latino populations grew and came to dominate schools and cities. Yet this growth did not result in "identity politics" among Latinos, although it did among alarmed non-Hispanic white voters, as will be described in chapter 5. Instead, it reflected the mundane, daily choices made by families—parents, children, relatives, friends, neighbors—as they went about the quotidian business of raising children, keeping a household functioning, going to work, establishing a business, enjoying weekends, finding spiritual solace, reminiscing about earlier days. The major difference was that these families had become largely composed of immigrant Latinos.

By sheer force of numbers and economic importance, immigrant Latinos forced the state's business community to take these wants, dreams, and fears into account as they developed products and services to sell to them. Increasingly, immigrant Latinos and their choices determined which businesses would live and which would die in the state's marketplace.

Immigrant Latinos, however, did not form a monolithic bloc. Immigrants from Central America, South America, and the Caribbean entered the mix during this period (1975–90). And even though the vast majority of immigrant Latinos were from Mexico, there is much diversity among the Mexican immigrants: they came from urban areas as well as rural ranchos, from the heavily Hispanicized northern states of Sonora, Chihuahuha, and Coahuila, as well as still-indigenous southern states such as Oaxaca and Chiapas. These internal segments were reflected in radio programs, musical choices, even the jokes used by the Spanish-language disc jockeys. But unlike the earlier wave of immigrants in 1910–30, these Latino immigrants could live most of their lives responding to Latino definitions of Latinos, rather than to Atlantic American ones.

The new definitions created by immigrants also had a profound—and hard to ignore—effect on U.S.-born Latinos. Some felt empowered to explore their "Latino side" and reveled in the opportunities to live large portions of their lives within the Latino cultural construct of the period. Others felt confused by it, at times a bit resentful that they were considered not sufficiently American by Atlantic Americans and not sufficiently Latino by immigrant Latinos. Whatever the individual reaction, the dominant dynamic had been put into place: Latinos were defining Latinos.

FIVE

Times of Crisis

Proposition 187 and After, 1990–2000

I was about twelve years old then [1994], just before the Proposition
187 vote. For weeks, on the rock stations that I listened to then, the
deejays were saying horrible things about Latinos and immigrants, and
I felt so bad. Then, one day I was in a theater in Westwood [upscale
non-Hispanic white section of Los Angeles], when an ad for Coca
Cola or something started, and there was Gloria Estefan on the
screen, and I was thinking, "Please, God, don't let her sing in Spanish.
I would be mortified." And sure enough, she sang in Spanish, and I felt
like the whole theater was watching me. Me, I felt ashamed to be
Latina. That's how bad it was.

C. Hayes-Bautista 2003

EVERY WAVE OF URBAN TURMOIL TO HIT THE COUNTRY during the late
1960s swept more and more whites out of urban areas, leaving behind an increasingly African American population to become the urban majority in
most U.S. cities. But this urban population, too, experienced change shortly
after that, in black middle-class flight from the urban cores. By 1990, much
of the black middle class also had fled the declining urban core, taking with
them their capital, skills, and businesses. In many American cities, such as
Detroit and Newark, the fleeing black middle class found no buyers for their
properties and simply walked away from them, leaving block after block of
uninhabited, derelict buildings. Nearly 80 percent of Detroit's urban white
population had left the cities, and less than half the remaining adult population was in the labor force (Jacoby 2001, 301, 328, 533).

By 1990, inner-city America appeared to be a nearly terminal case. But
in southern California there was life stirring in the urban wasteland. There
were people willing to move into areas abandoned by both the non-

Hispanic white and the black middle class; there were people willing to move into ghettoes, willing to put "sweat equity" into restoring houses and refurbishing businesses. These people were immigrant Latinos.

Latino immigrants changed the face of urban southern California by rehabilitating the social life of areas abandoned by non-Hispanic white and African American middle-class flight. After planting the seeds of new development and literally bringing southern California's cities back from the brink of social and economic death, the Latino community was punished by the passage of Proposition 187, the elimination of affirmative action, and the abolition of bilingual education. These were, indeed, times of crisis for California's Latinos.

THE LOS ANGELES RIOTS

As recently as the mid-1960s, Latinos in the Los Angeles region, like African Americans, had been legally restricted to home ownership in specific areas. In the case of Latinos, these were centered around East Los Angeles and the northern San Fernando Valley. Those who could not afford to buy houses were crowded into large rental complexes just west of the downtown core. With the repeal of covenants, which previously had restricted the sale of real estate to certain "races" and excluded others, previously all-non-Hispanic white areas changed. The Watts riots of 1965 panicked white home owners whose properties were "too close" to African American enclaves. Fearful that their property values would be hurt by an area that had become too volatile, white home owners around the center of Los Angeles County—Compton, Hawthorne, Inglewood, Fox Hills—sold their houses and fled to the outer perimeter of the county. Quite often, they sold to the newly affluent African American middle class, themselves seeking to flee the disorder of crumbling inner-city areas.

The same lifting of legal restrictions that opened African American home ownership outside the historic ghettoes also opened the door to residential mobility for Latinos. The more affluent, largely U.S.-born Latino middle class did as the African American middle class had done and bought directly from fleeing white owners, preserving the middle-class nature of areas such as Downey, Norwalk, and Montebello. Immigrants, who were largely not middle class, took another route. Initially lacking capital for down payments, they crowded into rental housing in densely packed core areas, such as the formerly elegant MacArthur Park and Pico Union just west of downtown. As black middle-class flight accelerated in the late

1970s and throughout the 1980s, rather than leaving behind hundreds of blocks of deserted, unproductive properties—such as happened in Detroit, Newark, and other cities—departing home owners found buyers who were willing to move into previously all-black ghettoes: Latino immigrants seeking their own piece of the American dream. So the immigrants poured out of rental housing into areas shunned by other, more middle-class buyers. The immigrant Latino population slowly moved outward from the downtown area, filling in the vacuum left by the fleeing black middle-class in areas such as South Central Los Angeles. Latino immigrants did not hesitate to buy in Watts, Compton, Inglewood, and other areas deemed undesirable by non-Hispanic whites and middle-class African Americans. And as they moved into what for two to three decades had been inner-city ghettos, they renewed life in that portion of urban America in southern California.

When abandoned property became derelict, no tax revenue was produced; when immigrants bought houses, they paid property taxes, thus providing a revenue base for city services. In addition, the houses were rehabilitated and remodeled. Although War on Poverty and Housing and Urban Development (HUD) programs had largely failed in their goal of urban renewal, immigrant Latinos, with their own private capital painfully accumulated from low-wage jobs, rehabilitated wide swaths of formerly declining properties in South Central Los Angeles. Beginning in the early 1980s, decorative wrought-iron fencing—a hallmark of Latino immigrant home ownership—began to appear outside of Huntington Park, moving farther and farther westward, marking the movement of immigrant Latino families into the former ghetto. Families returned to South Central Los Angeles; laughter was again heard in the abandoned parks, tricycles littered the sidewalk, chiming ice cream trucks appeared, and sidewalk taco stands brought life back to the streets. Enterprising Latino businesspeople bought abandoned businesses, unboarded the windows, and stocked the shelves. Commerce revived.

Quickly, South Central Los Angeles became Latinized. In 1980, two-thirds of that area's population was African American (66.7 percent), and only 13.7 percent was Latino. In only ten years, by 1990, Latinos were the majority population (50.1 percent) and African Americans a large minority (44.8 percent) (see Figure 24). The 1990 census showed—although almost no one noticed—that the African American population had become a minority in previously all-black areas such as Watts, Compton, and South Central. Continuing the trend, by 2000, Latinos were nearly two-thirds of

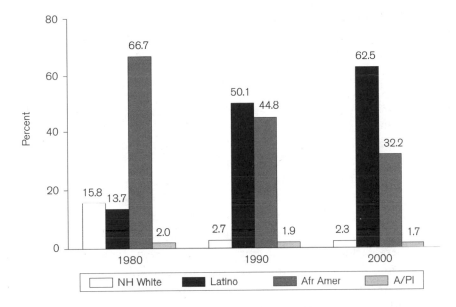

Figure 24. South Central Los Angeles Ethnic Composition, 1980, 1990, and 2000. Sources: 1980–90 (D. Hayes-Bautista, Schink, and Hayes-Bautista 1993, 431); 2000 (U.S. Bureau of the Census 2001a, map TM-P001H).

the population of South Central (62.5 percent), and African Americans were only one-third (32.2 percent) (see Figure 24).

During the 1970s and 1980s, when the American manufacturing regions of the Northeast melted down, California's economy seemed charmed. While unemployment soared in the rest of the country, California's unemployment rate was far below the national average and jobs were still being created. Aerospace provided high-wage, high-benefit jobs for the state's highly trained workforce. A great future was forecast for the new high-tech "Silicon Valley." Hollywood churned out epic stories of wars in the stars and aliens trying to telephone home. Yuppies were alive and well, and real estate boomed.

When the Soviet Union fell and America no longer needed to maintain a huge arsenal, defense spending was cut practically overnight. California was hit especially hard, because the state had enjoyed a disproportionate amount of defense spending on its military aviation and aerospace industries. As the aerospace industry imploded, many manufacturers went out of business or were acquired by others; hundreds of thousands of jobs were lost, while thousands of remaining jobs were downgraded and shuffled to new areas. For the first time since World War II, the state's economy was in worse shape than the national economy; unemployment was higher, jobs were lost at a higher rate, and bankruptcies were being declared at an alarming rate.

For nearly 140 years, California had been a magnet for the rest of the country. In the golden years after World War II, cheap housing and plentiful jobs had provided an irresistible attraction for the millions who moved in from Minnesota, Iowa, Illinois, Pennsylvania, and Ohio. In 1991, the Department of Finance announced the unthinkable: more non-Hispanic white population was moving out of the state than moving in (Morrison 1993). Dramatically, the department announced that, for the first time in nearly 150 years, the state could be losing population overall.

Southern California's social fabric unraveled even further during the spring of 1992, when long-simmering passions exploded in an uprising that recalled the "long hot summers" of the late 1960s. Recession and white flight had taken their toll on Los Angeles's inner city, but no one was prepared for what would happen on April 29, 1992, when white police officers on trial for the beating of African American motorist Rodney King were declared not guilty. The verdict stunned the remaining African American community of South Central Los Angeles and initiated a week of outrage and violence.

From the corner of Florence and Western avenues, just west of the Latino enclave of Huntington Park, members of the African American community poured into the streets, voicing their disbelief that the infamous videotape of King's beating had not been enough to convict the police officers of brutality. The crowd grew, and its mood turned ugly. Members of the crowd began shouting at passing cars, then banging with their fists on car fenders. A brick was thrown; shop windows shattered. A shop was torched, then another—and suddenly it was Watts 1965 all over again. A white trucker, Reginald Denny, was pulled from his truck and savagely beaten in an ironic replay of the Rodney King incident; although, unlike King, Denny was rescued and pulled to safety by a number of African American citizens. As flames jumped from shop to shop, hand-lettered signs provided an eerie reminder of the long, hot summers: "Burn, baby, burn." All through the night, block after block of inner-city buildings exploded in flames and death. Civil authority had essentially disappeared from South Central Los Angeles. The police had withdrawn, and fire fighters had to brave sniper fire without protection.

For the first two days, burned-out shops had been brazenly looted as an expression of contempt and anger. By the third day, the riot's dynamics began to change. As household food supplies ran low, the partly looted shops represented the only possible opportunity for survival. Residents of the area—since the late 1980s, predominantly immigrant Latinos—began darting furtively into burned shops to pick over the remaining stock. Far from demonstrating their solidarity with those protesting the not-guilty verdict, these looters took advantage of the breakdown of civil order only to establish some order in their own convulsed lives. Television camera crews broadcast images of Latino-looking looters with their arms full of diapers and milk cartons. The *National Review* ran a cover photograph of a Latino lugging an eight-pack of soft drink quarts across a parking lot (1992).

As the bulk of the area's residents, Latinos in fact were the primary victims of the Rodney King verdict crowd violence. About one-third of those who died in the riots were Latino (D. Hayes-Bautista, Schink, and Hayes-Bautista 1993, 429), largely the victims of crowd-driven violence. As Latino and Korean immigrants had been virtually the only entrepreneurs brave enough to risk their capital to restore commerce to the area, about 40 percent of the stores burned or damaged were Latino-owned (D. Hayes-Bautista, Schink, and Hayes-Bautista 1993, 429).

Glenn Spencer was an older non-Hispanic white whose first job had been in the aerospace industry. Raised and educated in Los Angeles public schools and universities, he had been fretting for some time about the growing Latino population. He felt as if his state were being taken away from him. As he later recounted (McDonnell 2001), these television images of Latino-looking persons scuttling away with their arms full of groceries were an epiphany to him. "I was stunned and thought, 'Oh my God, there are so many of them and they are so out of control'" (McDonnell 2001, 16). As he saw it, non-Hispanic white America was losing control of its borders, and the major cause was Latino undocumented immigrants. He felt it was his duty to awaken America to the danger, by whatever means necessary. Latinos had to be stopped.

In Huntington Park, East Los Angeles, Pacoima, San Fernando, and Wilmington, all long-standing Latino barrios, there had been little or no looting. During the third day of the riots, a number of Latino leaders gathered in East Los Angeles and congratulated the Latino community of the city for not taking part in the riots. While they were overtly proud that, by and large, Latino barrios had not burned, many privately expressed alarm that Latino prudence might actually be penalized, as untouched areas would not receive the kind of federal largess that had materialized in the wake of the 1960s riots (D. Hayes-Bautista, Schink, and Hayes-Bautista 1993). Mayor Tom Bradley appointed the 1984 Los Angeles Olympics Games czar, Peter Ueberroth, to lead a hastily convened committee called Rebuild LA (RLA) to assess the damages and recommend action. Latinos, indeed, were largely overlooked in the appointments to RLA.

I was asked to help write an alternative report, to provide the Latino perspective we feared would be left out of the RLA document, for an ad-hoc group of Latino leaders, the Latino Coalition for a New Los Angeles. Under the leadership of David Lizarraga, executive director of the East Los Angeles Community Union (TELACU) in East Los Angeles, the coalition met weekly to pore over data I had been extracting from the recently released 1990 Census files and to discuss what these data meant to the assembled coalition members.

Census tract by census tract, I walked coalition members through the new South Central Los Angeles, looking at a new topic each week: labor-force participation, education levels, unemployment, welfare use, family formation, language patterns, nativity, poverty, and the like. We analyzed how Latino populations differed from African American ones. A pattern quickly emerged: while Latinos in the South Central and Pico Union area had far less education and lived in far greater poverty than their African American neighbors, they had the strongest labor-force participation rates of any group in the county (D. Hayes-Bautista, Schink, and Hayes-Bautista 1993, 433) and they were far more likely to have households composed of a married couple with children (Latino Coalition for a New Los Angeles and the Latino Futures Research Group 1993, 65). Immigrant Latinos in Los Angeles County were also far less likely to use welfare (D. Hayes-Bautista, Schink, and Rodriguez 1994, 8). My analysis was a revelation to some Latino leaders.

Initially, some coalition members had wanted to argue that Latinos should have greatest claim on the federal funds that were expected to pour into the city, since their lower education and greater poverty placed them in greater need than African Americans. Presidential candidate Bill Clinton's visit to Los Angeles changed their mind about that argument. He had toured the burned-out areas of the city, then declared that the destruction was the result of an urban underclass that had taken root there, a population that bore virtually no relationship to the rest of the American population. "People . . . are looting [in Los Angeles] because they are not part of the system at all anymore. . . . They do not share our values, and their children are growing up in a culture alien from ours, without family, without neighborhood, without church, without support" (Brownstein 1992, A8).

Faced with this reiteration of the classic minority dysfunction equation, coalition members almost unanimously decided to demonstrate how Latino strengths, as documented by census data, could be used as a force to rebuild the city. Job creation was one area in which Latinos could help. The Ueberroth group had argued that the county needed 30,000 new jobs and lobbied for tax breaks for businesses willing to relocate in the affected areas. The coalition argued for a new, more cost-efficient use of federal aid funds. The coalition estimated that out of an estimated 103,000 Latino-owned firms in the county, there were 18,800 prosperous enough to have paid employees. If these locally owned firms each employed two additional persons, more than 37,000 new jobs would be created, quite a few more than the Ueberroth commission wanted. Although the recommendation went unheeded, it was a major breakthrough in policy thinking: the Latino community saw itself using its strengths to help rebuild the city.

In early 1993, the coalition released its report, *Latinos and the Future of Los Angeles*. Perhaps too far ahead of its time, it showed that in many areas pinpointed by RLA as needing attention—job growth, health services, employment, welfare—Latino patterns of behavior could provide the spark to rebuild Los Angeles into the city of the future.

PROPOSITION 187

One week after the riots, while the smell of burnt buildings was still in the air, the *Los Angeles Times* probed the mood of Angelenos in the aftermath of the country's worst race rioting in decades (*Los Angeles Times Poll* 1992a). They found it to be somber, pessimistic, wary. Nearly all Angeleno respondents—non-Hispanic whites, Latinos, and African Americans (Asians were not polled)—cited pressing problems that needed resolution. Racial tensions, unemployment, the economy, gangs, and violence were the top-ranked concerns. Immigration, curiously, was not in the picture; it was mentioned by just 1 percent of the sample. In a follow-up poll six months later, the *Times* confirmed the residents' concerns (*Los Angeles Times Poll* 1992b). Now suddenly referred to as illegal, immigration still was mentioned by only 3 percent of the sample. Governor Pete Wilson's reelection problems changed that radically; his reelection campaign managed to convince a majority of Californians that Latinos were indeed the problem.

During his term as mayor of San Diego, Pete Wilson had exhibited a willingness to work with city, state, and federal officials from Mexico on a number of issues, and he was viewed by some Latino leaders as moderate-to-liberal on matters relating to Latinos. When first elected in 1990, Wilson was a popular and moderate governor. The *Los Angeles Times* showed that in 1991 he had an approval rating of 52 percent (*Los Angeles Times Poll* 1994b, 2). But things in the state went terribly wrong on his watch. First the recession, then the riots, even earthquakes and firestorms—under Governor Wilson's stewardship, everything seemed to have gone wrong. His approval ratings plummeted, reaching a low point of 28 percent five months after the Los Angeles riots (*Los Angeles Times Poll* 1994b, 2). How could he run for reelection in 1994 with numbers so low?

A political consultant, holding focus groups for a governor in trouble, mentioned the topic of undocumented immigrants and their role in the state. Instantly, a focus group of non-Hispanic whites lit up. Angrily, they denounced the immigrants for ruining the state; they took away jobs, they crowded schools and hospitals, they sucked up government expenditures fueled by tax dollars, they overused welfare, they increased crime rates, they rioted and broke into stores. As wave after wave of invective poured out, the consultant realized he had found the governor's "red-meat" issue. Wilson's mildly pro-Latino posture was sacrificed in his quest for reelection, and he jumped onto the anti-immigrant bandwagon. As his campaign manager later described, Wilson's style was to "pound an issue until it registers," and thanks to his efforts to "beat the immigration drums," illegal immigration rose from not registering as a policy issue in 1992 to becoming the number-one policy issue by 1994 (Sherwood 1995).

Glenn Spencer provided Governor Wilson with an engine to pull that wagon: a state initiative that would bar undocumented immigrants from using almost any public service in health or education. Rather loosely worded, this initiative would require teachers and social service workers to deny services to anyone who "appeared to be illegal" or to be the children of illegal aliens. This would involve expelling suspected students from public schools and denying prenatal care to undocumented pregnant women. His group gathered the required 40,000 signatures in record time and began churning out inflammatory campaign literature blaming undocumented immigrants for nearly every one of California's woes. One such piece was addressed to the California taxpayer and was titled simply "OUR BORDERS ARE OUT OF CONTROL." It went on to charge that "every 24 hours, four to five thousand illegal aliens cross our southern border into California virtually unimpeded." The flyer concluded that close to one million undocumented immigrants crossed the border every year and would go on to appear on the state's welfare, public education, and criminal justice rolls, "funded by *our* tax dollars" (CCIR n.d.; emphasis in original).

Governor Wilson came out publicly in support of the newly qualified ballot initiative, henceforth to be known as Proposition 187. His poll numbers moved up, as the state's electorate found Latino immigrants a visible scapegoat for all of its recent problems. When asked by the *Los Angeles Times* to list the burning issues facing the state, Angelenos now ranked immigration in the top three, along with gangs/crime and unemployment (*Los Angeles Times Poll* 1994a, 1). Wilson was still in trouble, as his overall approval was only 39 percent, but Republicans liked his message; 66 percent of Republicans approved of the way he was handling events.

Supporters of Proposition 187 crafted an image of a state literally drowning in undocumented immigrants from Mexico. Commentators frequently mentioned on television shows that up to half of all Latinos in Los Angeles County were "probably" undocumented immigrants. Spencer's pro-187 group poured fuel on the fire by charging that "over 2/3 of births in county hospitals are to illegal aliens" (VCT 1995). Even Senator Dianne Feinstein (D-CA), fighting a close reelection campaign against novice Republican Michael Huffington, capitalized on the "drowning in immigrants" theme when she approved a televised cinema verité–style scare ad to show her tough stance on illegal immigration (Feinstein's TV Attack 1994, A3). The ad opened with a grainy black-and-white hand-held video footage of a few people on foot darting between the lines of cars awaiting inspection for entry to the United States at the San Ysidro border crossing station and continuing north into California, while a narrator announced in a loud, voice-of-doom tone, "And they keep coming! Two thousand each night" would cross, presumably to live in the state. The commercial itself was not specifically about Proposition 187; it touted the senator as being tough on illegal immigration. However, while later she did go on record as opposing Proposition 187, many viewers simply remembered the scary commercial and in their own minds attached it to the Proposition 187 campaign. The damage to the Latino image was done.

No public figure ever disputed the pro-187 campaign rhetoric, and many voters went to the polls fully convinced that millions and millions of illegal immigrants from Mexico were crossing the border and signing up immediately for welfare. Magazine covers constantly depicted an America being invaded by dreaded foreigners (see Leo Chavez 2001 for a detailed analysis of this phenomenon).

If two thousand or more Mexican immigrants indeed crossed the border every night, as Senator Feinstein's ads stated so convincingly, there would have been, by 1994, nearly 9 million undocumented Mexican immigrants in California alone. The California Coalition for Immigration Reform figure of five thousand border crossings a night would have resulted in 21.9 million undocumented Mexican immigrants in the state. Although these numbers were clearly untenable, many Californians were left with the impression that from ten to twenty million undocumented immigrant Latinos resided in a state of 27.8 million. Once they were convinced that this large number of undocumented Latinos was living in the state, their next logical conclusion was that any Latino was, ipso facto, an undocumented immigrant. Distinctions between U.S.-born Latinos, immigrant Latinos, and undocumented immigrant Latinos became lost in the popular discourse.

Then another round of accusations against immigrants began. Because of their large numbers, they were responsible for the water shortages during California's periodic droughts; they were responsible for clogged freeways; they were responsible for overcrowded schools. In this new view, Latinos in general came to be blamed for everything from firestorms to high taxes. Perhaps the most apocalyptic vision was supplied in 1995 by Voices of Citizens Together: "As illegal aliens flood in, schools are overwhelmed, wages fall, and *English becomes an unknown language in this city.* Seeing this, *Americans are fleeing Los Angeles,* leaving a collapsing real estate market and declining tax base behind them. We are importing poverty and exporting jobs" [emphasis in original]. On election night in November 1994, Proposition 187 was passed by an overwhelming majority. Governor Wilson was reelected by a comfortable margin, and Senator Feinstein squeaked by her opponent. Immigrant bashing had worked—for a while.

Though Proposition 187 passed overwhelmingly, a careful reading of the voting patterns provide a hint of the polarization to come. The measure passed easily in the non-Hispanic white electorate, with 59 percent approval. In 1994, the state's electorate was overwhelmingly non-Hispanic white. Yet Latino voters, who were U.S. citizens and theoretically not the target of the measure, overwhelmingly (78 percent) rejected the measure. It marked the first time the Latino vote had been so decisively for or against any state issue. The measure was also rejected, albeit by smaller margins, by the African American (56 percent rejected it) and Asian/Pacific Islander (54 percent rejected it) electorates (see Figure 25). Now that he had resurrected himself from near oblivion, Governor Wilson's aim moved to a possible

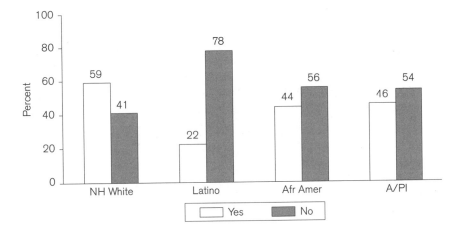

Figure 25. How Each Group Voted on Proposition 187, California, 1994. Source: Weintraub, Nov. 9, 1994.

presidential candidacy, and he decided to ride the anti-immigrant horse even harder. Early on the morning after the election, his office churned out faxes to nearly every hospital, clinic, school district, and other social service agency, citing the provisions of the proposition just passed and demanding immediate compliance.

In response, the Mexican American Legal Defense and Education Fund (MALDEF) filed an injunction, citing the many unconstitutional provisions of the measure. The injunction was granted, and shortly after the governor's office had faxed out its demand, MALDEF faxed out a copy of the injunction, with a request to the same agencies to continue providing services as before. For the four years of Governor Wilson's second term, the war of injunctions continued, with the governor demanding enforcement of a particular provision one day, and an array of civil rights groups, such as the ACLU, countering that the provision was unconstitutional and unenforceable the next day.

The Reality Behind the Image

Ironically, the same quadruple whammy of recession, riots, earthquake, and wildfire that had convinced many non-Hispanic whites to leave the state also led Latinos to pack their bags. For all the cries of "they keep coming," Latino in-migration (movement into the state) had already slowed tremen-

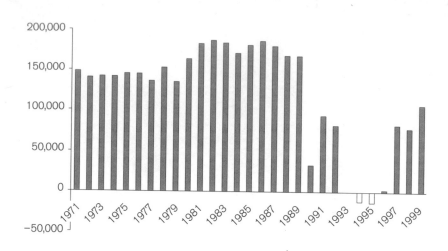

Figure 26. Annual Residual Latino In-Migration to California, 1971–1999. Sources: 1970–89 (CA DOF 1999); 1990–99 (CA DOF [2001b]).

dously by the mid-nineties (CA DOF 1999; CA DOF [2001b]). The peak period for Latino in-migration was 1982 to 1986, when an annual average of 182,575 Latinos moved into the state permanently; this figure does not include Latinos who moved through the state en route to another destination. In fact, anti-immigrant rhetoric to the contrary, estimates from the California Department of Finance (see Figure 26) show that Latino in-migration to the state not only had slowed tremendously during the late 1980s but had virtually stopped by 1993. In 1994 and 1995, as television ads warned of millions flooding into the state each year, California actually lost Latino population. More Latinos—around 12,000—left the state each year than entered it to stay (see Figure 26). By the late 1990s, Latinos were still moving into the state, but at an annual average (1997 to 1999) of 89,401, less than half the number of the peak period of 1982 to 1986.

Another pro-187 television ad panned over a classroom full of Latino-looking ten-year-olds, and a voice-over claimed that undocumented immigrant children were causing school crowding. This charge was repeated in print ads as well. Voices of Citizens Together charged that, as a result of illegal aliens flooding in, schools were overcrowded, and "Southern California has the lowest school ranking and the poorest educated young people in the U.S. . . . California taxpayers will *no longer be willing to pay taxes* if we are forced against our will to pay for *lawbreaking invaders*" (VCT 1995; emphasis in original). In 1994, Latino school-age children were predomi-

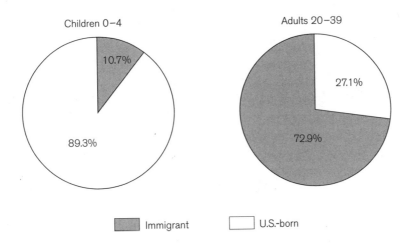

Figure 27. Percentage of U.S.-born and Immigrant Latinos Age 4 and Younger, and Age 20–39, Los Angeles County, 1990. Source: UCLA Institute for Social Science Research Data Archives 1996.

nantly U.S. citizens, by virtue of having been born in the United States. Data from the 1990 census show that Latino children four years old or younger residing in Los Angeles County—who would comprise the five-to-ten-year-old group by the time Proposition 187 passed—were 89.3 percent U.S.-born Latinos (see Figure 27). Only 10.7 percent were immigrants, and, of course, not all of those would have been undocumented immigrants. We do not have reliable census data about the immigration status of the relatively few immigrant children; but if we assume that as many as half were undocumented, more than ninety-four out of every one hundred Latino children still would have been either U.S. citizens or legal permanent residents. The paltry six undocumented children per every hundred certainly could not be the cause of school overcrowding, much less the other problems laid at their feet. Latino school-age children were overwhelmingly U.S.-born citizens, but they did usually have immigrant Latino parents. Nearly three-quarters of Latinos of child-bearing age (twenty to thirty-nine) were immigrants. One further data note is in order. While Voices of Citizens Together constantly raised concern about overcrowded schools in Los Angeles, the fact is that Los Angeles Unified School District enrollment in 1994 was actually 2.7 percent lower than it had been in 1969, when LAUSD enrollments peaked at 650,324, then declined sharply to 534,712 by 1980 (D. Hayes-Bautista, Iñiguez, and Chamberlin 2001). Starting in 1982,

LAUSD enrollments gradually recovered but by 1994 were still short of their earlier peak. Schools *were* overcrowded, but that was the result of LAUSD decisions to close schools during the 1970s rather than of the sudden appearance of vast numbers of undocumented children.

I had noticed that estimates prepared in 1992 by the Los Angeles County Board of Supervisors for the year 1990 (LAC ISD 1992, 16–28) were quite a bit lower than the figures being shown repeatedly on television. I wanted to create a new, independent estimate, using the newly released 1990 census Public Use Microdata Samples (PUMS) to see which "ballpark" estimate was most consistent with the census data. Therefore, I compared and evaluated different estimates of the Latino undocumented population, based on 1990 census data, for a report providing the immigrant Latino profile in Los Angeles County (D. Hayes-Bautista, Schink, and Rodriguez 1994). To maintain a constant base of comparison, I adjusted all state figures to Los Angeles County, which has 43.7 percent of all Latinos in the state, for 1990, so that I could compare census and Los Angeles County estimates to other estimates. Figure 28 provides the different estimates used at the time. The 1990 census counted only 3.3 million Latinos, U.S.-born and immigrant, in Los Angeles County.

The California Coalition for Immigration Reform's (CCIR) figure of over six million undocumented Latinos would have meant, first, that *every single Latino* would have been an undocumented immigrant, and second, that the census undercounted by 100 percent. Neither of these assumptions is viable. For Senator Feinstein's claim of 2.711 million to be true, eight out of every ten Latinos would have to be undocumented. Voices of Citizens Together (VCT) claimed that 20 percent of southern California's population consisted of undocumented immigrants. Applying that figure to 1990 census data would give a figure of 1.770 million undocumented Latinos in the county. Only if literally every immigrant Latino were undocumented could that figure have been valid.

Official estimates showed all these claims to be hyperbolic. The Los Angeles County study, based in large part on 1980 census data, estimated 0.408 million undocumented immigrants (LAC ISD 1992, 16–28). The INS estimate, based on visa issuances, estimated visa overstays, and "Entry Without Inspection," provided an estimate of 0.357 million (INS 1991; INS 1992). My own 1990 census PUMS estimate, based on response patterns to the 1990 census on birthplace, naturalization status, and year of entry, provided the lowest estimate, at 0.257 million (D. Hayes-Bautista, Schink, and Rodriguez 1994). Although the "official" estimates did not completely

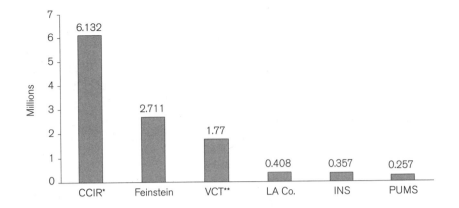

Figure 28. Comparative Estimates of Undocumented Immigrant Population in Los Angeles County, 1990. Sources: D. Hayes-Bautista, Schink, and Rodriguez 1994. *CCIR n.d. **VCT 1995.

agree, they certainly were far closer to one another than they were to the lurid, highly publicized estimates of anti-immigrant groups, which were based on guesses and suppositions but very little data. The actual number of undocumented immigrant Latinos was *not* in the tens of millions, though many California voters had the impression that it was.

In 1992, the Los Angeles County Board of Supervisors went further. It commissioned its Urban Research Section to estimate not just the number of undocumented and other immigrants but also the costs of providing county-funded services to them. They were also asked to estimate the tax base generated by that population. To summarize, the county report estimated that for every dollar in county-funded services provided to an undocumented person, that person paid $4.56 in taxes (LAC ISD 1992, 16–28). Accusations to the contrary, undocumented immigrants were *not* costing more than they paid in taxes; rather, they paid far more in taxes than they used in county-funded services.

Yet there was a rub. While the undocumented were generating taxes, the vast majority of those taxes went to federal and state coffers, not to the county, which provided the services. The Urban Research Section estimated that, of the $4.56 in taxes generated, more than half ($2.74) went to the federal level, and $1.29 went to the state. The county, which had provided the $1 of services, received only 38 cents. The undocumented were more than paying their own way, but the money simply did not go to the entities that provided the services.

The Effect on Latinos

After the electorate had overwhelmingly passed Proposition 187, there was some discontent that it was not being implemented with sufficient rigor; meanwhile, various civil rights organizations blocked every attempt by Governor Wilson to initiate implementation. Four months after the passage of the proposition, a *Los Angeles Times* reporter was interviewing an older, non-Hispanic white resident of Orange County about the state's strict tobacco laws. Complaining about its unfairness to smokers, she suddenly launched into an accusation about what was really bothering her: "Everyone in the country voted for Proposition 187 . . . the law against the Mexicans . . . and they still have those kids in the schools" (Kowsky 1995). Her comment illustrated the mind-set of many of Proposition 187's most ardent supporters and confirmed the worst fears of Latino voters who had rejected it. Her concern was not with undocumented immigrants, but with Latinos in general. From her comment, it appears she expected that most, if not all, Latino children should have left the region's schools after the passage of Proposition 187. The fact that at least 89.3 percent of those children were U.S. citizens in Los Angeles County—see Figure 27—apparently had not registered with her.

Pollster Mervin Field, pondering the many polls he had conducted before and after the vote, confirmed that the passion was not about immigration so much as it was about Latino population growth in general and its impact on daily life in the state. "How can you stop culture? How can you stop people from speaking the Spanish language or posting signs in Spanish? Here was a way to stop it—at the ballot box" (Hefner 1994).

Focus groups conducted with Latinos six years after the passage of Proposition 187 showed a smoldering resentment. Each set of participants—U.S.-born Latinos, immigrants, blue-collar workers, businesspeople, and political figures—described, in varying amounts of detail, the effects of Proposition 187 on the Latino community. Although most Latino immigrants were not "undocumented immigrants" during that debate, the very wide net cast by political advertisements and political debates during the period of "immigrant bashing" was perceived by legal permanent residents as having been aimed at them. "El gobierno sí nos ha marginado en ese aspecto, al latino, porque nos ha puesto en un status diferente a los demás, aunque estemos legalmente aquí" [The government certainly has marginalized us Latinos in this respect because it has given us a different status from everyone else, even though we are here legally] (CESLAC UW

1998, 5: Immigrant Latinos, 25). U.S.-born Latinos felt they too were targets of Proposition 187. Even though they were not illegal immigrants—in fact, were not immigrants at all, but U.S. citizens, by reason of birth—they perceived the policy debate to be about Latino presence in society, rather than merely the presence of undocumented immigrants. "I think that, as a note, [Proposition 187 was] telling us that we no longer belonged here" (CESLAC UW 1998, 2: U.S.-born Latinos, some college, 32).

They remembered picking up code words; for example, "illegal" or "undocumented" was a code word for "immigrant." "Immigrant," in its turn, was a code word for "Latino." "It's just like they say, 'Immigrant is always Mexican,' you know. If you're Mexican, you're an immigrant" (CESLAC UW 1998, 1: U.S.-born Latinos, high school only, 81–82). When the single word "undocumented" was used, the other words were often implied. "You sense that there's a race card, that, 'Oh, it's because they're undocumented; you know it's taxing our whole structure.' So, therefore, they don't like it. There is no 'Latino' mentioned" (CESLAC UW 1998, 7: Latino civic leaders, 31).

The negative effects were described as attempts to thwart the growth of Latino influence. "Están poniendo muchas leyes que están truncando a que el latino pueda superarse" [They are passing many laws that are keeping Latinos from getting ahead] (CESLAC UW 1998, 5: Immigrant Latinos, 19). A number of participants in different focus groups—immigrant, U.S.-born, high school educated, college educated—described the situation in great, macrolevel detail and saw the barriers in terms of recent public-policy decisions that would impede Latino access to education and decision-making power.

> La unión americana tiene miedo de que el latino se supere, se organice y llegue a tomar, algún día, las riendas del poder para lograr los cambios que nosotros estamos buscando. Por eso nos están poniendo esas trabas en el camino, para que no podamos llegar hasta allí. Ellos tienen mucho miedo de que el latino se supere. [The U.S. is afraid that Latinos might get ahead, get organized, and some day come to take the reins of power, in order to achieve the changes that we are seeking. For that reason, they are putting roadblocks in the way, so that we can't get there. They are very afraid that Latinos will get ahead.] (CESLAC UW 1998, 5: Immigrant Latinos, 36)

A survey I conducted for the United Way of Greater Los Angeles demonstrated the lasting hurt of Proposition 187 to U.S.-born Latinos (CESLAC 2000, 18). Nearly two-thirds (62.0 percent) of U.S.-born Latinos surveyed felt that "most Latinos are suspected of being illegal immigrants." A similar percentage of immigrant Latinos (60.7 percent) felt the lingering suspicions engendered by such polarizing debates. Nearly all Latinos had come to recognize that they themselves were the real target of Proposition 187, not the illegal immigrants, however many of them there might have been.

ENDING AFFIRMATIVE ACTION, BILINGUAL EDUCATION

Governor Wilson was riding a crest of great popularity. His eyes now firmly set on a run for the presidency, he decided to burnish his conservative credentials by pronouncing his intention to eliminate affirmative action programs. He created political pressure on the Regents of the University of California to follow the passage of Proposition 187 with the elimination of affirmative action admissions to the university system, a move that the polls indicated non-Hispanic white voters supported. At the same time, another statewide initiative had been placed on the ballot that would eliminate all affirmative action programs at the state level. Called the "Civil Rights Initiative," it forbade the state from providing any advantage to any person due to race, ethnicity, or gender. Even before the measure passed, the governor convinced the Regents to pass university-only measures (SP1 and SP2) that eliminated the use of affirmative-action admissions and simultaneously raised the bar for admission by mandating that a certain percentage of students must be admitted on the basis of Grade Point Average (GPA), test scores, and other such "objective" criteria alone.

The ballot measure, Proposition 209, passed, but a worrying trend had become quite visible in the voting patterns. As with Proposition 187, the initiative was quite popular among the non-Hispanic white electorate, winning by an even larger margin (63 percent) than Proposition 187 had. However, the polarization of the rest of the electorate was even clearer than in the 187 vote; 76 percent of Latino voters, 74 percent of the African American vote, and 61 percent of Asian/Pacific Islander voters rejected the measure (*Los Angeles Times Poll* 1996). These wedge issues were being used to pry the state's population apart, and while they were welcomed by the non-Hispanic white electorate, they were alienating Latinos and other minorities. And the latter groups, especially Latinos, were growing in number quickly.

Republicans were becoming increasingly nervous about this trend and did not endorse Governor Wilson's presidential aspirations. Still, feeling that immigrant-bashing and affirmative action elimination would get the job done, he campaigned in the Republican presidential primary. Wilson's wedge issues did not translate nationally, and his campaign ended in a rather resounding defeat in the Republican primary. He spent the rest of his term in office in a quixotic effort to have portions of Proposition 187 implemented. After his tenure, most of the measure eventually was declared unconstitutional. By 1996 his political fortunes had waned; the Republican National Convention pointedly did not offer him a role in its convention, feeling he was too divisive and alienating to the growing Latino bloc of voters.

Ron Unz, a self-made high-tech entrepreneur, had become convinced that bilingual education programs were handicapping immigrant children by preventing them from quickly mastering English. Using his personal wealth, he sponsored another initiative for the California ballot, Proposition 227; its simple purpose was to banish bilingual education from the state.

Unlike Propositions 187 and 209, the newly proposed Proposition 227 attracted a few high-profile Latinos to join in the campaign. Polls indicated that Latino parents supported the idea that their children should learn English, and Unz felt confident that he had the support of the Latino electorate. As with the other initiatives, Proposition 227 was passed overwhelmingly by the state's electorate, which, unlike the general population, was overwhelmingly non-Hispanic white. But the smaller number of Latino voters voted against it by a very wide margin. African American and Asian/Pacific Islander voters also voted against it, by narrower margins. The pattern of polarizing the electorate along ethnic lines was continuing.

Unz was right about one thing: Latinos support, very strongly, the idea that their children need to learn English. This trend can be seen in any poll taken over the last twenty years. In a 1990 poll I conducted along with Aída Hurtado and Robert Valdez (Hurtado et al. 1992), Latino parents overwhelmingly agreed that their children should learn English. In a 2000 reprise of that poll (CESLAC 2000, 35), modified for circumstances ten years later but exploring the same issues, I observed the same trend. Among U.S.-born Latino parents with children, 96 percent agreed, with 85 percent agreeing "very strongly," that all children should learn English at school. A slightly higher percentage (97 percent) of immigrant Latino parents also agreed, with a slightly higher proportion of 90 percent agreeing "very strongly." Not surprisingly, 97 percent of non-Hispanic white parents and 94 percent of African American parents also agreed (CESLAC 2000, 34). Basically, nearly all parents understand the value to their children of mastering English-language skills.

Mark Barabak, a *Los Angeles Times* reporter covering the Proposition 227 campaign, noted that while Latinos supported the idea of their children learning English, they were nevertheless wary of the tone of the debate. Again and again, he discovered that if the campaign took an anti-Latino tone, Latinos would turn against it (Barabak 1997). Some ardent Proposition 227 supporters did inject anti-Latino tones into the public debate, so that Latino voters perceived it as just another anti-Latino measure, not an educational imperative. They voted massively against it, continuing the trend of polarized voting.

Although perhaps well intentioned—and there was considerable debate about Unz's intentions—this proposition missed a chance to build on the nearly universal parental desire, irrespective of ethnicity, for California's children to become bilingual. Data from the United Way of Greater Los Angeles Survey (CESLAC 2000, 35) demonstrate a nearly universal desire for children to speak English *and* Spanish. It is not surprising that 96 percent of U.S.-born Latino parents and 98 percent of immigrant Latino parents wanted their children to speak Spanish. But 87 percent of non-Hispanic white parents and 88 percent of African American parents also wanted their children to speak Spanish. Our data indicate that non-Hispanic whites who were not parents were far less supportive of all children learning Spanish; only 65 percent agreed that it was desirable. As the vast majority of non-Hispanic white households do not have young children at home, this was the group most likely to have supported Proposition 227. In retrospect, a far better measure could have been prepared that would have brought together parents who wanted their children to be fluent in both Spanish and English, as well as nonparents afraid that Latino children were not becoming sufficiently fluent in English. This could have been a "win-win" situation. Instead, it became another wedge in the electorate.

THE POLITICAL GIANT AWAKENS

Noting in 1997 that more than 80 percent of newly registered Latino voters in the state were affiliating with the Democratic Party, Republican strategist Stu Spencer took his party to the woodshed. He felt that, unless Republicans made an effort to heal the rift these divisive issues had created, the party could be committing political suicide in a state so markedly moving toward minority-majority status. At this event, a former Wilson advisor remarked, "We walked over the sleeping giant on our way to [Pete Wilson's] reelection in 1994, but in the process, we woke it up" (Skelton 1997).

And indeed they had. The feelings of rejection and marginalization caused by Propositions 187, 209, and 227 created a Latino backlash. U.S.-born Latinos of voting age were not immigrants, nor were they always particularly fluent in Spanish. Yet they perceived that the initiatives were not really about immigrants but about the large Latino presence in the state. "[Proposition] 187 woke us up to ourselves as a community, and it made us aware that, yeah, we do contribute socially, economically, politically, and everything else to this community" (CESLAC UW 1998, 2: U.S.-born Latinos, some college, 32).

In focus groups we conducted with Latino businesspeople and professionals, they perceived that these measures were reactions to the sudden surge of Latino presence in the state. "We're in the middle of what I think is a historical transition in southern California and in California. Never have you seen, in the history of the planet, a European majority of an industrialized country become a minority. And we're right there, like the 'barbarians at the gate,' man. And we're still growing economically" (CESLAC UW 1998, 8: Latino business leaders, 30). In these participants' experiences, supporters of the initiatives were not willing to accept the demographic and social changes that were sweeping the state. "For some people, I think, they're in denial about the changes that are happening because they are so drastic and so they're coming up so fast" (CESLAC UW 1998, 7: Latino civic leaders, 24).

Some of the more politically involved focus-group members interpreted the initiatives as a power play, part of a contest over who could decide the future of the state. "People don't give up power gladly. And power is not given; it is taken. Notwithstanding the fact that we have a tradition in this country of peaceful transitions of power, we are witness to an unpeaceful transition in the form of Prop 187, etc." (CESLAC UW 1998, 8: Latino business leaders, 28). After tasting economic and political power, the U.S.-born in particular were not willing to be thrust back to the margins of society, as they had been while growing up in postwar America. "I think the power structure . . . [is] trying to retain what used to be, which is where the Latinos, mostly Mexicans, were properly humble and properly downtrodden and accepted their lives" (CESLAC UW 1998, 7: Latino civic leaders, 27). Some of the more admittedly cynical participants saw the initiatives as purposeful attempts to create obstacles to thwart Latino progress. "So it comes to . . . the system that is not helping, maybe deliberately, in order to stop us from taking over" (CESLAC UW 1998, 7: Latino civic leaders, 19).

Rather than distancing themselves from the reviled immigrant Latino, many Chicano-era groups rallied to them, providing invaluable legal and political support to a population they had not usually interacted with much before. MALDEF, for example, was instrumental in securing injunctions against blatantly unconstitutional portions of the measures. The Southwest Voters Registration Project increased its efforts to register new voters and encourage participation. The Latino Coalition for a Healthy California, a reprise of the 1970s National Chicano Health Organization, offered to find legal advice for health providers who would prefer to practice civil disobedience rather than comply with the provisions of Proposition 187. The Mexican American Grocers Association held fundraisers for candidates who opposed the measures. "So, as it happens, there are certain issues like 187 that awakes a few other souls and decides [sic] that they want to make a difference" (CESLAC UW 1998, 8: Latino business leaders, 33).

Each focus group expressed the opinion that Proposition 187 was a watershed moment. It forced the Latino community to stand alone and define its role in society, rather than allow itself to be, once again, defined by others. This self-definition took place in the face of strident opposition. "I think, after Proposition 187 . . . there was, I felt here, within the church, we started banding together, Latinos. And we had some groups get together and talk about what we need to do in our community" (CESLAC UW 1998, 3: U.S.-born Latinos, some college, 17).

In responding to questions about the initiatives, focus-group participants recounted weaving tighter strands of community. In a way similar to the World War II experience that had marked a generation of non-Hispanic whites, the five years of anti-Latino invective marked this generation of Latinos. "I saw a change around the time [of 187] . . . where Hispanics started to get together and to kind of band together and, I think, to make a better [life] for themselves" (CESLAC UW 1998, 3: U.S.-born Latinos, some college, 21–22).

Historically, immigrant Latinos, especially from Mexico, have been extremely reluctant to become naturalized U.S. citizens for many reasons: fear of having to desecrate the Mexican flag (ever since the early 1970s I have been told by many immigrant Latino respondents, erroneously, that part of the naturalization process requires a person to step on, spit on, or urinate on the Mexican flag), the desire to own property in Mexico (noncitizens could not, up until the late 1990s, own property in Mexico; they had to have property held in trust for them), or the desire to retire and return to Mexico for good. In 1990, only 5,671 Latinos living in California became naturalized U.S. citizens (INS 1991), and they represented only 9.2 percent

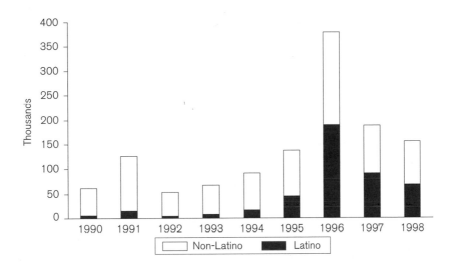

Figure 29. Annual Number of Immigrants Naturalizing, California, 1990–1998.
Sources: 1990–98 (INS 1991–99).

(of a total of 61,736) of all those immigrants from around the world in the state who became U.S. citizens that year.

Until 1994, only around 8,500 Latinos became naturalized citizens per year. But, spurred by the negative imagery of the Proposition 187 debates, those numbers soared thereafter (see Figure 29), to reach a peak of 188,627 in 1996, at which point immigrant Latinos were almost exactly half (49.9 percent) of all the immigrants who naturalized that year (INS 1991, 152; INS 1992, 130; INS 1993, 140; INS 1994, 142; INS 1995, 144; INS 1996, 148; INS 1997, 156; INS 1998, 152; INS 1999, 184). Not only were many more immigrant Latinos becoming naturalized, but also they were registering to vote. In the eight years from 1992 to 2000, the number of Latino registered voters increased 38.7 percent, from 1.4 million to 1.9 million (NALEO 2002a). They were joined by U.S.-born Latinos in the registration process. Thanks to their anger at Governor Wilson, they were registering for the Democratic Party in proportions never previously seen. In a William C. Velásquez Institute survey conducted of Latino registered voters one month prior to the 2000 presidential election, 79.9 percent of respondents declared an affiliation with the Democrats, only 12.0 percent with the Republicans (WCVI 2000).

The drumbeat of negative political campaigns—Proposition 187, the elimination of affirmative action, the ending of bilingual education—awoke the sleeping political giant as nothing else had before. Yet, some focus-group participants wondered, wistfully, if this effect could have been achieved without wedging apart the state's electorate. "It is unfortunate, for example, that it takes Proposition 187 to get Latinos to become citizens, to get Latinos to go and vote. I'd like to find other ways, that [we] don't have to be attacked from outside the community" (CESLAC UW 1998, 7: Latino civic leaders, 53).

An almost inevitable result of the growth of the Latino population and the Latino electorate was an increase in Latino holders of elected office. This growth was spurred by another Republican move to curtail minority political power, the term-limits initiative, designed to break the grip that Willie Brown, an African American assemblyman from San Francisco, had held on the state legislature for nearly twenty years. The measure moved him out of the state legislature, but it also moved out many incumbents from their comfortable sinecures, suddenly opening the way for an emerging generation of Latino candidates. Latino officeholders in the state legislature grew from seven in 1990 to twenty-seven in 2002 (Guerra 2003). Now, one out of every four state assembly members is Latino, a proportion close to Latino representation in the state's adult population (see Figure 30). There has also been a tremendous increase in the number of Latino local officials. As recently as 1990, cities with a majority Latino population rarely had Latino council members or mayors (Latino Coalition for a New Los Angeles 1993, 107). For example, the cities of Bell, Bell Gardens, Cudahy, Huntington Park, and South Gate were more than 90 percent Latino in 1990, yet that was not reflected in the composition of the city councils. In that year, Bell had no Latino council members; Bell Gardens, Cudahay, and South Gate had one, or 20 percent of the city council members; Huntington Park had three council members, for a 60 percent Latino council composition. By 2002, in four of the cities—Bell Gardens, Cudahy, Huntington Park, and South Gate—80 to 100 percent of the city council members were Latino (NALEO 2002b, 26–35).

Lieutenant Governor Cruz Bustamante, the first Latino to be elected Speaker of the Assembly, recently told me an anecdote that might well be repeated by many Latino politicians. A newspaper reporter wanted to know if Bustamante, as newly elected Speaker, was going to follow a "secret Latino political agenda." Wanting some good press, Bustamante replied that yes, absolutely, he had a secret Latino political agenda. The reporter, sure of a scoop, asked the then-Speaker what that agenda consisted of. Tick-

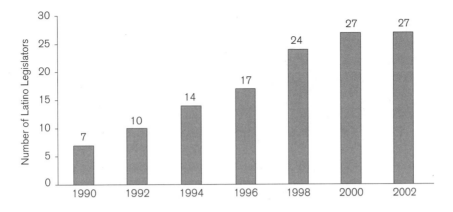

Figure 30. Latino State Legislators, California, 1990–2002. Source: Guerra 2003.

ing the points off on his fingers, Bustamante listed the topics on this secret Latino political agenda: good schools, safe streets, and good jobs for everyone. Disappointed at such a pedestrian agenda, certainly not the agenda for an ethnic political takeover, the reporter remonstrated that such an agenda did not seem particularly Latino or very secret—in fact, it seemed very ordinary. To which the then-Speaker replied that such was indeed the case. The Latino agenda is California's agenda, and vice versa. As far as Bustamante was concerned, there was no difference (Bustamante 1999).

Early in the George W. Bush administration, the president addressed Latinos nationwide by radio in Spanish. Some critics grumbled that his pronunciation left much to be desired, but that a sitting president would even attempt such a feat demonstrates how much Latino political fortunes have changed since the dark immigrant-bashing days of 1994. The Battle of Puebla was celebrated in the White House Rose Garden on Cinco de Mayo with strolling mariachis, and the popular singer of Mexican *ranchera* songs, Vicente Fernandez, made a statement of support of a Republican politician that would have been unthinkable earlier in the decade. Democratic Governor Gray Davis made a point of appearing at the Mariachi USA Festival at the Greek Theater in Los Angeles when appealing for Latino votes.

"IT'S OKAY TO BE LATINO NOW"

In the 1930s, strident anti-Latino rhetoric and massive deportations had served to intimidate many Latinos, forcing them to bury their cultural behavior. As recounted earlier in chapter 2, the children of deportation-era Latinos stated that the period from 1940 to 1965 was one in which being Latino was definitely not validated; some focus-group participants remembered feeling that they had to hide the Latino side of themselves.

Although the attacks on Latinos in the 1990s were as vicious as they had been in the 1930s, the result was quite different. Rather than creating another generation of "silent Latinos," the effect was to galvanize pride in being Latino, which in turn resulted in political participation and higher visibility. Focus-group members recounted how they felt: "I think that, as a note, 187 woke up that sleeping giant . . . that was dormant, not only in the political aspect but in the social aspect, the education aspect, because they were telling us that we no longer belonged here. . . . As a Latino community, as a whole, it woke up and said, 'Wait a minute!' " (CESLAC UW 1998, 2: U.S.-born Latinos, some college, 32). Repeatedly, U.S.-born Latino focus-group members recalled the difference between being Latino as children in postwar America and being Latino in the late 1990s. Being Latino had once been invalidated, but by the late 1990s, it was a validated experience. "You know, it's okay to be a Mexican. Now it's okay [laughter], but back in the forties and fifties, it was not. My mother raised me so that I wouldn't have to go through what she went through" (CESLAC UW 1998, 3: U.S.-born Latinos, some college, 26).

The validation in being Latino came from within the group, certainly not from outside. Indeed, the external drumbeat of negative imagery was a deliberate attempt to invalidate Latinos, leaving Latinos no choice but to validate themselves. "You go from here [downtown Los Angeles] all the way down to 120th [Street] . . . and it is thriving. You see stores, you see cafeterias, you see everything. And you see people on the streets, and you think, 'Wait a minute, this is the future of LA, and it's an entrepreneurial spirit that's dynamic and resilient' " (CESLAC UW 1998, 7: Latino civic leaders, 43). Participants perceived that this pulsing, vibrant economic engine had spread out from small barrios, to be influential in almost every area of Los Angeles. "During the past fifteen years, particularly the last ten years, I think that Latinos have established themselves in Los Angeles" (CESLAC UW 1998, 7: Latino civic leaders, 13). The same pattern could be seen in the rest of California.

The sea change in political representation created a corresponding high tide of Latino validation. While the political conflicts were painful in the early 1990s, by 2002 it was another area in which Latinos could point, with pride, to significant representational accomplishments. "It's a fact that we are now coming into positions of power, I think" (CESLAC UW 1998, 7: Latino civic leaders, 12). Although the road ahead might not be seen as smooth—for example, the Los Angeles mayoral campaign of 2000, in which the non-Hispanic white candidate ran commercials that attempted to present his Latino opponent as another Latino linked to the drug trade—focus-group members expressed a sense of empowerment. "I believe very firmly that Latinos are going to be running this place" (CESLAC UW 1998, 7: Latino civic leaders, 9). That both Republicans and Democrats were now courting and wooing their vote was not lost on Latinos. "In fact we're becoming the strongest political people you want to get on your side" (CESLAC UW 1998, 3: U.S.-born Latinos, some college, 96).

The political arena provided one locus for eventual validation. Just as important, however, was corporate America's validation of the Latino consumer base. Interested in profiting from that base, businesses paid the attention to Latinos that many politicians had tried to deny them.

> What we have going for us now that we've never had before is the growing recognition, on the part of those people who have historically been biased against us, that we are an economic power and that we are a major source, potential or present, of revenue for them. And they want to do that. In order to do that, they have to find out what our needs, our wants, our preferences, our ways of doing business are. (CESLAC UW 1998, 8: Latino business leaders, 44)

Although many U.S.-born Latinos were not fluent in Spanish, advertising in that language nevertheless was a source of validation for them. Immigrant Latinos saw Spanish-language advertising as a recognition of their presence. A participating Latino executive of a Fortune 500 corporation reported how his company saw the issue: "We, as a company . . . have no choice but to do our business in Spanish. We have no choice but to do that if we wanted to retain the consumer market" (CESLAC UW 1998, 7: Latino civic leaders, 17).

Spanish-language commercial advertising also presented the public with more positive imagery of Latinos. In contrast to contemporary English-language news portrayals—gang members, welfare mothers, illegal immigrants—these new images treated Latinos as human beings with dreams and ambitions. "Businesses . . . say, 'Hey, we're making money out of the Latino community.' You see commercials now that you wouldn't see before, like [department store, fast-food outlet]; and not only are they doing the commercials, but they're doing it *[sic]* with, like, values and cultural traditions that are addressed in these commercials" (CESLAC UW 1998, 2: U.S.-born Latinos, some college, 30).

Corporate efforts went far beyond simple Latino-oriented marketing. Adapting to specific Latino patterns of consumer taste, nimble businesses created completely new products that were more in tune with Latino self-images. These efforts have been quite successful. "I mean, it was nice for me to find a magazine, *Latina,* that I can buy, and I can actually read something in there and say, 'Oh yeah. okay.'. . .Yeah. No more *Glamour,* no more *Vogue,* no more *Housewives* [laughter]" (CESLAC UW 1998, 3: U.S.-born Latinos, some college, 99–100). These new commercial images resonated with Latino aspirations, and the corporations that aired them reaped financial rewards. The contrast with Proposition 187's images could not have been greater. "Our image is changing. We're not by the cactus anymore with the sombrero on. . . . We're college students, we're senators, we're congresspeople. We're people who are moving up" (CESLAC UW 1998, 3: U.S.-born Latinos, some college, 96).

Where, once, being Latino had been a source of shame, as a result of responding to the negative campaigns of the 1990s, now it had become a source of pride and satisfaction. "When I was going to college, there was *[sic]* very few Latins . . . and now I look at the colleges that I visit, or whatever, and you see a lot of Latinos, and that's beautiful" (CESLAC UW 1998, 2: U.S.-born Latinos, some college, 29).

❦

The 1990s were indeed times of crisis for Latinos in California. Immigrant Latinos, who had been largely responsible for the renovation of large swaths of inner-city Los Angeles, were thanked poorly for their efforts by the passage of a string of initiatives meant, in part, to limit Latino participation in the state. Yet they stayed the course. Having made their investments in family and home, immigrant Latinos chose to protect them politically by taking the heretofore unprecedented step of becoming naturalized U.S. citizens, then registering and voting in extremely high numbers.

U.S.-born Latinos did not shrink from immigrant Latinos, by and large, but joined with them to defend the Latino presence in the state from outside attacks. In doing so, together, both U.S.-born and immigrant Latinos have created a new political power base and are beginning to capture statewide offices. "You can be a Latino and keep doing that and live here very successfully, as opposed to have to hide it or lose it" (CESLAC UW 1998, 7: Latino civic leaders, 36).

Although Proposition 187 caused Latinos to feel uncomfortable in the public sphere, it also galvanized that community into action. Nevertheless, regret was expressed that it took such a drastic, negative, and divisive action to create the subsequent positive reactions. Latinos did become citizens, they registered, they did vote, and they changed the face of elected officialdom. Rather than shrink from being Latino, they expressed pride in it, strength in it, and fulfillment in it. California will never be the same. "[N]ow I can say, 'Yes, I'm a Mexican.' You know, it's okay now" (CESLAC UW 1998, 3: U.S.-born Latinos, some college, 90).

SIX

Latinos Define "American"

2000–2020

I think they [Latinos] want to be Americans, but . . . they want to be Americans on their own terms.

CESLAC MALDEF 1998, 2: Non-Hispanic whites, 22

EVER SINCE THE EMOTIONAL CAMPAIGN WAGED IN 1994 to pass Proposition 187, Mexican American Legal Defense and Education Fund (MALDEF) attorneys had been hearing a low-level drumbeat, the sound of a negative public perception of Latinos. They overheard comments, made in various meetings and functions, reflecting the feeling that it must be true, as had been depicted in the television ads, that most Latinos were undocumented immigrants, that immigration from Mexico and Latin America was ruining the state, and that Latinos refused to become part of American society. MALDEF attorneys were astounded by the residual ill-will still expressed in many quarters years after that measure had passed.

At about that same time, I was visited in Los Angeles by a former academic colleague from Berkeley. Much to my surprise, he told me he had voted in favor of Proposition 187. He was a bona fide red-diaper baby, whose father had been involved in numerous liberal causes during the cold-war period. He himself had been an early Peace Corps volunteer, serving in a severely underdeveloped country for two years, then marrying a health professional from Latin America. It seemed out of character to hear such a self-described political liberal mention that he had voted in favor of 187. I asked why he had done so, and he proceeded to repeat the images from the various television ads that had run for months—the state was awash in millions of undocumented immigrants, who increased crime rates, relied on welfare, and the like. He was concerned for the state and truly wanted to help "Save Our State"; hence his vote.

I then shared with him data from my research on the relatively small numbers of undocumented Latino immigrants and their positive role in society, and his eyebrows shot up. Why had no one shared any such data during the campaign? he remonstrated. He had been shown only one side of the debate and had never been offered an alternative argument. His shoulders slumped; he felt he had been duped, and he wondered how many liberals like himself had been sold an image of Latinos that was not sustained by the data. How many of his friends, he wondered, were in his position regarding their perceptions of Proposition 187—and were now lapsed liberals?

While the vote on the actual proposition receded into the past, the vivid images that had been broadcast for months still remained and were poisoning the political atmosphere. In 1997, Antonia Hernandez, MALDEF's president and CEO, decided to counter this negative tide with an alternative view of Latinos. She called together an advisory group of key Latino business and communications leaders, who concluded that constantly televised negative images were responsible for much of the public's jaundiced view of the Latino community. Thus, a television message that presented a more positive view of Latinos and their role in the state was needed. The target audience for the spot was the "lapsed liberal," a non-Hispanic white not necessarily negative about Latinos but lacking a positive Latino image. What should MALDEF say to such "lapsed liberals" about Latinos?

MALDEF asked CESLAC to conduct the background research that would identify the content of the message. We were invited into this process because we specialize in developing messages, usually about health, tailored to create awareness in Latino populations. We applied our methods to discover how to create a similar awareness in a non-Hispanic white population.

NON-HISPANIC WHITES DEFINE "AMERICAN"

We began by assembling focus groups of the target population of non-Hispanic white "lapsed liberals." The only selection criterion for participation in the focus group was that those selected not be overtly anti-Latino. Participants were told only that they would participate in developing a television commercial, a frequent activity in Los Angeles, where television-show pilots and movie plots are routinely tested.

We began by asking the groups to define what it means to be an American. Perhaps reflecting the groups' liberal composition, participants were initially a little reluctant to provide a specific definition. "I hear over and over again that no one can say what "American" is. . . . I don't think there is an American identity" (CESLAC MALDEF 1997, 4: NH whites, 8). Over time, though, a range of opinions about the nature of American society and identity emerged. Yet, in all the groups, there was always a small core that refused to be pinpointed on the nature of American identity.

Those who felt that there was an American society and identity also felt that it had changed over the past few decades. "There's a lot of question about what is it [American] anymore. What I grew up with doesn't . . . exist anymore. I tell my brother that it doesn't exist anymore" (CESLAC MALDEF 1997, 3: NH white evangelical young adults, 40).[1] The participants did not regret the changes in American society and identity but felt that their parents, the World War II generation, were having difficulty accepting and adjusting to the changes. "Definitely, I think my parents' age [group], the senior citizens, they're just frustrated because their world is changing. It used to be, say, the community where my parents lived, [was] 99 percent English-speaking" (CESLAC MALDEF 1997, 3: NH white evangelical young adults, 38).

We probed the non-Hispanic white focus-group participants: "When you say 'American,' how does that make you feel? What images come to your mind?" In all of the focus groups, participants eventually described some core civic values that to them were American values.

A feeling of pride in one's country, a sense of emotional commitment to the country's welfare, was described by members of various focus groups as a part of being an American. "It is the greatest country in the world, and I think most Americans agree—not all of them, but most of them" (CESLAC MALDEF 1997, 4: NH whites, 30). Although not predisposed to describe themselves as "flag-waving" types, these group members described the pull of classic American symbols on them. "The underlying values are, 'I believe in God, family, the American flag'" (CESLAC MALDEF 1997, 3: NH white evangelical young adults, 41).

1. Members of this particular focus group were young, non-Hispanic whites who lived in a predominantly Latino neighborhood close to the University of Southern California (adjacent to downtown Los Angeles) and were members of an integrated evangelical church. Although they were evangelicals, their daily lived experience with Latinos was not typical of evangelicals in more suburban areas.

For some participants, the classic "American Dream," the desire to aspire a level of well-being that is not possible elsewhere, is a central part of being an American. "But, I say, definitely part of American life is the sort of American Dream mentality. Like, you have this dream of what you want. You always want more. [It's an] individual-achievement mentality. 'I can get this if I work hard enough'" (CESLAC MALDEF 1997, 3: NH white evangelical young adults, 7).

Part of this achievement is for one's self, but part is also for one's children, to provide for them the opportunities one did not always have personally. "Yeah, working towards, 'Someday I can buy my own house if I work hard. Someday, you know, I can send my kids to college. . . . I can have a decent car'" (CESLAC MALDEF 1997, 3: NH white evangelical young adults, 7).

The desire to achieve, as described above, must be matched with actual accomplishment in order to be truly American. "I would term that as the American culture, that wanting to get ahead, wanting an education, wanting to buy a house, a hard work ethic" (CESLAC MALDEF 1997, 4: NH whites, 25).

The "rugged individual" has been an American archetype for at least two centuries. These groups shared that image enthusiastically. "['American' means that] I am an individual, I am unique, I am different" (CESLAC MALDEF 1997, 4: NH whites, 12). This individualism, the ability to define one's self and one's own life, is an American virtue, even if carried to the extreme of going against the crowd. "American is, if I want to go on, I will go" (CESLAC MALDEF 1997, 4: NH whites, 23).

Once the groups had defined their views of what was American, we gradually and subtly turned their attention to Latinos. The bottom-line question was: Are Latinos Americans? And the non-Hispanic white participants were horribly confused about Latinos as Americans. Their primary dilemma was: How could Latinos be Latino and be American at the same time? For, in their view, if Latinos still retained some sense of emotional commitment to Mexico or other home countries, this might interfere with their loyalties to America. "It's hard for us to identify with how you can have two homelands. . . . How can you love America and still love Mexico? . . . I love it here [in America], and if you're going to be a citizen, don't you want to love it, too?" (CESLAC MALDEF 1997, 4: NH whites, 31).

They expressed concern that a continuing desire by Latinos to maintain their culture might cause some harm to American society. "If you are going to be Mexican first and American second, what is that going to do?" (CES-

LAC MALDEF 1997, 4: NH whites, 33). Such a cultural continuity, they feared, might threaten the cohesion of American society. "What is the common identity that we are going to have that's going to keep us from falling to pieces?" (CESLAC MALDEF 1997, 4: NH whites, 34). In the worst case, they expressed fear that a continued emotional attraction to things Mexican might lead to the physical collapse of American society, such as happened in the former Yugoslavia, at that point torn apart by ethnic fighting and "ethnic cleansing." "Look at what happened to Yugoslavia—do we want the balkanization of America?" (CESLAC MALDEF 1997, 4: NH whites, 32). Arriving at the bottom line of their fears, there was concern that Latinos might not be willing to fight this country's wars if they were waged in Mexico or Latin America. "If we went to war, like, if we went to war with Cuba, a Mexican might have some affiliation or ties to Cuba because of the whole Latino-bonding thing and . . . [I wonder] whose side are you on?" (CESLAC MALDEF 1997, 4: NH whites, 29).

The depth of the emotions, particularly the fears expressed, left no doubt that the non-Hispanic white participants were quickly able to move beyond the fact that Latinos were facilitating these focus-group sessions. Their greatest concern was: Can Latinos truly be Americans if they feel a bond to things Latino?

U.S.-BORN LATINOS AS AMERICANS

After hearing the concerns of the non-Hispanic white "lapsed liberals" focus groups, we felt it important to assemble some Latino focus groups, to probe if they saw themselves as Americans. For U.S.-born Latinos, there was usually not a second's hesitation in describing themselves as Americans. "I love being an American" (CESLAC MALDEF 1998, 2: U.S.-born Latino professionals, 10). Some described "American" as being a transcendent description that could, and should, bridge over other group identities, including Latino. "I definitely do [feel American], and I think that's very positive. . . . The problem is that a lot of people . . . are always identifying themselves as one thing or another, but we are all Americans, you know" (CESLAC MALDEF 1998, 1: U.S.-born Latino blue-collar workers, 11).

Some Latinos in the focus groups traced their families' presence in what is now the United States to the original de Oñate expedition to New Mexico in 1598 (Villagrá 2001), twenty-two years before the Pilgrims landed at

Plymouth Rock. With their ancestors antedating nearly every other population except American Indians (who, as seen in chapter 1, were also partially their ancestors) in this country, they expressed quite proudly that,
while Latino, they, too, are part and parcel of the American landscape.
"One of the things about Hispanics is that, as Americans, some of us have
been here for a long time. We're part of this land" (CESLAC MALDEF
1998, 2: U.S.-born Latino professionals, 34).

The more affluent respondents who had traveled outside the United
States had discovered that even if other non-Hispanic white Americans
viewed them as not quite American, overseas they felt more American than
anything else. "I had the experience of being able to live out of the country for a long time. . . . I felt foreign when I left. . . . Once you leave this
country, you realize that you're not a foreigner" (CESLAC MALDEF 1998,
2: U.S.-born Latino professionals, 31).

The fact that non-Hispanic white Americans might not see Latinos as
Americans grieved some, for they wanted to be seen, and appreciated, as
Americans. "When I see the word 'American' . . . that's who we are. . . . It
needs to be engraved [sic] to the other ethnic groups out there that that's
who we really are, and they need to accept that" (CESLAC MALDEF 1998,
1: U.S.-born Latino blue-collar workers, 10).

Continuing their stories about feeling American, the U.S-born Latinos
recounted their personal histories with the term. Although they accepted
the term, they often felt that they were excluded from that identity by others, usually non-Hispanic whites. The exclusion process was a lifelong experience but was described as concentrated in the late adolescent early
adult period. Respondents remembered their childhood feelings, when they
naively assumed that they were simple, unhyphenated, unadorned Americans. "Other people impose artificial separation. . . . As a child, you identify yourself as an American first. Later on, you start learning [that] you are
different, kind of Hispanic" (CESLAC MALDEF 1998, 2: U.S.-born
Latino professionals, 26). In late childhood or early adolescence, they were
made aware that some elements in their daily experience were not part of
the "American" experience. Classes in American history that left out Latino
experiences were cited as an early example of feeling excluded from the term
"American." "Part of it happens when you take history classes and you learn
about the Pilgrims, and you think that is not part of your family, that came
over on the Mayflower" (CESLAC MALDEF 1998, 2: U.S.-born Latino
professionals, 27).

As they emerged into adulthood, the sense of exclusion from an "American" identity continued. One respondent recounted his sense of loss of childhood certainties that he was simply "American."

> Before college, I never questioned my identity. We lived in a Mexican community, and we did everything that everyone around us did, so the issue of identity never bothered me. Until we got to college. Excuse my language, all hell breaks loose, and you are being thrown all these terms . . . of . . . who you are. And then you ask yourself, "Wait. Wasn't I American to begin with?" (CESLAC MALDEF 1998, 1: U.S.-born Latino blue-collar workers, 19)

Over time, a few described how they developed a reluctance to use the term "American," as the process of exclusion continued. The reluctance is more the product of being excluded than of active rejection of the term, and things, American. "We are not racist. We want to be part of it. We don't want to separate ourselves; they separate us" (CESLAC MALDEF 1998, 2: U.S.-born Latino professionals, 18).

In the popular discourse about immigrants, a wide net is often cast that mixes nearly all Latinos together, irrespective of whether they were born in the United States. Claims about the undesirability of undocumented immigrants can be quickly generalized to all Latino immigrants, then to all Latinos. The following letter to the editor illustrates how quickly and effortlessly the distinctions between undocumented and all Latinos can be made. "You can call me a racist or anything else you want. . . . Mexicans don't have the right to force their values, standards and way of doing things down our throats in our own country. In fact, illegal aliens don't have the right to be here at all" (Letters 2001, 4). The widespread immigrant bashing of the early 1990s was felt by U.S.-born Latinos to be an extreme example of becoming excluded from the category "American." "In the late seventies, early eighties, we became the enemy again, the target" (CESLAC MALDEF 1998, 2: U.S.-born Latino professionals, 13). The repeatedly shown images and the heightened political rhetoric of those times gave the final shove to some respondents, who described feeling that they did not belong any longer. One participant showed the depth of her feelings when she mocked "typical" statements she sarcastically attributed to supporters of the various 1990 initiatives. " 'We gave them too much opportunity, we're opening too many doors for them. Stop them! Cut their health care, everything! Make it impossible for them to succeed!' " (CESLAC MALDEF 1998, 2: U.S.-born Latino professionals, 38). Such immigrant-bashing has often been interpreted by U.S.-born Latinos as being directed at them, and they gradually began to feel resentment.

At the end of the process of describing becoming excluded, some respondents expressed resentment at not being considered fully American. One expressed that he felt "distanced" from the term, although he would prefer to use it. "A lot of people, when they think of Americans, they equate that with Anglo Americans. So it is sometimes very difficult to call yourself Americans . . . because you have been distanced from that word" (CESLAC MALDEF 1998, 1: U.S.-born Latino blue-collar workers, 18–19).

Finally, after being so excluded for so long, some respondents were reluctant to use the term, as the struggle to be included had become too painful. "I just wanted to say [that] when the word 'American' comes up, I don't feel like an American. I feel, sometimes, I'm treated as second class. . . . The label "American", it's like it doesn't fit me" (CESLAC MALDEF 1998, 1: U.S.-born Latino blue-collar workers, 9).

U.S.-born Latinos have usually felt that they were American, but as they grew up, they felt pushed to one side, excluded from this definition and not accepted by non-Hispanic whites as truly American. Yet when members of this group travel internationally, it is clear to them they are American.

IMMIGRANT LATINOS AS AMERICANS

Immigrants from Mexico have been migrating to the state of California in sizable numbers for more than 150 years. When they first arrive, they have been made acutely aware of their Mexican-ness, often more so than when they were in Mexico. "Según ellos, nosotros somos diferentes a ellos; costumbres latinas son diferentes" [According to them (non-Hispanic whites), we are different from them; Latino customs are different] (CESLAC MALDEF 1998, 4: Immigrant Latinos, 13).

The dream that brought many respondents to California included putting down roots, marrying, buying a house, and raising a family. It was a reprise of the classic American Dream as described by the non-Hispanic white focus groups. "Así como uno viene del extranjero . . . y el sueño de uno de formar familia, de educar a los hijos, comprar casa, ese es uno de los sueños fundamentales" [When one comes from a foreign country . . . one's dream of starting a family, of educating one's children, buying a house; that is one of the fundamental dreams] (CESLAC MALDEF 1998, 4: Immigrant Latinos, 2). Their trajectory was to go from feeling they were strangers and foreigners to finally feeling an emotional attachment to the United States and engagement with their new identity as Americans.

Over time, they engaged in activities that helped to anchor them to the daily life of their communities in the United States. These could range from finding stable employment to learning English, which helped them begin to feel part of a larger community. "La actividad cuando ya sentí que era parte de este pais, pues, aprender el inglés y trabajar" [The activity that (I did) when I felt I was part of this country, well, learning English and working] (CESLAC MALDEF 1998, 4: Immigrant Latinos, 10). These activities could be as mundane as participating in a child's schooling, helping a neighbor, or paying taxes (CESLAC MALDEF 1998, 4: Immigrant Latinos, 11, 13).

> Incluso, fuí voluntaria de la escuela por un año, y me sentí muy satisfecha poder ayudar y poder servir a los niños. [I was even a volunteer in the school for a year, and I felt really satisfied that I could help and serve the children.]
>
> Participar en actividades comunitarias. [Participating in community activities.]
>
> Pagar impuestos. [Paying taxes.]

Voting was routinely described as the culminating activity that signaled they had dedicated their lives to the United States. "Cuando dí un voto allí y me dieron un sticker y que pude ir a la urna, dije, 'Ya soy parte del poder' " [When I voted and they gave me a sticker, and I could go to the ballot box, I said (to myself), "Now I am part of the powers-that-be"] (CESLAC MALDEF 1998, 4: Immigrant Latinos, 10).

In increasing numbers, Latino immigrants began becoming naturalized U.S. citizens. Although in the past there was great hesitation to do so, one after-effect of both the Immigration Reform and Control Act of 1986, which facilitated the amnesty and naturalization process, and of the Proposition 187 debate, which was often perceived as challenging the roots they had put down, was that more and more Latino immigrants have become naturalized citizens. "Cuando la tomé la residencia . . . yo tambien me considero . . . ciudadana americana; no sería ciudadana hispanoamericana" [When I started living (here) . . . I considered myself . . . an American citizen also; I would not be a Hispanic American citizen] (CESLAC MALDEF 1998, 4: Immigrant Latinos, 6).

Latino immigrants remarked in focus groups that after about a decade in the United States, when they returned to their home countries, they begin to realize that they were no longer simply Mexican or Salvadoran. They had developed some new habits of the heart. They felt that they were American, and they felt a surge of pride when seeing the American flag. The focus-group facilitator asked one group how the members felt when they saw the U.S. flag in the MALDEF television advertisement:

FACILITATOR: Una vez me dijeron que sienten un poquito de tristeza y confusión. ¿Me pueden decir que es lo que sienten con la bandera [de los Estados Unidos]? [They once told me that you feel a bit of sadness and confusion. Can you tell me what it is you feel when you see the (U.S.) flag?]

GROUP MEMBER: Cuando uno mira, le da a uno alegría. [When a person beholds it, it gives him joy.]

FACILITATOR: ¿Les faltó ver la bandera de México y El Salvador en este comercial? [Did you miss seeing the Mexican and Salvadoran flags in this commercial?]

GROUP MEMBER: ¡No!

GROUP MEMBER: ¡No!

GROUP MEMBER: ¡No!

GROUP MEMBER: ¡No hay necesidad! . . . Nosotros no somos de aquí, pero la sentimos así, como también los niños, nuestros hijos, han de sentir la alegría de la bandera. [It's not necessary! . . . We are not from here, but we feel as if we were, just as the children, our children, must feel the joy of the flag.] (CESLAC MALDEF 1998, 3: Immigrant Latinos, 30–32)

Whereas, years earlier, they felt that they were immigrants and foreigners, by the time they became naturalized citizens, they described a deep emotional attachment to the United States. In essence, they had finished the transfer of their loyalties from their country of origin to the United States and considered this country now to be their adopted homeland. "Entonces ésta es una segunda patria" [So this is (now) a second homeland] (CESLAC MALDEF 1998, 3: Immigrant Latinos, 31).

In spite of being the direct targets of the anti-immigrant campaigns of the 1990s, respondents expressed very little resentment about the treatment they had received. Rather, they wanted other Americans to learn to accept them as fellow Americans, as the following dialogue demonstrates (CES-LAC MALDEF 1998, 4: Immigrant Latinos, 28).

> Para demostrar que nosotros también estamos aquí, y que luchamos con ellos, y que hacemos cosas con ellos. [To let them know that we are here too, and that we fight alongside them and we do things together with them.]
>
> Que lo tienen que aceptar. [They have to accept that.]
>
> Les guste o no les guste. [Whether they like it or not.]

More information about how Latinos see their attachment to this country was revealed by a survey for the United Way of Greater Los Angeles, which CESLAC was asked to conduct between 1999 and 2000. I asked a sample of U.S.-born and immigrant Latinos to respond, point blank, to the assertion: "I am proud to be an American." The question was intentionally provocative, designed to polarize the respondents. I did not want respondents to be vague about their feelings, so I included the qualifier "proud." Figure 31 provides the patterns of response, from agreeing somewhat to agreeing strongly. U.S.-born Latinos were nearly unanimous: 95 percent replied "yes" to the question, with 82 percent agreeing strongly, and this after nearly a decade of Latino-bashing in the popular press and the public scourging of Proposition 187 (CESLAC 2000, 4). Immigrant Latino responses to the question largely reflected the emotional investment they had made in the United States. Naturalized citizens were nearly as unanimous as U.S.-born in answering positively: 88 percent replied "yes," with 70 percent agreeing strongly. Legal permanent residents, who had been in the United States a shorter period of time than the naturalized citizens, were understandably a little less likely to answer in the affirmative. Yet nearly two-thirds of them (64 percent) also responded "yes." The most ambivalent group included those immigrant Latinos on visas and other temporary statuses; only half (53 percent) responded positively. By way of comparison, when asked the same question, 97 percent of non-Hispanic whites and 96 percent of African Americans also agreed that they were proud to be Americans.

An earlier study, the California Identity Project (Hurtado et al. 1992, 59), designed to understand how Latinos constructed their social identity, provides further information of American-identity formation among Latinos. The phenomenon of Latino identity change and continuity from one generation to the next interested us especially, so we oversampled second- and third-generation U.S.-born Latinos; that is, we included more of them than

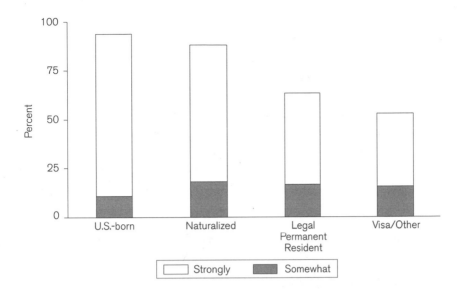

Figure 31. Percentage of Latinos Who Agree: "I am proud to be an American," Los Angeles County, 2000. Source: CESLAC Social Attitudes Survey 2000.

would be encountered in a straight population-based sample, so that we could better see their responses. This way we could see changes in how Latinos viewed themselves from the immigrant Latino (first generation) to the U.S.-born Latino child (second generation, adult at the time of the study), to the U.S.-born Latino grandchild (third generation, also adult at the time of the study). Although the study was conducted more than a decade ago, the general pattern is still valid today.

We gathered the responses of a statewide sample of 1,086 Latino adult heads of household (average age thirty-eight years) who had been asked to describe themselves using "descriptors" such as "Democrat" or "blue-collar worker." Included in the list were "immigrant," "foreigner," "American," "U.S. citizen," and "U.S. native." Not surprisingly, most of the immigrant Latinos saw themselves as immigrant or foreigner. Seventy-seven percent of first-generation Latinos still called themselves immigrants, and more than 63 percent still called themselves foreigners. But by the second generation, the sense of being an immigrant and being foreign had dropped substantially: only 18 percent of this group called themselves immigrants, and 13 percent called themselves foreigners. By the third generation, these terms had nearly disappeared from Latino self-identity: 4 percent of third-generation U.S.-

born Latinos called themselves immigrants; 4 percent called themselves foreigners. They no longer saw themselves as being separate from other Americans (Hurtado et al. 1992, 59).

In 1990, only 18 percent of immigrant Latinos described themselves as Americans. Their children, however, saw themselves as part and parcel of the American landscape, describing themselves as U.S. natives, U.S. citizens, and Americans. In the second generation, 85 percent described themselves as U.S. citizens, 76 percent as U.S. natives, and 74 percent as plain, unadorned Americans. By the third generation, 90 percent described themselves as U.S. citizens, 84 percent as U.S. natives, and 83 percent as unhyphenated Americans.

The results of ten years of surveys and the specially commissioned focus groups pointed to one conclusion: Latinos feel that they are Americans. The longer Latinos are in the United States, the more likely it is that they consider themselves to be American. As more immigrant Latinos have become naturalized in the last decade, a much higher percentage of this community considers itself American sooner, as the 2000 United Way data confirm. Yet their emotional connection to America was not clearly perceived by even the most sympathetic non-Hispanic whites, the "lapsed liberals" in our focus groups. As the MALDEF advisory group pored over the research, dissected non-Hispanic white concerns, and felt stung by Latino frustration over exclusion, we decided on the advertisement's core message: Latinos are Americans like anyone else.

THE MALDEF PUBLIC ANNOUNCEMENT

MALDEF asked Hector and Norma Orcí, principals of La Agencia de Orcí, one of the largest Latino advertising agencies in the country, to help craft a message that could provide a more positive, healthy, productive, and realistic image of Latinos. They immediately agreed and committed key agency staff members to the project. Two staffers, given in-depth briefings on the focus-group findings, developed a series of storyboards for presentation to the community advisory committee. Once the message was agreed on, all the necessary work for shooting and showing a commercial began, from writing the script and getting permission to film on location around the city of Los Angeles, to finding volunteer actors, to editing the film and layering in the voice-over narration, music, and optical effects, to raising funds to buy prime-time broadcast hours from the major television stations. Between February and April 1998, southern California viewers of news-commentary programs and upper-end sports events such as golf and tennis saw a thirty-second commercial that caught many of them off guard: "A message from Hispanic Americans." While an off-screen narrator reassured listeners that Latinos shared the same goals, dreams, and problems as everyone else, a number of images flashed across the screen:

two white-coated Latinos peering through a microscope

a business-suited Latino presenting at a meeting

a Latino construction contractor on the job with his workers

a gaggle of multihued children sliding down playground equipment

a multicultural neighborhood birthday piñata party

a group of young Latino children wearing antidrug T-shirts

Latinos washing out and painting over graffiti

a grainy television news archive shot of a Latino soldier wounded in action

a Latino soldier returning home to his family

a Latino Cub Scout and a Latino Boy Scout

a multicultural group of children playing baseball

a young Latino couple buying a house

a diversified group of students graduating from college

The closing shot showed a ten-year-old boy saluting the American flag, as the announcer signed off with "America. It's home. For everybody."

MALDEF's office received scores of calls about the television spot. The ad, some callers said, went by so fast that they were a little confused. Was MALDEF trying to sell them something? If so, it wasn't clear what that thing was. Was it presenting a position on another proposition about immigrants? Latinos also called, enthusiastic about what they had just seen. Was this a motivational, inspirational message for Latino immigrants? If so, was it available in Spanish? Was it going to be shown on Univisión or Telemundo, the Spanish-language networks?

MALDEF asked us at CESLAC to call another round of focus groups to evaluate the public-service announcement and provide suggestions for a follow-up campaign. In La Agencia de Orcí's focus-group facilities, we convened groups of non-Hispanic whites and Latinos, both U.S.-born and immigrant.

NON-HISPANIC WHITE REACTIONS

First, we convened groups of non-Hispanic whites, most of whom had not seen the commercial on television. To commence our sessions with the groups, we showed the spot to them twice in succession and then asked them to discuss how it made them feel.

Initially, the emotional responses were uniformly positive. The spot's high production values showed and set the desired emotional tone. The short commercial gave an unprecedented message of hope. Unlike ads of the 1994 Proposition 187 campaign, which were specifically designed to make people feel uneasy and upset about Latino presence in the state so as to stampede them into supporting the measure, this commercial provided a sense of hope. "I think initially I was, like, 'What is it selling?' but at the end I was, like, 'Oh, I had hope. That was good'" (CESLAC MALDEF 1998, 5: NH whites, 42). The combination of high production values, soothing voice-over narration, and soft but peppy salsa background music created a feel-good atmosphere. "It threw me off. I actually felt good about it" (CESLAC MALDEF 1998, 5: NH whites, 42).

The repetition of images of Latinos doing things that non-Hispanic whites also did—working, playing, celebrating, buying houses, graduating, fighting the country's wars—provided an unusual sense of commonality. "You look at this, and you're saying, 'Yeah, they look like us; they are doing the same things we do; they are appreciating the things we appreciate'" (CESLAC MALDEF 1998, 6: NH whites, 27).

Then the serpent appeared in the garden. As the non-Hispanic whites reflected a little, they began to notice a discrepancy between the commercial and what they had momentarily forgotten they "knew" about Latinos: Latinos are not middle class at all. "Is this what you would call middle-class Latinos?" (CESLAC MALDEF 1998, 6: NH whites, 27). Their daily images of Latinos were not of middle-class persons with whom they had a lot in common, but of a different class of people, who probably did not have many things in common with them. The constant images of middle-class Latinos did not square with their perception that Latinos are rarely middle class. "It's a nice, pretty picture, but it's not what we read about all the time in the *LA Times*" (CESLAC MALDEF 1998, 5: NH whites, 35).

A few respondents, after reflecting about the discrepancies between what they saw in the commercial and what they "knew" about Latinos, began to reject the commercial. "I got this sense of looking for the Latino in the picture, and I couldn't find them" (CESLAC MALDEF 1998, 5: NH whites, 30). Rather than perceiving that Latinos could be scientists, teachers, builders, and soldiers, they reverted back to what they "knew" Latinos did: menial labor that was poorly remunerated. "The people that connect with your conceptual center are the Latinos you see that bus dishes, nannies, who do the car wash" (CESLAC MALDEF 1998, 6: NH whites, 36).

One respondent provided a partial analysis of the genesis of the discrepancy, blaming the policy debates for the creation of the picture of Latinos as non-middle-class. "In political culture, we don't talk about the middle-class Hispanic. We talk about the barrios and gangs and the violent, the people who don't have opportunities" (CESLAC MALDEF 1998, 6: NH whites, 27). As the focus-group respondents talked about their sources of information about Latinos, they began to describe extremely limited inputs, which perhaps had led them to feel that a spot that showed middle-class Latinos was unusual. "I actually have no information, so I don't have any way of knowing what Latinos want or say. I mean, I don't live in a very integrated world. I don't really have many [Latino] social contacts" (CESLAC MALDEF 1998, 6: NH whites, 23). Up to this point in their lives, they had not seen a Latino middle class.

In the non-Hispanic white focus groups conducted prior to and after the release of the MALDEF commercial, our focus-group facilitator noticed that the participants kept developing a particular line of thought related to the perceived lack of Latino accomplishment and their subsequent ability to be considered American. After participants had articulated that a key element of the American Dream was the desire to achieve more, to accomplish more, to better oneself, they were not sure that Latinos really wanted to progress, particularly into the middle class.

The non-Hispanic white participants, who all lived in California, certainly had noticed that Latinos are hard workers. "They do the jobs that nobody else does. And you know what, I wouldn't want to hire anyone else, because they are hard-working; they take pride, whether they are a dishwasher or a turkey carver. In California, the restaurant industry would die without Latinos" (CESLAC MALDEF 1997, 6: NH whites, middle age, 44). They recounted personal experiences with Latino labor: gardeners, nannies, mechanics, odd-job workers. "My son had a babysitter, a Mexican lady. Gosh, I love her to death. She doesn't speak very good English" (CESLAC MALDEF 1997, 6: NH whites, middle age, 11).

Yet, for all the admiration they expressed about Latinos' strong work ethic, in their perspective all this hard work did not seem to get Latinos anywhere. In particular, it seemed as if Latinos were perpetually mired in poverty, in spite of working hard. "When you think of the Mexican Spanish, you think of the barrios, of lower class" (CESLAC MALDEF 1998, 6: NH whites, 28). Participants speculated that maybe this lack of upward mobility, in spite of the hard work, was an indication of a Latino lack of higher aspirations. "They [Latino parents] are giving mixed messages. On one level, 'My kid is important; I will work one hundred hours, and I will be responsible for them.' On the other is, 'I can't verbalize anything beyond that'" (CESLAC MALDEF 1997, 3: NH white evangelical young adults, 13).

An important part of being American was aspiration to improve one's lot: getting an education, buying a house, wanting to improve oneself. When the participants watched televised news at night, however, what they saw was a lack of Latino mobility. The pictures they constantly described were of Latino low-income workers, gang members, school dropouts, and poverty. "One thing I see prevalent among the Latino parents, especially in this community, is sort of a hopelessness, like, 'We are stuck here and there is no getting out of this' . . . and I see the same thing translated to their kids" (CESLAC MALDEF 1997, 3: NH white evangelical young adults, 11).

Participants discussed the idea that all immigrant groups are poor when they arrive, including their own ancestors. But modern Latino immigrants appeared not to be moving up, or their children either, and this concerned them.

This seeming lack of achievement was bothersome for the non-Hispanic white participants; they felt that such a lack could be un-American. "If they [Latinos] express, 'No, I'm stuck in a barrio, I can't get out,' then they [Anglos] don't like that; it's not in line with their American Dream" (CESLAC MALDEF 1997, 3: NH white evangelical young adults, 5).

Rarely did the participants describe Latinos who had achieved. If anything, after some discussion among themselves, they described suddenly being aware of not seeing Latino achievement. "If you had a hundred Latinos, maybe five to ten would be in that [middle-class] category. . . . [They] are the exception, more invisible" (CESLAC MALDEF 1998, 6: NH whites, 37). And if most Latinos were not achieving, given that the United States offers opportunity to everyone, then might it not be possible, they mused, that Latinos are not, or do not want to be, or possibly cannot be, American?

Because MALDEF had received so many calls from Latinos, asking that the spot be run on Spanish-language television, focus groups were also held with Latinos to evaluate that possibility. We held separate groups, in English for U.S.-born Latinos and in Spanish for immigrant Latinos. As with the NH white group, the participants only knew that they were testing a television commercial. We showed the video twice, once without sound, to ask what message they thought the images were trying to convey, and once with sound, to get their reactions to the voice-over and music.

The U.S.-born, in particular, did not generally watch Spanish-language television; hence, they had seen only English-language eleven o'clock news images of Latinos. When shown this spot, they were at once overwhelmed by the simple fact of positive images of Latinos. "It was, like, wow! They are actually portraying people graduating and people happy and working, and these are all Latinos. I thought that was really cool, and I felt really proud" (CESLAC MALDEF 1998, 1: U.S.-born Latino blue-collar workers, 1). Especially after nearly a decade of consciously negative portrayals of Latinos in the pro-Proposition 187 campaigns, U.S.-born Latinos described their feelings of emotional catharsis when presented with a positive image created for mainstream television. "Initially, I felt kind of like I wanted to cry, but not because I was sad but because it was the first time I had seen a collection of so many positive things" (CESLAC MALDEF 1998, 1: U.S.-born Latino blue-collar workers, 1).

Both of the U.S.-born groups spent a considerable amount of time describing how validating it felt to see positive Latino images. They also consistently commented on the absence of such imagery from English-language television. Most often mentioned was the news treatment of Latinos. "I felt good, like some people said, that they knew it existed, but I was surprised to see it on TV, you know, because in the news you don't see that" (CESLAC MALDEF 1998, 1: U.S.-born Latino blue-collar workers, 6).

Immigrant Latinos who have learned English (and most of them eventually do) also watch English-language news and notice the constant negative imagery, which on Spanish-language television news is balanced out by portrayals of the rest of the Latino community news, including human-interest stories, political events, business news, and entertainment news. "Todo le echan al latino. Mira al latino como está destruyendo" [They blame everything on Latinos. Look at the Latino, how he's destroying (things)] (CESLAC MALDEF 1998, 3: Immigrant Latinos, 13). After further reflection, this lack of positive imagery was also noticed in the programming itself. "Images are so powerful, and so far I can't think of one TV program that portrays positive images of Latinos" (CESLAC MALDEF 1998, 1: U.S.-born Latino blue-collar workers, 40). Even commercial advertisements managed to present a less-than-flattering portrait of Latinos. Popular in the late 1990s was a commercial for a fast-food chain that used a talking Chihuahua dog to ask for Mexican-style food. "You can have something like this [MALDEF spot], versus us being [depicted as] gang members, prostitutes, and being sex symbols or jumping the border, or being a Chihuahua. This is ridiculous; this is 1998, and we are still categorized as that, and we are going to become the majority in California" (CESLAC MALDEF 1998, 1: U.S.-born Latino blue-collar workers, 40).

Whereas non-Hispanic white respondents were eventually put off by not seeing the Latino images they were most familiar with, Latino respondents, both U.S.-born and immigrant, saw nothing out of the ordinary in the images provided. These were common scenes for them. "There were a lot of images that were familiar to me" (CESLAC MALDEF 1998, 1: U.S.-born Latino blue-collar workers, 38). Even English-dominant U.S.-born Latinos who no longer lived in the barrios could relate to these images, for these were seen in their family life.

Whereas non-Hispanic whites could not imagine that immigrants could possibly live as portrayed in the short announcement, immigrant Latinos had no problem identifying themselves in the various images. The facilitator asked one group of immigrants if the people in the spot seemed authentic to them.

> FACILITATOR: ¿La gente que vieron, es gente real? [The people you saw, are they real people?]
> GROUP MEMBER: ¡Sí! [Yes!] [multiple responses]
> GROUP MEMBER: Son personas como nosotros. [They are people like us.]
> GROUP MEMBER: Casos de la vida real. [Examples of real life.] (CESLAC MALDEF 1998, 4: Immigrant Latinos, 3)

They contrasted the negative images shown on English-language television with the ones provided in the spot and felt that the spot reflected their community far better. "Nuestra comunidad es más como ésta" [Our community is more like this] (CESLAC MALDEF 1998, 3: Immigrant Latinos, 22). The emotional connection to the various images was quite strong for the immigrants. "Se siente como si uno fuera parte de la vida de ahí" [One feels as if one were part of the life (depicted) there] (CESLAC MALDEF 1998, 3: Immigrant Latinos, 10).

In stark contrast to the bewilderment expressed by the non-Hispanic white respondents, caused by the perceived differences between the spot's Latino images and the ones they were more familiar with, Latino respondents said that the announcement provided an accurate representation of their everyday life. The images that were so disconcerting for non-Hispanic white respondents provided a comfort level for Latinos. "What I remember about the ad is that it is almost colloquial, in that it's like everyday, like the events that happen in the course of a normal day for people. . . . This is . . . what happens in our homes, our parks, our churches, our neighborhoods. . . . Really, what I liked about it was its everyday kind of quality" (CESLAC MALDEF 1998, 2: U.S.-born Latino professionals, 7). Immigrants, who loomed so large in the negative depictions of a California on the road to wrack and ruin, likewise felt that these images were simply a reflection of their daily life. Interestingly, the very images that caused a dissonance for non-Hispanic white respondents were seen as realistic and ordinary for Latinos.

The dissonance described by the non-Hispanic white focus-group members is a product of nearly exclusive media and policy attention on the recently arrived immigrant. Immigrant Latinos, like most immigrants to the United States, arrive with few financial resources and start at the bottom of the job and socioeconomic ladders. They take the least desirable jobs, busing tables, selling oranges on freeway on-ramps, and working as nannies. Over time, most immigrants work their way out of poverty, learn English, and eventually become home owners. But this movement up the socioeconomic ladder is rarely seen by most media and policy shapers. Television news prefers dramatic images, catastrophes, immigrants dying forgotten in a box car in Iowa. It is not surprising that many people feel that Latinos are not moving up, and so they ask if Latinos really have what it takes to be Americans.

One answer comes from the 1996 Current Population Survey national oversample of immigrants (U.S. Bureau of the Census 1997). Latino immigrants do indeed move up. The survey shows that about half (53.3 percent) of the most recently arrived immigrants from Mexico, those who arrived between 1990 and 1996, live above the poverty line. Those who have been in the United States a little longer, arriving in 1980–89, have moved further out of poverty; 63.2 percent are above the federal poverty level. Those who have been here yet longer, arriving in 1970–79, are even further

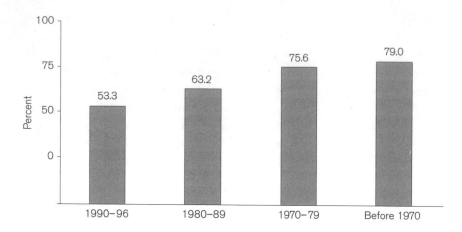

Figure 32. Movement Out of Poverty by Year of Entry, Mexican Immigrants, United States, 1996. Source: U.S. Bureau of the Census 1997.

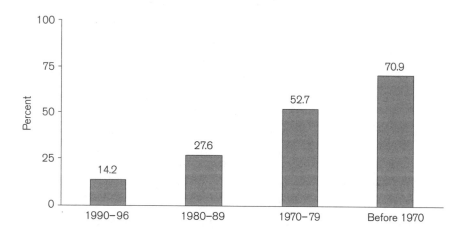

Figure 33. Home Ownership by Year of Entry, Mexican Immigrants, United States, 1996. Source: U.S. Bureau of the Census 1997.

out of poverty; 75.6 percent earn above poverty levels. Those who have been in the United States for twenty-five years or more, with entry prior to 1970, have moved the furthest; 79.0 percent live above the federal poverty level (see Figure 32). The dynamic is very clear. Given enough time, most immigrants will move out of poverty.

Home ownership is another indicator of stability and long-term commitment. The longer Mexican immigrants are in the United States, the more likely it is that they will have bought homes. The most recently arrived, after 1990, were the least likely to have bought a house (14.2 percent); those who arrived a little earlier, in 1980–89, were more likely (27.6 percent); those who arrived yet earlier, in 1970–79, even more likely (52.7 percent); and those who arrived prior to 1970 have home ownership rates not too different from those of U.S.-born Latinos (70.9 percent) (see Figure 33). The reassuring, unambiguous finding of more than a decade of research is: yes, most Latinos do want to enter the middle class, and in fact, given enough time, most do.

BELMONT HIGH SCHOOL, CLASS OF 1989

In the 1950s, California's public education system was one of the wonders of the country, consistently ranking among the top five in the United States. By the 1990s, however, it had fallen nearly all the way to the bottom of the U.S. ranking, by almost every measure. Some districts manage to function, and some function well, but on the rock bottom are some of the large urban districts that seem to exist in chaos. The Los Angeles Unified School District (LAUSD) seemed to lag so far behind other school districts in the state that the superintendent of LAUSD, Ramon Cortines, called it the most dysfunctional district in America (Sahagun 2000, A1; Sahagun and Smith 2000, B1). Within that discouraging context, Belmont High School has the reputation for being the most overcrowded, understaffed, lowest-performing high school in one of the nation's most dysfunctional school districts. How bad is it? Even though the Belmont High building is overcrowded and physically decaying by the week, the Board of Education cannot decide whether, or how, to finish building a replacement for the school, the foundations of which have already cost more than $1 billion but which may be sitting on top of a pocket of methane gas. Three different school superintendents in three years have not been able to break the deadlock.

The area around Belmont High epitomizes the demographic changes that time has wrought in Los Angeles. Fifty years ago, the formerly genteel MacArthur Park, just west of the concrete corridors of downtown Los Angeles, was ringed by refined hotels and upscale medical offices. Elegantly dressed ladies walked carefully groomed dogs around the lake. Pico Union was the shabbier relative, but it provided affordable housing for those waiting to be discovered at Schwab's drugstore.

After the 1965 Watts riots panicked the non-Hispanic white residents into leaving the core downtown area, hundreds of thousands of Central American political refugees and an equal number of immigrants fleeing Mexico's economic turmoil filled the population vacuum. The neighborhood now has the dubious distinction of being the most overcrowded in the county, with one of the lowest adult education attainment levels, one of the highest rates of poverty, and some of the highest rates of stubborn tuberculosis. For over a decade now, MacArthur Park has been taken over by drug dealers and gang members. Across the street, *pupuserías* (shops selling *pupusas*, a traditional Salvadoran dish) occupy spaces once rented by jewelry stores.

In June 1999, Robert Lopez, a young reporter covering the urban beat at the *Los Angeles Times,* wondered what had happened to his classmates from Belmont High, class of 1989. Was he, he wondered, the only one of his class to become a modest success? Was his story unique? Did most of his classmates wind up prey to drugs, gangs, dropout pressures, and teen pregnancy? He convinced his editor to use the *Times*'s surveying capabilities to find out, ten years later, what they had done with their lives.

Finally, after nearly five months of polling—including tracking one classmate down to an Indian reservation in Arizona—the sample was complete. What the reporter saw in the results both surprised and did not surprise him (Lopez and Connell 2000). More than two-thirds of his classmates were Latinos, nearly all of them either immigrants or the children of immigrants, primarily from Mexico and El Salvador. Very few of their parents had graduated from high school, and they themselves had spent four years at the most dysfunctional school in the most dysfunctional school district in a state ranked near the bottom nationally in education. It sounded like a formula for a vicious cycle—a poster school for the urban underclass—if there ever was one.

Yet the data from the survey showed that the class of 1989, especially the Latino population, was solidly middle-class, only ten years after their senior year, in spite of all they had had to contend with at Belmont High. The Latinos in the class of '89 had greatly improved on their parents' educational levels. While only a little more than one-third (39 percent) of their parents had graduated from high school, close to all (85 percent) the Latinos in their class had graduated. More than three-fourths (77 percent) had gone on to study in college, and over one-fourth (28 percent) had received a bachelor's degree. We can best appreciate the magnitude of this increase in educational attainment under such dysfunctional conditions when we realize that, in the state of California, an identical percentage of non-Hispanic white adults aged twenty-five and older (27.9 percent) (D. Hayes-Bautista 1996, 38) also earned a bachelor's degree in 1990, but they came from families with far greater income, far higher parental educational levels, and, of course, superior mastery of English.

Robert Lopez was not alone in achieving a middle-class job. In fact, nearly all his Latino classmates (87 percent) were active members of the workforce, and over three-fourths (80 percent) worked in either white-collar or managerial positions. Almost half (45 percent) earned $40,000 or more per year, while still relatively young in their careers; college graduates would only have been five years in the workforce. Despite their youth, however, Latinos of the class of '89 did not copy the television sit-com yuppie formula of eternal dating without commitment, but demonstrated a very Latino pattern of marrying and having children. Nearly half (47 percent) were married, and slightly more than half of those couples (58 percent) already had children. It is unlikely that their low-income, poorly educated parents could have given them much help in buying a house, but well over one-third (34 percent) were already home owners, so young in their careers.

If improvement in life is a cornerstone of the American Dream, Belmont's 1989 Latino graduates are extremely American. Virtually unanimously (94 percent), they believed they had much better opportunities in life than their parents had. While still getting their professional feet under them, over three-fourths (75 percent) already had improved on their parents' economic situation, while 19 percent were still on a par but probably looking to move ahead eventually.

The fact that some of his classmates had become middle-class did not surprise Lopez. He had kept in contact with a few old high school friends, and they had risen together. What did surprise him was that nearly *all* his classmates had moved up into the middle class. What might they all have accomplished, he wondered, if they had gone to a *good* high school, one that had had enough books, teachers, and space for everyone?

"AMERICAN" AS DEFINED BY LATINOS

In spite of being educated at one of the most problematic schools in the state, Belmont High School's class of 1989 is typical of Latino high school students. In fact, their lives ten years after graduation provide a basis for some speculation about how Latinos are defining what it means to be American.

Through our work on the health of the adolescent Latino population—

including the relatively small, but important, percentage of Latino adolescents who become involved in teen pregnancy, substance abuse, and other risk behaviors—we have observed Latinos making the vital transition from dependent children to autonomous, individualized adults within the context of Latino family and community dynamics. A basic process of adolescent transition can be observed in any group of teenagers in the United States, but Latino adolescents demonstrate some distinctive characteristics. Very little work has been done on Latino adolescents, and the following observations are essentially anecdotal, although illuminated by some data (D. Hayes-Bautista, Hsu, Hayes-Bautista, Iñiguez et al. 2002).

Generally, adolescence is a time of testing limits of parental knowledge and authority. It is the rare adolescent who does not, at some point, question the parental way of life and experiment with alternative dress, music, behavior, and the like. During this period, the foundations for future civic identity and participation also are formed, as adolescents begin to define themselves and explore ways of expressing their uniqueness and individuality. In so doing, they start to define their relationships with the rest of society.

Of course, this does not take place in a vacuum. While parents recede into the background, peers and youth culture loom large, providing new sources of socialization. When Latinos were a small minority, they frequently felt rather isolated at this important period in their lives. Because there was virtually no media-delivered, Latino-oriented youth culture to relate to up through the 1970s, Chicano-era Latinos essentially created their own.

But by the early twenty-first century, the social environment has changed radically. In 2004, among California's population of children and adolescents seventeen years of age and younger, the Department of Finance projects that the largest single group—comprising nearly one out of every two children and adolescents (45 percent)—is Latino. In Los Angeles County, the predominance of Latino adolescents is even more striking; at 62.4 percent of the young population, there are three times as many Latino youths as non-Hispanic whites, nearly six times as many Latino youths as African Americans or Asian/Pacific Islanders (CA DOF 1998).

The peer groups that loom so large in adolescent development are now largely Latino in California; in major urban areas such as Los Angeles, Fresno, and others, Latinos form the overwhelmingly predominant element of youth peer culture. Latino cultural expression is driving media markets in many parts of the state. A Latino adolescent–young adult culture is emerging, delivered daily via radio, television, and the Internet. Away from adult supervision, away from xenophobic initiatives, Latino youth are defining who they are vis-à-vis American society. How do they view themselves as Americans?

Data from the previously mentioned 1990 California Identity Project (Hurtado et al. 1992, 59) provide some clues as to how the "average American" of California in twenty years will likely describe him- or herself. Earlier, we saw that while first-generation immigrant Latinos were not likely to call themselves plain, unadorned "American," their second- and third-generation U.S.-born Latino children and grandchildren almost unanimously saw themselves as "American," with no modifiers added; that is, they did not describe themselves as "hyphenated-American." This sense of being American is a major change over the three generations of Latinos.

It is equally important to note, however, that there were some descriptors as likely to be chosen by first-generation immigrants as by third-generation U.S.-born Latinos. These seem to be consistent elements in the self-perception of these Latino Americans, passed unchanged from one generation to the next.

The family orientation of Latino populations has become almost a marketing cliché. Yet sixty years of census data, from 1940 to 2000, confirm it, so there is some basis to this marketing shortcut. In the CIP survey, in fact, nearly all Latinos in all three generations identified themselves as a member of a family: 91 percent of the first generation, 96 percent of the second generation, and 95 percent of the third generation chose this descriptor. Unwittingly, they were repeating Fernand Braudel's contention that families "provide the geology beneath history" (1988, 106–7); that is, the basic "ways of being and doing" are learned first in the family, and those constructs are used to create larger social organizations.

Although Latinos often have difficulty describing Latino culture, they are very likely to describe themselves as being formed by it. Eighty-eight percent of first-generation respondents described themselves as being Hispanic, as did 83 percent of second-generation and 83 percent of third-generation Latinos. In spite of assertions that Latinos are largely becoming Protestant, data from this 1990 study, confirmed by the 2000 United Way study, show that this movement is fairly minor. Most Latinos, over all three generations, define themselves as Catholic: 79 percent in the first generation, 74 percent in the second, and 77 percent in the third.

One social-identity element, however, did change significantly over the three generations. Eighty-seven percent of the first generation, 79 percent of the second generation, and 65 percent of the third generation called themselves Spanish-speaking. Yet while there is a significant decline over the three generations, this change needs to be taken in the context of the official discouragement of Spanish-language ability and lack of Spanish-language media during the lives of the third-generation respondents from 1940 to 1970. The fact that almost two-thirds of third-generation U.S.-born Latinos used this item to describe themselves shows the tenacity of the language.

From the surveys and focus-group work it is clear that Latinos, particularly those born in the United States, see themselves as Americans, are proud to be Americans, and identify with the "American Dream." These Americans, however, differ from Atlantic Americans in some fundamental ways. They form very large, strong family networks; they like to speak Spanish in addition to English; and they feel very comfortable with the mores and values they learned at home. But they are American and resent any implication that they are not.

CONVERGING DEFINITIONS OF "AMERICAN"

By the end of each MALDEF focus-group session, the non-Hispanic white participants began to reflect on how much the definition of "American" has expanded, possibly enough to include Latinos whose lives are still anchored in the Latino cultural experience. The participants wondered if their expanded definition of America was a product of living in southern California, with its diverse population. California, now, provides an opportunity to glimpse American identity as it might be defined later in the twenty-first century. "For someone living in Los Angeles, it [American] seems more blurred for us than it is for somebody in the Plain[s] states, Idaho, or Iowa" (CESLAC MALDEF 1997, 4: NH whites, 6). It is this very blurriness that provides a glimpse into the future of American identity.

Whoever aspires to be an American, according the focus-group discussions, has to demonstrate an emotional commitment to the country. There has to be no doubt as to whose side such a candidate would fight for. "If you say someone is assimilated, they may love the country they came from, but they also have that sense of 'I love America'" (CESLAC MALDEF 1997, 3: NH white evangelical young adults, 9). Although the non-Hispanic white respondents did not know it at the time of their focus-group sessions, Latinos agreed with that definition.

These baby-boomer and Generation X non-Hispanic whites could see that their parents' generation had required a nearly complete assimilation of immigrants in order to be considered American. "This is one of the things that drives [older] Americans crazy because they feel that immigrants should drop their culture" (CESLAC MALDEF 1997, 2: NH whites, 20). These younger participants, however, leaned more toward an acculturation than a total assimilation. They thought that Latino immigrants should not have to give up their culture completely but that they should have to learn how to navigate the local host culture. "It doesn't mean necessarily losing your own culture but coming and coexisting with the culture that exist[s] in a neighborhood" (CESLAC MALDEF 1997, 3: NH white evangelical young adults, 2).

In cases in which the vast majority of the local host culture might already be Latino, acculturation meant learning to navigate outside the Latino cultural shell. "I think assimilation does have to do with being involved with [a] different culture other than your own. Not necessarily moving out of a culture that's purely Hispanic, but involved with the [other] culture" (CESLAC MALDEF 1997, 3: NH white evangelical young adults, 45). Again, they did not know it at the time, but Latinos agreed with them.

Living in an environment where the top-rated radio and television stations are aimed at the Spanish-language market, these non-Hispanic white participants did not expect that Latinos would stop speaking Spanish. However, they did expect that Latinos should learn enough English to facilitate communication. "Well, if you are coming to my country, the United States, our country, I think you should have to learn some English, enough to get by" (CESLAC MALDEF 1997, 6: NH whites, middle age, 8).

Given the ubiquity of Spanish-language communication in southern California, these respondents also had come to accept the idea that their own personal economic success might in large part hinge on their learning enough Spanish to communicate. "I definitely see that the schools are pushing bilingual education to Anglos. They're saying, you're not going to have a future in economics, in business, in teaching, et cetera, unless you know English and Spanish" (CESLAC MALDEF 1997, 4: NH white evangelical young adults, 11). Once again, Latinos agreed with them.

Although the non-Hispanic focus-group members were not sure that Latinos were American, some eventually expressed the opinion that perhaps Latinos do indeed want to become American. "I do think and feel very strongly that the Latinos want to be American" (CESLAC MALDEF 1998, 2: NH whites, 20). They could see that immigrants were attracted to this country, and from what they could tell, the opportunities provided to them here were far greater than they could have encountered in their home countries. Thus, it seemed logical that Latinos might have a desire to become American.

Any person interested in the economic well-being of southern California quickly understands how vital the Latino market is to the economy. Not only have radio and television stations aimed themselves at this population segment, but entire chains of grocery stores, clothing stores, and consumer electronics stores have staked their future on this market. Far from being a minority culture in danger of extinction, Latino culture is alive and well in the region's marketplace. The strength of the cultural dynamics that now drive major market decisions impressed the non-Hispanic white respondents. "This group has a very strong culture" (CESLAC MALDEF 1998, 2: NH whites, 20). Of course, the sheer size of the Latino population segment—nearly eight million strong in southern California, from Ventura to San Diego counties—helps propel the cultural dynamics. In the area of music, for example, internal changes in Latino musical tastes keep entire genres of music profitable, such as rock en español, banda, and *romántica* music. "They are large enough to be able to keep their culture" (CESLAC MALDEF 1998, 2: NH whites, 20).

—

The non-Hispanic white focus groups came to conclude that Latinos might want to be American, but it appeared that Latinos would be Americans in ways that included the retention of large portions of Latino culture. "They want to keep their culture, I do believe, but I also think that . . . many, if not most, Latino immigrants, they would want to be Americans" (CESLAC MALDEF 1998, 2: NH whites, 21). There seemed to be ways of being and doing that were not associated with Atlantic American culture but that were part of the Latino culture. "[They become American], but they want to keep those ways of behaving, those ways of expressing themselves that don't seem to be part . . . of [non-Hispanic] white culture" (CESLAC MALDEF 1998, 2: NH whites, 30).

Given the sheer size of the Latino population and the ubiquitousness of Latino culture, Latinos might turn out to be Americans in precisely the ways that Latinos want to develop, independent of non-Hispanic white desires. One respondent nicely summarized this thought about Latinos becoming Americans in a slightly different way: "They want to be American, as Latinos" (CESLAC MALDEF 1998, 2: NH whites, 20). Latinos in the focus groups agreed with the non-Hispanic whites on this point. Indeed, Latinos today are defining what it is to be American.

SEVEN

Creating a Regional American Identity

2020–2040

LATINO OR AMERICAN?

I come from Texas. What a Texan views as American is very different from somebody here [in Los Angeles].

CESLAC MALDEF 1997, 4: NH whites, 6

A SENIOR REPORTER FROM A LARGE EAST COAST NEWSPAPER decided that for one of his last professional columns before retiring, he wanted to write about something that was new to him: Latinos. He traveled to Los Angeles, to the epicenter of Latino population growth, to embark on a series of interviews with a variety of Latinos. He arranged to have breakfast with me to provide himself with some background before getting started in LA. During our breakfast at a glitzy Westwood restaurant noted for its popularity in the movie business, the reporter kept prodding me to define myself: Was I primarily a Latino, or primarily an American? I frustrated him by refusing to state an unequivocal choice. He appeared to think I was evading the question. But I too felt frustrated: I could not explain to him in a way he could understand that, particularly for U.S.-born Latinos, there is no difference between the two.

Suddenly, an analogy came to mind, a way of explaining my position so that he could grasp that the very asking of the question has already posited a false polarity. I replied (I am reconstructing this exchange from memory), "You have to look at it like this. When you ask me that question, you're implying that Latino is not American, or that maybe it's un-American, and that's not it. Think of it like this: being Latino is not un-American. It's not being anti-American; it's like being . . . being . . . a Texan. It's a *distinctive* way of being American."

"Oh, I see." The reporter eased back into his chair, reflecting on this insight. The analogy was new to me too, having just flashed across my mind. Thinking out loud, I continued, "Look, you know how Texans are; they're different. With their accent and vocabulary, they talk differently; they walk differently in those cowboy boots; they wear those cowboy hats. They are very proud to be Texan. You know some Texans, don't you?"

"Yes," he replied, still pondering my comments.

"Well, would you ever ask a Texan to choose between being a Texan and an American? Of course not. For a Texan, that's a ridiculous question. Texans are Americans. They will refuse to separate the two. You won't find any more patriotic group than Texans. And that's the key. Texans aren't un-American or anti-American; they're Americans, but Texas style, and proudly so. Well, think of Latinos the same way. Sure, we're Latino. And we're American. It's that we're American, Latino style. It's not a choice between the two. Being Latino is like being a Texan; it's a *distinctive* way of being American."

The quintessential cultural icon of Texas is the cowboy, a figure nearly synonymous around the globe with America. Yet the evolution of the American cowboy provides a case study of how societies, cultures, and traditions blend, modifying themselves to suit local circumstances. It also provides a clue to the future role Latinos may play in American identity and society.

From the beginning, cattle raising was a key element in defining the identity of the region that came to be known as Texas. British colonists brought cattle with them across the ocean, as well as cattle-tending methods—farmers on foot, aided by herding dogs prodding cattle to pasture by day and back to an enclosure by night, became the norm in the Atlantic colonies (Jordan 1993, 43–55). On the Iberian Peninsula, however, a different form of cattle raising had developed. There, men on horseback drove herds of cattle from one open range to another. Once a year, herds would be separated and animals branded with a hot iron to establish ownership. This form of cattle tending was also established in the Americas, giving rise to many local variants: the *gaucho* in Argentina, the *huaso* in Chile, the *llanero* in Venezuela, and the *vaquero* (literally, "men who work with cows") in Mexico (Slatta 1997, 74–98). Vaqueros operated as far north as Texas, New Mexico, Arizona, and California.

In Texas, Mexican vaqueros adapted Iberian techniques and equipment to local conditions. They wore broad-brimmed hats to protect themselves from the burning sun and leather *chaparreras* to protect clothing from spiky mesquite branches (Sandler 2001, 23), and they carried a rope called *la reata* that formed a noose called a *lazo,* with which to capture cattle on the open range (Jordan 1993, 102; Sandler 2001, 43). The finest rope was made from *mecate* (hair from horses' tails), which they used to form a bitless bridle, called a *jáquima,* to begin the process of taming a wild *bronco.* Astride a trained *mesteño,* they herded cattle into a *corral,* roped one animal and stopped it in its tracks by quickly snubbing the rope around the saddle horn in a maneuver called *dale vuelta* (give it a turn), letting the horse's weight serve as an anchor (Sandler 2001, 45; Jordan 1993, 256, 262). After a *rodeo,* vaqueros celebrating with too much liquor would be picked up to spend a few days in the local *juzgado.*

When settlers from Virginia, Tennessee, and Kentucky moved to Texas during the 1820s, they quickly discovered that tending cattle on foot, British style, was not suitable for the sparsely vegetated, wide-open plains. In a feat of cultural borrowing, they picked up the technology developed by Mexicans for Texas conditions and even adapted the Spanish terminology. They became cowboys, *buckaroos* (a mispronunciation of vaqueros), with ten-gallon hats adapted from the wide-brimmed Mexican sombrero, wearing *chaps* (chaparreras) to protect their clothing, using a *lariat* (la reata) to *lasso* (lazo) cattle. They used fine rope made out of horses' tails called *McCarthy* (mecate) to make *hackamore* bridles (jáquima) for the early stages of *bronc*-busting (bronco). Once astride a trained *mustang* (mesteño), they would rope a calf in the *corral* (corral) and stop it in midstride by snubbing one end of the rope around the saddle horn in a maneuver known as *dally roping* (dale vuelta). Using a Mexican saddle with a horn, they participated in *rodeos* (rodeo), and when they celebrated and got drunk, they sometimes would spend a night or two in the local *hoosegow* (juzgado).

That most American of images—the cowboy on the lone prairie—was the product of the meeting and partial merging of Latino and Atlantic American civil societies and cultures. British cattle technology alone never would have given rise to the cowboy; yet the social and cultural mix created a regional culture and identity that today is distinctly Texan, yet wholly American.

This cultural mixture became an unconscious part of the daily life and self-image of people—non-Hispanic whites, Latinos, African Americans,

American Indians—living in the Texas region. So strong was this bicultural influence that it created a distinctive regional identity. One hundred and fifty years later, a similar type of cultural blending process is at work in California, most likely creating the foundation for a future regional identity. To see that process at work, we need to develop a new way to view Latinos: neither as a dysfunctional minority nor as simply an immigrant group, but as creators of a civil society. Such a view allows us to understand better the continuity and change that are at once California's history and its future.

With Latinos already comprising more than half of all children born in California, Latinos cannot be considered a numerical minority. And, as we have seen in earlier chapters, Latinos do not fit the definition of "dysfunctional minority" as used in policymaking. Rather than exhibiting endlessly dysfunctional behavior, Latino social behaviors have been the strongest of any group, and their health outcomes are surprisingly good. Some (Linda Chavez 2001) have tended to see Latinos as just another immigrant group and have suggested the Latino future will resemble that of Italian or other immigrant groups. Yet the European immigrant experience is of limited value in understanding Latino social dynamics. To begin with, for most of the past 150 years, the majority of Latinos in California have been U.S.-born. At times in the company of immigrant Latinos, at times by themselves without immigrant accompaniment, U.S.-born Latinos have been making their lives in this state, doing so in very "Latino" ways.

Latinos are not just a minority, or immigrant group. To understand Latino paradoxes, we need to look into the thoughts and behaviors of Latinos, both those born in the United States and their immigrant relatives, over the past 230 years to discern their possible future, as well as the influence of immigrants on them. We need to look for the "Latino habits of the heart" that have been passed from generation to generation, constituting the "stock of knowledge" that an individual Latino uses in her or his daily life.

LATINO CIVIL SOCIETY

Tocqueville . . . speaks of . . . "habits of the heart"; notions, opinions and ideas that "shape mental habits."

BELLAH 1996, 37

Civil society is, essentially, the world of daily life—the world of primary relations such as are found in family, friends, neighborhood, faith communities, small businesses, workplace networks, and voluntary associations—

upon which rests the larger institutions of society, such as governmental and marketplace organizations (Spragens 1995; Hollenbach 1995). Over conversations at the dinner table, through behavior modeled while performing household tasks, through silent example and spoken word, this primary network provides a place for daily conversations about the guiding values of life: the good and the bad, the desirable and the undesirable, the just and the unjust, the beautiful and the ugly, and so on. These countless family conversations also provide important first notions of self and the sense of the "we" in society. Family tales, lore, traditions, and practices provide the initial notions. The larger network of relatives, friends, neighbors, and parishioners provides additional ideas.

Civil society is a human product, an ongoing human production. Experiences are shared between individuals in a primary group, and the accumulation of these experiences and their meanings gradually constitute a "stock of knowledge" (Berger and Luckmann 1966, 41). This stock of knowledge is transmitted from generation to generation and is available to each individual in daily life. Almost unconsciously, an individual develops, within the primary web of social relationships, de Tocqueville's "habits of the heart," the unexamined mental and emotional framework that guides an individual to actions because they "feel right," not because a rational decision has been made.

The twelve million Latinos in California by 2004 present a seeming paradox. In spite of low income and poor educational levels, they present social behaviors and a health profile equal to, or stronger than, groups with far better education and far higher incomes. These profiles cannot be attributed to income and education or access to care; hence, we must look at the one area left for investigation: the moral discourse and mores that lie at the core of Latino daily life—in other words, at Latino civil society, based on "habits of the Latino heart," the product of a civil vision emanating from processes and dynamics brought to California by Mexican colonists from 1769 to the present day.

Latino civil society provided not only place names now world-famous—San Francisco, Sacramento, San Diego, Los Angeles—but also patterns of daily behavior that are, once again, forming the core of social life for half the babies born in the state. Temporarily overshadowed by a century of Atlantic American numerical dominance, Latino civil society once again provides a framework for behaviors that may come to be seen as "typically California behavior" by the middle of this century. Latino civil society will be at the center of a new regional identity.

Health Indicators

For more than thirty years, I have researched Latino experiences in health care in California. The disease areas I have researched are many: HIV/AIDS, diabetes, asthma, arthritis, obstetrics, breast cancer, osteoporosis, teen pregnancy, and youth risk behavior, with special attention to the issues of children, adolescents, immigrants, the elderly, and farmworkers. Research in these areas has given me the privilege of being able to look deeply into Latino values and daily behaviors concerning issues that are very basic to the human condition, stripped of superfluous noise about identity politics, political correctness, or ethnic pride. Instead, I have heard Latinos grappling with the fundamental issues of human existence: illness, pain, suffering, death, relief, hope, birth, and life. Listening closely, I have heard them describing their values, their culture, and their sense of moral development while they described daily activities related to health. These activities and conversations provide the framework of meaning that yields the strong health and social behaviors so at odds with the low income and low educational levels common in most Latino populations.

And, as I continue to research Latino health, I am convinced that these daily conversations around the kitchen table, on seemingly mundane, unimportant topics, provide the cultural and intellectual resources for a strong, productive, harmonious California society for the twenty-first century: the habits of the Latino heart, with roots that go back hundreds, sometimes thousands, of years. Although the research that would "prove" the influence of Latino civil society in this respect remains to be conducted, I nevertheless want to share some observations that have led me to recognize the persistence of that civil society.

In a class that I teach each spring to around sixty Latino premed students, I routinely ask the aspiring physicians, dentists, epidemiologists, biostatisticians, nurse practitioners, and health educators to describe the last pregnancy in their family. Usually they allude to a sister's or a close cousin's experience. Then I ask them what sorts of beliefs and behaviors these urban Latinos engaged in when pregnant. A number are mentioned year after year: they avoid chewing gum, avoid "cold" foods and drinks, shun smoking and alcohol. Also mentioned, year after year, is the fact that pregnant Latina women wear red underwear adorned with a safety pin. Their mothers and grandmothers feel this ensures the birth of a healthy baby.

The wearing of red material around the belly during pregnancy dates back to pre-Columbian times. Unlike Europeans, who saw a "man in moon," the indigenous Náhua (Aztecs) of Mexico saw a rabbit in the full moon. They believed that if a pregnant woman exposed her fetus to the rabbit-faced full moon, her child risked a hare-lip or other deformity. Náhua prenatal practices suggested that a pregnant woman could protect her baby from the deleterious effects of the moon by suspending an obsidian blade over her swollen belly, tied by a red string—red being one of the Náhua cardinal colors. This advice was passed from mother to daughter in Náhuatl or other Indian languages. After the arrival of the Spaniards, a metal blade was substituted for the obsidian, and the advice came to be passed from mother to daughter in the Spanish language. Once underwear was developed, the red string fell into disuse, replaced by a full set of red underwear; the blade, over time, was replaced by a metal key. This custom has been observed by anthropologists studying modern-day Mexican birth behaviors (Madsen 1964, 70; Clark 1959, 122).

In twenty-first-century California, a safety pin stuck through red bikini underwear does the trick, and the advice now is passed from mother to daughter in the English language. When I ask if the students believe what their mothers and grandmothers have told them, they usually laugh nervously and reply that, while it does not make rational sense, they will indeed wear red underwear with a safety pin when they are pregnant. "Better to be safe than sorry," one student inevitably replies.

Diabetes is the bête noire of the Latino community, the major disease for which the Latino Epidemiological Paradox does not hold true. Latino mortality from diabetes is two to three times as high as the rate for non-Hispanic whites. Because of its intractability in the Latino community, I have conducted a number of studies regarding diabetes knowledge, beliefs, and behaviors, with both Latino and non-Hispanic white populations. In 1997, I conducted a population-based telephone survey of Latino and non-Hispanic white elderly persons (sixty-five years or older) in Los Angeles County (CESLAC Roybal 1997). Among other items, we asked our respondents an open-ended question: What did they think caused a person to become diabetic? The response patterns, for immigrant Latino and non-Hispanic white elderly, shown in Figure 34, are fascinating and reveal once again the persistence of Latino civil society in the world of health beliefs. It surprised the study's funders, the Centers for Disease Control in Atlanta, to find that immigrant Latino elderly persons were about as likely as non-Hispanic white elderly to mention the roles of heredity, diet, and being overweight as factors in the onset of diabetes. Yet, unlike their non-Hispanic white counterparts, immigrant Latino elderly were nearly as likely to at-

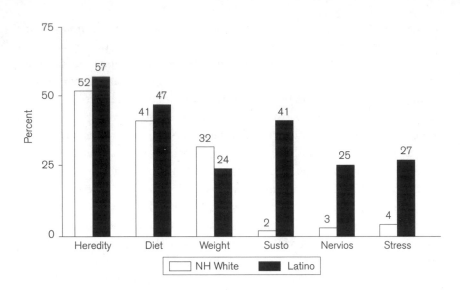

Figure 34. Causes of Diabetes, Latino Immigrant and NH White, 65+, Los Angeles County, 1997. Source: CESLAC Roybal 1997.

tribute the onset of diabetes to emotional factors as well: *susto, nervios,* and stress (see Figure 34).

Susto is a classic Mexican folk disease, having its roots in indigenous Náhua beliefs about the relation between the body and spirit. It is caused by an emotional trauma, a sudden emotional shock, and is often cited by Latinos as the reason for the onset of diabetes in an adult. "Con el susto que me dieron cuando me volvieron a decir que tenía cancer, me asusté y me volvió a subir el azucar . . . precisamente porque me asustaba" [Because of the fright *(susto)* they gave me when they told me again that I had cancer, I became frightened, and my sugar (levels) rose again . . . precisely because of the fright that I had suffered] (CESLAC Diabetes 1997, 2: Immigrant Latina, 1–2). Nervios and stress are two additional emotional causes of diabetes perceived by Latino respondents. The specific source of the emotional stress—susto, nervios, stress—is less important than the larger causal view, that an upset to a person's emotions can cause either the onset of diabetes, or, if one already has diabetes, an increase in blood-sugar levels.

Sí, es emocional, porque el diabetis pega de gusto, de susto, de tristeza; de todo pega el diabetis. . . . Entonces, si a usted le da gusto, le puede subir el

diabetis, si tiene tristeza, puede subir el diabetis, si hace coraje . . . se
sube . . . el diabetis. [Yes, it is emotional, because diabetes comes from an
intense desire for something *(gusto)*, from a fright *(susto)*, from sadness; diabetes comes from all of that. . . . So, if you really want something, your
diabetes can go up; if you are sad, your diabetes can go up; if you get
angry . . . your diabetes . . . can go up.] (CESLAC Diabetes 1998, 5: Immigrant Latinos, 8)

The Náhua believed that the link of *tonalli* (soul) and body could be tenuous at times, and it could be endangered by proscribed activities such as
drunkenness or inappropriate sexual intercourse. An emotional shock also
could separate soul from body (McKeever Furst 1995, 111–12). Bolton (1981)
noted that indigenous descriptions of susto—shaking, debility, fainting,
loss of consciousness, and anxiety—could also be descriptions of a diabetic
suffering from hypoglycemia. Interestingly, although anthropologists (Kay
1977, 139; Clark 1959, 175–78; Madsen 1964, 77) have described susto as an
illness that must be treated in its own right, none have cited it so far as a
factor in the onset of diabetes.

The existence of many folk cures for diabetes reflects a continuation of
Latino civil society into the world of medicine. Perhaps the most commonly mentioned herbal cure is a nearly unshakable belief in the efficacy
of nopal, a cactus found in Mexico.

Cuando como nopales me baja [el nivel de azúcar], cantidad. Cantidad!
El nopal me ayuda cantidad. Hasta voy a buscar pastillas de nopal, que
me dijeron que hay cápsulas de nopal. Porque cuando como nopales me
baja. Cuando me sube, inmediatamente como nopales y al otro día se me
quita, me baja. [When I eat nopales, my (blood-sugar level) goes down a
lot. A lot! Nopales help me a lot. I am even looking for nopal pills, because they told me that there are nopal pills. Because when I eat nopales,
it goes down. When it goes up, I immediately eat nopales, and by the
next day, it goes away, it goes down.] (CESLAC Diabetes 1997, 2: Immigrant Latina, 6)

Nopal can be eaten raw, cooked, strained into a juice, or mixed into a
"smoothie" in a blender. Although our surveys did not ask about the preva-
lence of nopal usage, its constant mention in focus groups and testimony
from physicians managing Latino diabetics lead us to see it as another re-

minder of how deeply rooted Latino civil society remains in twenty-first-century California.

Another chronic condition, arthritis, is also routinely treated by Latinos with an astounding array of home remedies for pain: a tincture of alcohol and marijuana leaves, *ventosas* (cuppings), rattlesnake meat, uncontrolled *nostra* purchased in Tijuana pharmacies, and the like. Not surprisingly, we also have heard variations on an age-old Mexican hot-cold theory as a source of arthritis: a too-rapid change from warm to cold—throwing ice water on someone perspiring in the Mojave Desert or moving too quickly from the summer warmth into a cold meat locker—is believed to bring on the disease. But others described arthritis as being a result of *bilis* (bile), supposedly produced when a person is emotionally angry or upset. A *bilioso,* an easily angered, Type-A sort of personality, was described as being more susceptible to arthritis and other diseases (CESLAC Arthritis 2001, 3: U.S.-born Latino males, 31–34).

GROUP MEMBER: Another one [type of arthritis] is from your mind. . . .

GROUP MEMBER: And one is people who get mad easily.

FACILITATOR: Who get mad easily?

GROUP MEMBER: Sí. Es muy bilioso. [Yes. One who is a very angry personality type.]

GROUP MEMBER: It also is when you're angry and you hold it in.

GROUP MEMBER: Biliar. [Biliary.]

GROUP MEMBER: And nerves. Emotional, emotional.

These angry types of people expose themselves, in many Latino respondents' views, to adverse health outcomes, including arthritis, rheumatism, and other diseases.

GROUP MEMBER: Le pegó a mi suegra el reumatismo bilioso. [My mother-in-law got bilious rheumatism.]

FACILITATOR: Bilioso? Hay reumatismo bilioso? [Bilious? There is bilious rheumatism?]

GROUP MEMBER: Ese le vino de un susto. . . . Se puso amarillo . . . se enmoheció la coyuntura porque se le derramó la bilis. [It was because of a susto. . . . She got all yellow . . . her joints got all rusted . . . because her bile spilled over.]

GROUP MEMBER: Yo he sabido que sí derraman las bilis de un susto. De un susto hasta muda queda la gente. [I have known that susto causes bile to spill over. Because of a susto, people even have been struck mute.] (CESLAC Arthritis 2001, 10: Immigrant Latina females, 32–33)

Again, these health beliefs have their origin in pre-Columbian Mexico. Mc-Keever Furst (1995, 129–30) described the Náhua belief that the somatic location of the tonalli was in the joints; an injury to the joint could cause an injury to a person's soul. López Austín (1980, 218) has examined medical manuscripts written in Náhuatl and pointed out that the joints of the body—wrists, elbows, shoulders, knees, ankles, hips, and neck—were considered to be minor *"centros anímicos,"* or places where life-giving forces resided. Although the Náhuatl manuscripts did not specifically state that anger would cause an arthritis flare-up, the relation between an angry state (bilioso) and arthritis has been reported so consistently that I consider it as a primary indication of a pre-Columbian belief, related to the Náhua vision of the body and its relation to the universe.

Latino civil society is also present in the operating room. Dr. Ismael Nuño, chief of Cardiac Surgery at the Los Angeles County/University of Southern California Medical Center, talks extensively with his patients and their families about the possibility of death during a heart transplant, a procedure designed to save life. But when Dr. Nuño counsels Latino patients, their concern usually is not with possible mortality (Nuño 1999, 166). Still believing, as did the Náhuas, that the soul resides in the heart (López Austín 1980, 252–57; McKeever Furst 1995, 17–19), Latino patients are more concerned about the transplant's effects on a person's character—kindness or meanness, astuteness, love and passion. Removing the diseased organ that contained one soul and replacing it with another could be risky. They fear that a totally new person will awake from the operation, and they wonder if this person will recognize the family.

In our research on the relation between Latino culture and health, we have uncovered scores of similar examples that illustrate the persistence of a deeply rooted, fundamentally influential Latino civil society in the world of health and illness. The growing Latino population has distinctive views of health and illness, life and death, which can be traced back over centuries and which are alive and well in examination rooms in today's California. They are part and parcel of the larger cultural dynamic that has been the experience of most of the Western Hemisphere. And by virtue of the size of the Latino population, they are becoming part of the daily experience of health and illness of the average person in California.

Origins

The concept of "Latino civil society" should be used to view the past, present, and future roles of Latinos in California. The other definitions used in the past to describe Latinos simply have not been useful: a minority, a race, a linguistic group, a traditional society, or an urban underclass. Latinos defy all these attempts to be boxed into a single category. From all the data we have seen in this book, clearly Latinos are more than a group practicing identity politics. Viewing Latinos as a civil society allows us a larger, more comprehensive, more dynamic framework for viewing Latinos sui generis. In order to see the future role of Latino civil society, we need to appreciate its origins.

For non-Latinos, perhaps the most recognizable and familiar elements of Latino civil society are the Iberian ones, for example, the use of the Spanish language and the presence of Catholic symbols. The Iberian Peninsula was, and is, part and parcel of Western Christian civilization. Itself an amalgamation of various peoples—Celts, Phoenicians, Romans, Goths, Arabs, Berbers, and Sephardic Jews—and several religions—Catholicism, Islam, and Judaism—the Iberian region presented a mosaic of languages, cultures, genetics, and politics, all tucked by 1492, sometimes none too tidily, under the covering tent of militarily triumphant Catholicism.

Yet, this amazing diversity was, officially at least, artificially reduced to an imposed homogeneity when brought to the New World. Of the many languages spoken on the peninsula—Catalan, Euzkadi, Galician, and Asturian, among others—Castilian, the language originating in the region of Castile, was mandated, by the mid-sixteenth century, as the official language of the Spanish colonies (Cuevas 1914, 59). This somewhat artificial linguistic uniformity has resulted, five hundred years later, in the relative linguistic unity that allows Argentine and Venezuelan *novelas* (televised soap operas) to find a lucrative audience among the thirty-five million Latinos in the United States alone.

A key element of Latino civilization was, of course, Catholicism. Yet this unity of religion was tempered by the nature of Catholicism; it is by its nature a religion of diversity, encompassing a wide variety of opinions manifested in the multiple religious orders—Franciscans, Dominicans, Jesuits, and so on—that were given authority over different regions of Latin America.

The multicultural Iberian society was artificially reduced when brought to the Americas, and this artificially homogeneous reflection was overlaid on the even more diverse indigenous societies of the New World.

To understand the future regional identity of California, it is important to understand a major difference between the British and the Spanish approaches to indigenous societies. While neither asked the indigenous what their desires might be, the British, and later Atlantic Americans, generally saw Indians as an obstacle, a nuisance that should be moved out of the way as rapidly as possible. The Spanish Crown, however, saw the Indians as subjects and citizens of the realm—under certain restrictions, of course, but also deserving of certain protections. Thus, rather than seek ever-more-remote reservations for Indians, the Spanish Crown sought to incorporate them into the regime. The results were quite different from the British colonial experience.

In the Americas, the tongue of Castile encountered hundreds of indigenous languages and dialects, and it did not always win out as the main vehicle for communication. Many Indian languages, such as Náhuatl, actually gained in influence by now being written in the Roman alphabet and used in a wide variety of settings: religious instruction, theater, lawsuits, wills, music, and poetry. The Jesuits, in particular, were assiduous in learning native languages—especially Náhuatl, which they considered the lingua franca of Mesoamerica—and wrote grammars of eleven indigenous languages for use in translating religious materials (Martinez 2001, 30). Thanks to these linguistic efforts, the Castilian language was often held in abeyance, and for a while indigenous languages flourished. In a process lasting three centuries, Indians learned Spanish, but Europeans also learned indigenous terms for native plants, animals, foods, and social behaviors.

The Crown's Catholicism likewise confronted the diverse religious beliefs of the different indigenous societies. Some key Catholic beliefs—finding salvation in community, the importance of ritual, the sacramentality of life's events—proved to be critical points of nearly immediate convergence with indigenous traditions. This convergence and blending of European Catholic and indigenous spirituality can be seen in the reported apparition in 1531 of the Virgin of Guadalupe to the Náhuatl-speaking Indian Juan Diego (canonized by the church in 2002). Not coincidentally, the brown-skinned, Náhuatl-speaking Virgin Mary appeared at the spot where the Aztec earth-goddess Tonantzin ("Our Mother") had been venerated for centuries (León-Portilla 2000). For nearly three centuries, efforts to inculcate Western Catholicism into the indigenous experience of God yielded a vigorous publishing industry in Náhuatl, providing narrative, plays, music, and poetry in the language of the Aztecs, as well as in Castilian Spanish and Latin.

The extent to which the various indigenous societies should, or should not, be influenced by the Europeans was constantly debated by the Spaniards. Some argued that the indigenous peoples should be assimilated as a source of labor and commerce, expecting that they should completely adopt Iberian ways of life. Others, for example the first generation of evangelizers, argued that the corrupting Iberian influences should be kept away from Indians. They advocated the formation of Indian utopias, protected areas in which indigenous languages and traditions could flourish and into which the Spanish should not be allowed to intrude.

Indigenous societies could not continue to be unaffected by the Spanish presence for one simple reason: the epidemiology of the conquest, especially of smallpox, which was unwittingly unleashed on a population that had no related immune defenses. When the ravages of epidemic *cocolixtli* (smallpox, probably) took the lives of an estimated 95 percent of the indigenous population of Mexico over the course of the sixteenth century, a demographic vacuum resulted. A new, diverse population—the mestizo, the offspring of Spanish, Indian, African, and Asian—filled the void. Ultimately, the various waves of cocolixtli may be said to have created the population dynamics of twenty-first-century California. Mestizo society was more than simply a bridge, or mediator society, between the Spanish and Indian. It was a fusion of the two, more than simply an Iberian transplant, yet very different from the indigenous cultures.

The mestizo paid reverence to both the Iberian and the indigenous in the spiritual realm. While the recently converted Indian might be suspected of hiding pre-Columbian gods beneath a supposed conversion to Christianity, the mestizo was rarely suspected of this. Life for the mestizo was filled with sacrament, the presence of the sacred and a joyful release into ritual. The complementarity of indigenous and the Catholic religions found full, unquestioning expression in the religious beliefs and practices of mestizo society.

Meaning in mestizo society was created and sustained by two sources: the formal, institutional church; and popular Catholicism independent of, but linked to, the institutional church. Often called "popular religion" or "popular spirituality" (Matovina 1998, 82), Latino faith expressions are "those religious traditions which the majority of a people celebrate voluntarily, transmit from generation to generation . . . with the clergy, without them, or even in spite of them" (Elizondo and Matovina 1998, 3). More important to daily life was popular Catholicism, the unconscious welding of pre-Columbian moral discourse with a pre-Tridentine Catholicism, largely unaffected by the search for individual perfection unleashed by Martin Luther and John Calvin. Mestizo popular religion built on indigenous ritual and Iberian popular cults of saints. Only occasionally reinforced by the formal sacramental life of the institutional church, the mestizo worldview—what was desirable or undesirable, acceptable or unacceptable, beautiful or ugly, good or bad—was built up over centuries of everyday life. Nearly five hundred years of civil society in Mexico sprang from this worldview, which we might term a moral-spiritual matrix.

The demographic-cultural formation of mestizo society was repeated up and down the mountainous spine of Latin America and across its wide, low plains. There were subtle variations, depending on the characteristics of the indigenous society—language, urban or nomadic social structure, religious beliefs, and so forth—and on genetics; some parts of Latin America have a more indigenous genetic heritage, others a more European or African heritage, and most have a soupçon of Asian, as well. Despite variations at the local level—one is not simply Mexican, but is more proudly a *poblano* from Puebla, a *jarocho* from Veracruz, a *tapatío* from Guadalajara—the overarching presence of formal and informal Catholic religion provided a basis of continuity from region to region.

LATINO CIVIL SOCIETY IN CALIFORNIA

Beginning in April 1769, colonizing expeditions from Mexico brought California into the modern age. As with earlier colonization efforts in Texas, New Mexico, and Arizona, dating from 1598, the very demographic composition of the early parties of settlers reflected a Mexican, not merely a Spanish, experience with life. There were, in fact, relatively few pure Spaniards among the colonists of the Southwest. The bulk of them were a very racially mixed group from the northern regions of Mexico. By Mason's recent reckoning (1998, 66), 61 percent of the colonists present in Alta California by 1790 had come from Sinaloa and Baja California, where the need for skilled labor outweighed scruples about racially mixed background in terms of employment and economic mobility. Added to this mix were Indians from the central regions of Mexico, speaking Náhuatl, Otomí, Seri, and a variety of other indigenous languages (Sego 1998). There were also Mexicans of African heritage, Mexicans of Asian heritage, and their mestizo offspring (Cano Sánchez, Escandell Tur, and Mampel González 1984, 252–53). Mason indicates that, apart from the missionaries, there were probably no more than twenty peninsular Spaniards in Alta California at any time prior to 1821 (Mason 1998, 69). When the pueblo of Los Angeles was founded in 1781, only two of the forty-four settlers were putatively Spanish; the overwhelming majority, including the wives of the two Spaniards, were Indians, Africans, and mestizos.

The most important element the colonists brought was their living civil society. As single colonists sometimes married local California Indian women, local indigenous cultural elements were added to the already heady mix. From 1769 to the present day, a constant inflow of population from Mexico has continuously contributed a "centering" function to this developing civil society, moving it back to the Mexican experience—in essence, regressing to the Mexican cultural norm, such as the health beliefs we have so often observed. Meanwhile, new elements came in that gave Latino civil society in California a flavor slightly different from that of Arizona, New Mexico, and Texas. For example, being open to the sea instead of landlocked, Latino civil society in California developed a very cosmopolitan cast, with Latinos from Peru, Argentina, Chile, Colombia, Costa Rica, Cuba, and Puerto Rico adding their experiences to the California mix.

This Latino civil society set about creating a modern way of life in California, by eighteenth- and nineteenth-century standards. Medical services were provided by a number of surgeons-major appointed from 1769 onward, and periodic public health campaigns were undertaken. The Bancroft Library at UC Berkeley possesses the oldest medical license in California, dated 1799, awarded to Dr. Manuel Gutiérrez y Quixano by the examining board of the Protomedicato in Mexico City, prior to his nomination as surgeon-major in California (Bancroft Library 1799). Elementary schools were established before 1796 in Santa Barbara and by 1797 in San Diego (Bancroft Library 1767–1822, 8:28, 8:102, 9:169–70), and scientific expeditions roamed the countryside. A printing press was established in 1834, and the first book published in California was a mathematics text. An early publication was a health education booklet ordered by Comandante Mariano G. Vallejo (1838).

Californios, as the Latinos born in the state came to call themselves, debated the political and philosophical issues of the day: divine right of kings, independence, democracy, slavery, suffrage, trade, and the lingering effects of the Enlightenment. Eager to support George Washington and his Continental Army, Californios donated two pesos each to be sent to support his efforts (Boeta 1977, 106). To further support Washington, Governor Bernardo de Gálvez of Louisiana, nephew of José de Galvez, Comandante General of New Mexico and Texas and organizer of the California colonizing expeditions, led up to seven thousand troops from Mexico, Cuba, Puerto Rico, Spain, and Hispaniola in a flanking maneuver against the British, first marching up the Mississippi as far as Lake Michigan, then along the Gulf of Mexico seaboard to the harbor of Pensacola, where they defeated the British holding the fort, disrupting their plans to embargo the nascent United States into submission by a tight naval blockade anchored from that port (Caughey 1934, 187–214).

These mestizo Californios built towns, established blacksmith shops, constructed waterworks to irrigate fields and fill fountains, and tended their cattle from horseback. While doing so, they also formed families, worshipped in churches, socialized with one another, and stitched together a primary web of relations into which each succeeding generation of children was born. Several times a day, they all sat down around the family table for meals, and in thousands of hours of seemingly idle chitchat, they recreated the social and moral world as they gossiped, providing models of the desirable and the undesirable, the good and the bad, for their children. Just as in New Mexico, just as in Guadalajara, just as in Mexico City and Puebla, Latino civil society provided a framework of meaning for the daily, unthinking activities of the state's growing population.

In 1829, the Yankee Abel Stearns sailed from Massachusetts (Monroy 1990, 156) and arrived in California to continue his life, but in an area being formed by Mexican-Catholic Latino civil society rather than one by British-Protestant Atlantic American civil society. He established himself as a trader, learned Spanish, and became a practicing Catholic. An eligible bachelor, he fell in love with Arcadia Bandini, the daughter of a prominent Californio, Juan Bandini, married her, and built her the "handsomest house" in the Pueblo de Los Angeles, with a ballroom one hundred feet long (Nunis 1998, 307), where his parties and balls became legendary. He was typical of these early generations of Atlantic Americans in California, who physically melded British-derived Atlantic American culture with Mexican-derived Latino civil society. A contemporary described Stearns as "a Yankee . . . who had been a resident in the country for so many years, and who had become, in manner and appearance, a complete Californian" (Monroy 1990, 161).

California had created a unique response to the issue of multicultural society, one that built on the experience of the native soil: the formation of "Latin-Yankee society," as Kevin Starr termed it (1973, 26). For more than fifty years, from the late 1820s, when California was a state in the Republic of Mexico, to the mid-1880s, thirty years after it had become the thirty-first state in the United States, adventurous young men from the Atlantic seaboard, as well as a few women, traveled to the Spanish-speaking Pacific coast region, fell in love with charming, darker-skinned women or men, married them, and raised generations of families that exhibited an easy blend of both Mexican-Catholic-based Californio society and British Protestant–based Atlantic American society. Toward the end of this era, in 1882, Johnny Adams, one such young man of modest means living in Santa Barbara County, was reported by a local newspaper as being "severely smitten by the beauty of one of the fascinating native señoritas . . . to the extent that is soon likely to lead him into the ranks of the benedicts. Should such be the case, we have no doubt of the cross between the Irish and the native Californian improving the character and physical ability of the population of Santa Barbara" (*Santa Maria Times* 1882, 1).

Without realizing they were forming a new multicultural society, hundreds of young Atlantic American single men arrived in California, married Latinas, and formed bilingual, bicultural families whose children moved effortlessly from Spanish to English, read books from Boston and Mexico City, ate tortillas and (post–gold rush) sourdough. The vision for the first fifty years of interactions between Latinos and non-Hispanic whites was that of an organic integration of California's Latino people into the American commonwealth, Mexican in culture but with American political institutions (Starr 1973, 33, 29).

When Richard Henry Dana, also from Massachusetts, visited California in 1835, he took a jaundiced view of the Californios. He and other early visitors, such as Thomas Jefferson Farnham, described the Latinos in California as "unfit to control the destinies of that beautiful county" (Nunis 1998, 306) and urged Atlantic Americans to immigrate and populate the country with a more enterprising breed of human. Dana was careful to warn his East Coast readers to avoid "going native." "The Americans (as those from the United States are called) and Englishmen . . . are fast filling up the principal towns . . . yet their children are brought up Mexicans in most respects, and if the 'California fever' (laziness) spares the first generation, it is likely to attack the second" (Dana 1981, 237). In 1841 John Bidwell heeded their advice and led one of the first covered-wagon parties overland from Missouri to California. He shunned intimate contact with Latinos and settled far away from the Latino-dominant coast, in the sparsely populated hinterlands of the northern Sacramento Valley. His account of the journey, published in 1843 or 1844 (Nunis 1998, 136), encouraged other overland parties. Wave after wave of settlers from the United States arrived. Unlike earlier settlers, such as Stearns, this new wave shunned contact with Latinos, expressing rather racist views about the "greaser" population. They did not marry local Californio daughters but married other Atlantic Americans, remained Protestant, and refused to become citizens.

The gold rush of 1849 changed the dynamics of civil society in the north of the state. Tens of thousands of Atlantic Americans sailed around the Horn, poured through the port of San Francisco, traveled up the river to Sacramento, then out to the "Mother Lode" in the Sierras. Tens of thousands more trekked across the continent, across the plains, deserts, mountains, and valleys. Within a matter of months, the sudden increase of Atlantic Americans swamped the Latino population in the north of the state, and the core of society in that northern region ceased to be built around Latino civil society. Atlantic American civil society thereafter formed the core of daily life in northern California.

In the southern part of the state, however, in the "cow counties"—so called because of the preeminence of ranching in the economic life in Los Angeles, Santa Barbara, Riverside, and San Bernardino counties—Latino civil society continued to provide the core for another three decades. Latinos outnumbered Atlantic Americans for more than thirty years; Spanish was predominant; Latino businesses continued to be established; and Latino families went about their daily routines.

Overlooked in most histories of early California has been the spiritual dimension of daily life. Although economics and demographics have been well studied (Romo 1983; Griswold del Castillo 1979), and the political organization of the years 1848 through 1965 fairly well documented (Acuña 1972; Rosales 1997), underneath all these activities is a spiritual dimension, one that provides meaning to all the other activities. Mestizo Catholicism was part and parcel of daily life in Alta California, a strand of Latino civil society from Mexico present since the beginning of modern California. After California had become the thirty-first state of the union, Pablo de la Guerra described in his journal Holy Thursday as celebrated in Santa Barbara in 1851, an event that demonstrated the depth of such spiritual and social bonds, even after the U.S. annexation.

> [T]he procession arrived at the sepulcher, amidst the clouds of aromatic smoke born[e] aloft by the various censers, the Blessed Sacrament was deposited with all reverence, while the multitude remained prostrate for a long time offering its acts of adoration and raising its fervent prayers to the Divine Prisoner. . . . I was so overcome by feeling and so tenderly was

I moved that I could not refrain from making in that instant [an] entreaty. (cited in Matovina and Poyo 2000, 62)

De la Guerra described in great detail the church and its decorations, the choir and its music, the priests and their vestments, the worshipers and their feelings. After describing the service, he depicted the families engaged in subsequent social activity.

They went prepared with everything necessary to spend the day in the open. Soon they began to move toward the Arroyo Pedregoso . . . the people formed into a reunion and while some prepared food, others spread carpets and mats about the place to enjoy themselves. Others began to put out plates, tablecloths, napkins, while others still (the majority) played, ran about the rocks, talked, flirted or went visiting and walking with companions. (cited in Matovina and Poyo 2000, 62)

In these small acts of worship and companionship, Latinos continued weaving and reweaving their civil society out of the strands of the Latino Catholic civilization they had carried with them to California. Their expressions of faith were deeply rooted, their devotions motivated them, and their festivities strengthened their social bonds.

People also continued to move into the southern part of the state from Mexico and Latin America. In fact, the largest in-movement of Mexicans took place after California had become part of the United States. The same 1849 gold rush that had attracted hundreds of thousands of Atlantic Americans also attracted tens of thousands of Latino miners from Mexico, Chile, Peru, and Argentina. Quite often, these immigrants stayed in California and married Californios, both male and female, as they shared a language, religion, music—in short, an entire civil society. On February 21, 1859, for example, Jayme Vila, the parish priest at the mission in Santa Barbara, married Leandro Martínez, who had immigrated from Zacatecas, Mexico, to Josefa Váldez de Gamón, who had been born in Santa Barbara, California (Santa Barbara County 1859, fols. Lv.–Mr. [19v–20r]). The cultural influence of Mexico continued, with newspapers, circuses, musicians, and books from Mexico constantly circulating among the majority Latino population. In addition to patriotically celebrating the Fourth of July, Latinos also celebrated Mexican Independence Day and (after 1863) Cinco de Mayo.

By the mid-1880s, southern California finally was connected to the continent-spanning U.S. rail system. Land speculators bought large tracts of land from the rancheros, subdivided the properties, then advertised in the Midwest for buyers. Lured by the promises of cheap land and healthful living, settlers from Ohio, Indiana, Illinois, Iowa, and other midwestern states poured in, and within a decade, they outnumbered the local Latino population. Thanks to cheap rail fares, during the 1880–1910 period southern California, especially Los Angeles, became the most homogeneous Atlantic American region in the United States, with the lowest European immigrant population of any metropolitan area in the country (Starr 1990, 120).

But the local Latino population, while ignored, did not disappear. It continued living its life, going to its churches, celebrating its holidays, forming its families. A constant flow of immigration continued to anchor these communities to the larger Latino civil society operating in Mexico and Latin America, for example, when Chilean immigrant Benigno Gutiérrez opened up a homeopathic pharmacy with his wife, Soledad, a Californiana who had been born in Santa Barbara (U.S. Bureau of the Census 1880, 12, Family number 147). Nevertheless, Latinos begin to feel the effects of restriction and segregation, as they were gradually moved to the margins. The lives of three Latinos whose lives spanned the post–1848 events to the beginning of this book's narrative (1940) illustrate the continuity and vitality of Latino civil society, even as it was being actively ignored by the incoming waves of settlers from the Protestant Midwest.

The life of Pío Pico, the last Mexican governor of California, illustrates this continuity and vitality. In 1775, his father, José María Pico, then only eleven, accompanied his grandfather, Santiago de la Cruz Pico, a soldier of Indian and African ancestry (Monroy 1990, 135), on the historic de Anza expedition to California. Pío Pico, the fourth child, was born in 1801 near San Gabriel. He married María Ignacia Alvarado in the church (still standing) close to Olvera Street in Los Angeles in 1834, and together they raised their children. He owned ranches in southern California and grew wealthy and influential.

Imbued with a strong regional identity as a Californio, after Mexican Independence Pico chafed, along with many other native Californios, under a series of governors sent from the unstable governments in Mexico City to set policy with little input from the citizens. Forced to extreme measures by the imprudent actions of another Mexican Governor Micheltorena, Pico led a successful uprising of Californios at the Battle of Cahuenga Pass (close to the site of today's Hollywood Bowl), deposed Micheltorena, and sent him packing back to Mexico. Pico then was acclaimed governor of Alta California. Rather than rejoicing, however, he sensed changes coming from the east. "We find ourselves threatened by hordes of Yankee immigrants who have already begun to flock into our country and whose progress we cannot arrest" (Monroy 1990, 163).

When U.S. troops landed in San Pedro (now the port of Los Angeles), Governor Pico once again led his mounted troops into battle. Although he won the initial battle, the Californios lost the war, and the Treaty of Guadalupe Hidalgo ratified U.S. possession of the northern half of Mexico. In disgust, Pico removed his household to Mexico for a while, but then returned to California, to his ranches. Subsequently, however, nearly endless litigation, mortgaging, and ownership squabbles reduced his holdings to virtually nothing.

Retired from public life, thereafter he lived until 1894 at Mission San Fernando, greeting visitors with a bow and a smile, "saying in his broken English, 'I am de gentleman always' " (Monroy 1990, 228), dispensing wisdom he accumulated over nearly a century of life lived in Latino civil society. He witnessed the celebrations held in honor of Mexican Independence ever since the 1830s, the founding of the Los Angeles–based Spanish-language newspaper, *El Clamor Público,* in 1855, the first celebrations of the Cinco de Mayo victory of Mexican troops over the French at the Battle of Puebla in 1862, the founding of La Sociedad Hispano-Americana de Beneficencia Mutua in 1875 (Monroy 1990, 275), and doubtless greeted some of the tens of thousands of new immigrant Latinos arriving from Mexico during that period. He saw both the first centenary of the American Revolution in 1876 and the 400th celebration of Columbus's arrival in the New World in 1892. More than ninety years of age when he died, he had been witness to the emergence, then temporary swamping, of Latino civil society in California. But that entity did not die when he did. Instead, it was just beginning its Whitmanesque emergence into "broadest flow and permanent action."

Symbolic of the Mexican immigrants who arrived after the U.S. takeover of California, María Amparo Maytorena Ruiz was born in La Paz, Baja California, where her grandfather had been governor, and in 1848 arrived in Monterey, California, a town whose social core was still formed around Latino civil society (Ruiz de Burton 2001, 58–74). Embodying the emergent Yankee-Latin society, she married Captain Henry S. Burton of the U.S. Army and began a lifelong comradeship with prominent Californios such as Mariano G. Vallejo. Although her husband spoke fluent Spanish, she dedicated herself to learning English; their two children were bilingual.

With the American Civil War looming, Captain Burton was posted back to the Atlantic coast, and Ruiz de Burton followed with their children. She stayed there for nearly ten years, polishing her English and learning Yankee mores, while following unfolding events in Mexico: the French invasion of Mexico, the heroic Battle of Puebla on May 5 (Cinco de Mayo), and the eventual restoration of democracy to Mexican soil.

When her husband died in 1869, she returned to California. Her daughter Nellie married a Mexican, Miguel de Pedrorena, and went to live in Mexico. Her son stayed on the East Coast for his education and married Minnie Wilbur. Ruiz de Burton had had ample opportunity to observe Latino civil society's interactions with Atlantic American civil society, and she wrote two novels that examined this dance of social mores: *Who Would Have Thought It?* (1872) and *The Squatter and the Don* (1885). The latter work was based on her own experience with land title litigation over her ranch in Jamula, near San Diego. It must be noted that she, who had learned English as a second language, wrote her novels, as well as plays and newspaper columns, in English, while maintaining a flow of correspondence in Spanish. She died in 1895.

Symbolic of the post-1848 generation, Reginaldo del Valle's life (Griswold del Castillo 1980) shows the continuity of Latino civil society up to the early twentieth century. In 1839, his great-grandfather had been deeded a large ranch in what is today Ventura County. When he died, Reginaldo's father, Antonio, was bequeathed a portion of that property, which he named Rancho Camulos. It was large enough that Antonio del Valle was able to survive and prosper—despite disputed land titles, floods, drought, and depression that wiped out the holdings of many other Californio families between 1848 and 1865—by selling off portions of the ranch to raise cash.

Educated at Santa Clara University, a Jesuit institution, Reginaldo del Valle studied law and was admitted to the California bar in 1877. He used his talents to continue the family ranching business, forming the California and Mexican Land Company to sell one family holding, Rancho Temescal, in 1886, and another corporation to manage Rancho Camulos in 1908. The author Helen Hunt Jackson visited Rancho Camulos in 1883, and charmed by its ambience, "as Mexican and un-American as heart could wish" (Griswold del Castillo 1980, 3), used it as the setting for her famous novel *Ramona*. Although mildly upset at the depiction of Californios in her book, del Valle nonetheless was astute enough to recognize a business opportunity. He held stock in the Mission Play Association, which gave annual performances for more than twenty years, based on Jackson's somewhat overdrawn romance (Griswold del Castillo 1980, 10).

Eager to participate in civic life, he ran as a Democrat for Congress in 1884 but was defeated by an opponent who harped on the undesirability of a Latino in government, as "no decent man has ever been born of a Mexican woman" (Griswold del Castillo 1980, 11). Turning to less political venues, he helped Charles Fletcher Lummis found the Landmarks Club in 1887, to restore crumbling adobes and missions for future generations to enjoy. In 1914 he became a member of the Public Service Board, which later became the Los Angeles Board of Water and Power.

While familiar with the new corridors of power, he spent large portions of his life in the Latino civil society. One of the few bilingual attorneys in the state, he represented monolingual Spanish-speaking clients in court. Working with a group of middle-class Latinos, both California-born and Mexican emigrants, he helped form the San Gabriel Spanish-American League, and in 1925 he was given an award by the Liga Protectiva Latina, an early civil rights organization advocating full Latino participation in the state's society, for his years of outstanding service to the Latino community.

When he died in 1938 of a heart attack, just two years before the data used in this book begin, the *Los Angeles Times* praised his accomplishments and noted dryly that he had disliked being called "Spanish" (Griswold del Castillo 1980, 13).

Even Latin-Yankee society continued in some corners of the state. As recently as 1912, an English author, J. Smeaton Chase, wrote a book in which he described an evening he spent with one of the last remnants of this Yankee-Latino experiment, the Danas of Nipomo in San Luis Obispo County. "Seeing three generations of Yankee-Latins gathered around the huge table, hearing the laughter, the talk in Spanish and English, Chase felt in the presence of bygone Yankee-California, the civilization that Thomas Oliver Larkin and others had long ago hoped would be the pattern for the future. It had not been the future, but somehow, it had held on" (Starr 1973, 436).

The flow of people back and forth between Mexico and California was constant from 1848 to the present. As newcomers from Mexico and Central and South America arrived, they joined the spiritual and social activities of the ongoing Latino civil society. Thus, even though outnumbered after 1880 by in-migrants from Atlantic American civil society, the Alta California variant of Latino civil society continued forming and shaping lives of an important portion of the state's population.

The Latino population of the state now finds itself once again drinking deeply of the "mother wine," to use Baltzell's imagery, of Latino civil soci-

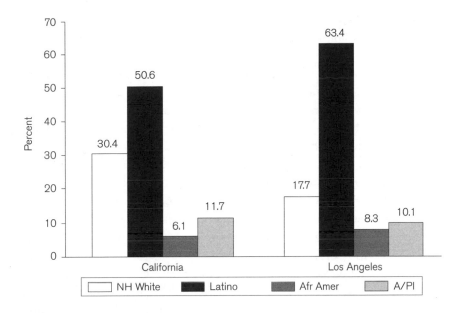

Figure 35. Composition of Births, California and Los Angeles County, Fourth Quarter, 2001. Source: CA DHS 2001a.

ety, due to demographics, technology, and proximity. With such a large population base, a critical mass of Latinos has been established, creating an economic base that is self-sustaining. This economic force is nearly 50 percent immigrant. Each immigrant brings a small reinforcement of the Latino Catholic civilization, bolstering not just the language but also values, behaviors, and popular religiosity. Modern radio, satellite television, and two-hour flights to Guadalajara weave into the California Latino population the same effects they do in the rest of the Americas, bringing Mexico City, Caracas, Santiago, Buenos Aires, and Rio de Janeiro into millions of living rooms in the state every night.

California's future adult population already exists (see Figure 35), in the babies born since the fourth quarter of 2001. Latinos were over half of all babies born in the state (50.6 percent), and non-Hispanic whites were less than one-third (30.4 percent), African Americans were 6.1 percent, and Asian/Pacific Islanders were 11.7 percent. Projections for the year 2040 (see Figure 1 on page 2) show that the state's population will closely resemble this young population of 2000. The state's future 58.7 million persons will be composed of 47.8 percent Latinos, 30.7 percent non-Hispanic whites,

15.5 percent Asian/Pacific Islanders, and 5.5 percent African Americans. No large-scale immigration will be necessary to cause these momentous changes.

To a certain extent, the future of California can be seen in Los Angeles County, its largest, most populous, and some might say most vibrant county. Its 10.2 million inhabitants showed a racial or ethnic composition in 2004 virtually identical to the projected composition of California in 2040: less than one-third non-Hispanic white, nearly half Latino, with smaller African American and Asian/Pacific Islander populations (CA DOF 1998). More revealing is the current composition of the babies born in Los Angeles County. Since the fourth quarter of 2001 (see Figure 35), nearly two-thirds of the county's children (63.4 percent) were Latino, and close to eight out of ten babies (82 percent) were what used to be called "minorities" (CA DHS 2001a).

Southern California is becoming a region with a Latino population majority. The way that Latinos define the activities of daily life—family, work, diet, religion, music, dreams, fears, the common good—soon may become characteristic of the entire region, not just of Latinos. The stock of knowledge (Berger and Luckmann 1966, 41) that more than half the children in the state are raised with now comes from Latino experience with civil society.

ATLANTIC AMERICAN REACTIONS: PURITANS AND QUAKERS

The lives of Abel Stearns and John Bidwell, recounted briefly above, illustrate the responses of representatives of two major Atlantic American population segments to cultural diversity: the Puritan segment, which is uncomfortable with diversity, and the Quaker segment, which embraces it. Baltzell (2001) uncovered these two patterns in studying the seedbed civil societies of Puritan Boston and Quaker Philadelphia that have greatly influenced Atlantic American life. I find it instructive to transplant these paradigms to California, in order to understand past, and potential future, interactions between Latinos and Atlantic Americans in California.

Atlantic America's cultural foundations were laid by intensely religious people, participants in the theological, and sometimes physical, Reformation warfare that swept across the green, rolling hills of England and Scotland. Once the genie of Protestant sectarian fission was out of the bottle, men and women burning with the conviction that God had chosen them to create a New Jerusalem on earth gathered converts around their unique views of the relation between God and humankind. Ranters, Levellers,

Diggers, Separatists, Independents, Seekers, Mugglestonians, Ethringtoni-ans, Grindelstonians . . . the list of new sects that appeared in seventeenth-century England seemed endless, not unlike the endless new religious sects of twenty-first-century America.

The Calvinist foundations of the first English Puritans were evident in their views of predestination; though humans were hopelessly sunk in sin, an elite few were predestined for salvation. That elite was to impose a moral order on sinful humans by dint of all-encompassing laws and vigilant polic-ing. The greatest threat to this view was dissent: different opinions, lifestyles, philosophies. That which was different was simply not tolerated, for fear of upsetting the tenuous hold of the saved elite over sinful hu-mankind. Law and an unsleeping vigilance for deviant behavior were a principal means of holding diversity at bay (Baltzell 2001).

As if to prove the frequent observation that each generation must rebel against its parents, the Quakers arose in England a generation after the flow-ering of Puritan hegemony, openly electing to disagree with the Puritan worldview in almost every respect. The Puritans believed that only an elect few were to be saved. The Quakers believed everyone could achieve salva-tion. The Puritans thought that sinful humans had to be legislated and po-liced into righteous behavior. The Quakers felt that each individual's "inner light" would provide guidance to salvation without external coercion. The Puritans were convinced that humankind was basically sinful. The Quakers believed in the potential for perfectibility of every individual in the world. The Puritans sought to create an educated, elite leadership. The Quakers showed compassion for the down and out, for society's marginal groups.

Most importantly, while Puritans were fixated on maintaining purity in theology, behavior, culture, and race, Quakers felt that their settlements in the New World were a Divine Experiment in diversity. While Puritan set-tlements drove away those who dissented in any fashion, Quaker settle-ments purposely invited settlers from different languages, cultures, and re-ligions to live among them. Rather than rely on law to avoid diversity, Quakers relied on the individual "inner light" to negotiate the inevitable conflicts diversity brings.

Although descendants of the Atlantic American colonial settlers largely have lost the spiritual dimensions of these differing approaches to the rela-tionship between God and human, they have maintained the cultural pat-terns established by their forebears three hundred years ago. It has been cus-tomary for minority scholars and leaders to perceive a single, monolithic Atlantic American cultural pattern, yet it is important to recognize the diversity within that cultural group. On matters of diversity, the 1990 survey described in detail in chapter 4 (Hurtado et al. 1992, xi) showed that, with regard to their comfort level with diversity, non-Hispanic whites in California were nearly evenly divided between the Puritan exclusionary approach (almost 50 percent) and the Quaker inclusive approach (again, nearly 50 percent). Continuing this historic cultural pattern, modern secular "Puritan" Anglos raise shrill voices about the dangers of diversity, while secular "Quakers" welcome and feel comfortable with diversity.

In many of the ballot issues the non-Hispanic white electorate faced in California during the 1990s, the Puritan streak was active. If "different" people weakened Atlantic American cultural strengths, then they should be stopped from entering the country. If these "different" people spoke a strange language, the state should legislate the sounds they were allowed to make. If too many were sneaking into the New Jerusalem by becoming citizens, then their sincerity was in question and the process should be made more difficult. If the voices raised against today's diversity sound like an echo of the Salem witchcraft trials, it is because they are, indeed, descended from the Atlantic American cultural segment that invented the scarlet letter.

Given the size, purchasing power, and growth of the state's Latino and multicultural population, marketers, driven by the quest for larger shares, have taken up where Quakers, driven by an immanent God, left off. Market forces are not consciously and introspectively trying to create a new society, as the early Quakers were. Indeed, they seek profit from today's market, and these forces are creating a new norm concerning the nature of the "we" in American society. Tortillas are advertised daily in Spanish on billboards that fill the landscape.

The Puritans' descendants do not face an appealing future. Given their rigid inability to concede the existence of the "other," they will most likely be unable to adapt to new market needs, will certainly find themselves at an increasing competitive disadvantage, and probably will end up voting with their feet by leaving the state. The more Quaker-oriented Atlantic Americans likely will remain comfortable in the state, reveling in its diversity and making a good living by allowing the "other" an autonomous "inner consumer light."

DEMOGRAPHY AND REGIONAL IDENTITY

In early Texas, incoming Atlantic Americans rarely intermarried with Latinos, yet an amazing amount of intercultural penetration still occurred. By contrast, in early California there was a significant amount of intermarriage between the Latino Californios and incoming Quaker-like Atlantic Americans, creating a hybrid "Yankee-Latin" society, until the more Puritan-like overland settlers came to outnumber more Quakerish coastal non-Hispanic whites. Subsequent miscegenation laws made interracial marriages unlawful in most states of the country. State by state, these laws were repealed in the last half of the twentieth century.

The 2000 PUMS files are not available as of this writing—however, files from 1990 indicated that intermarriage was somewhat rare in the United States; less than 2 percent of couples nationally were composed of individuals from different racial or ethnic groups (D. Hayes-Bautista and Rodriguez 1996). In Los Angeles County, however, couples were nearly five times more likely to be racially intermarried than in the United States as a whole. But there is a large generational difference. Whereas older couples, age sixty-five and over, in Los Angeles County had an intermarriage rate equivalent to the rest of the United States (around 3 percent), younger couples had progressively higher intermarriage rates. Twenty-six percent of young non-Hispanic whites, nineteen years and younger, were married to partners from other racial groups, and 45 percent of young African Americans were married to non-African Americans. The partner of choice for an out-marrying black or white was a Latino.

More important for the formation of civil society is the child-bearing couple, for they create the next generation of Californians. Data from the 2000 California Master Birth File indicate the race or ethnicity of both the mother and the father of each child born in the state. Data from Los Angeles County are presented in Table 6. A trend similar to the intermarriage trend is seen in the interpaternity patterns. Younger non-Hispanic white, African American, and Asian/Pacific Islander mothers are far more likely than older mothers to have a partner from a different racial or ethnic group. There is a generational difference in the choice of the father. In all three of these groups, the most frequent out-group father for young mothers under twenty-five years of age was a Latino. Among older mothers, twenty-five years and older, however, for African American and Asian/Pacific Islander mothers the preferred out-group father was a non-Hispanic white, while older non-Hispanic white mothers preferred Latino fathers. In a stunning example of "retro-assimilation," more than one-third (39.8 percent) of older U.S.-born Latina mothers (forty years or older) had an out-group father for their child, while younger U.S.-born Latinas were more likely to have a Latino father for their child. Immigrant Latina mothers almost universally

TABLE 6

Percentage of Mothers by Age and Race/Ethnicity with Fathers of Child from Different
Racial/Ethnic Group, Los Angeles County, California, 2000

Age	Non-Hispanic White	African American	U.S.-born A/PI	Immigrant A/PI	U.S.-born Latino	Immigrant Latino
Under 20	55.6	32.2	46.6	32.7	18.4	16.4
20–24	39.5	24.6	53.0	22.0	17.1	10.1
25–29	24.5	18.4	49.7	14.0	19.8	7.9
30–34	16.0	18.8	50.0	13.8	31.1	9.2
35–39	15.2	19.5	52.7	18.9	38.7	10.5
40+	15.8	21.0	57.1	21.4	39.8	12.2

SOURCE: CA DHS 2000c.

had Latino fathers for their children. Not only are Latinos becoming an increasingly large percentage of the state's population, but through intermarriage and interpaternity Latinos also are exerting an influence on non-Latino populations.

These families most likely will raise their children in a combination of Latino and Atlantic American civil societies. This combination will not be new; it is, in fact, probably the unique California contribution to a multicultural society—the Yankee-Latin society discerned by Kevin Starr, which flourished from the 1830s to the 1880s. It is likely that the non-Latino spouse of a Latino or Latina will be very close to the non-Latino spouses in Latin-Yankee society of the nineteenth century. "They remained Yankees . . . but their values and lifestyles were modified. They went by Spanish names, used Spanish in daily conversation (even in private correspondence), dressed as Mexicans and fathered Mexican families. Their children, felt William Heath Davis, were the eugenic beginnings of a new people, a Latin-Yankee California stock partaking of the best of both strains" (Starr 1973, 26). Young adults in California of the early twenty-first century appear to be completing the work begun in 1830. These children will grow into adults and start their own families. Seamlessly, unconsciously, they probably will finish the cultural creation begun, then sidelined, in the nineteenth century. The daily activities of home and kitchen will form the core of the new civil society, emerging out of the two major inputs, and will create a new regional American identity: the twenty-first-century Californio identity, in a situation analogous to, but different from, the creation of the distinctive Texas regional identity.

The "stock of knowledge" (Berger and Luckmann 1966, 41) that undergirds civil society may be likened to a stone quarry supplying building materials. Each individual uses the quarry but shapes the stones a little differently and builds somewhat different structures. Yet the structures share the same stone material, and that very stone guides the outer limits of the buildings constructed; a building of granite can take forms impossible for one made of sandstone. In the Texas analogy that opened this chapter, the experience of Texas regional identity is passed on to each child raised in Texas, forming part of the society-wide Texan "stock of knowledge." Each young Texan uses the building material as part of her or his daily, meaningful life. We may appreciate that each Texan fashions the elements from the stock of knowledge in slightly idiosyncratic ways, so that no two Texans are identical; yet nearly all Texans share some elements of the stock of knowledge in common, marking them as Texans, not Bostonians or Minnesotans.

In California, two major stocks of knowledge undergirding two distinctive experiences with civil society—the Latino Catholic and the Atlantic American experiences—are once again interdigitating with one another, as they did before, when they combined to form the Yankee-Latin shared stock of knowledge for the fifty years between 1830 and 1880. Neither of these two stocks of knowledge is likely to disappear. Instead, we are likely to see a combining of the stocks in the near future, just as occurred in the past.

The influence of Latinos on the regional identity of all Americans living in the state may finally wash away the "original sin" of Atlantic American cultural domination, the destruction of one California that another might take its place (Starr 1973, 21), by returning to the old, historical Latin-Yankee pattern, similar to that experienced before, from 1830 to 1880, when "the American community had achieved a blending of cultures, a lifestyle which pointed in the direction of a California sadly destined never to flourish, or at least never to unfold naturally. Later generations would be haunted by its memory" (Starr 1973, 25). The haunting may now be over, as the younger generation goes about its daily business of creating "La Nueva California" for the twenty-first century, with Latinos once again contributing substantially to what may be the creation of a new regional American identity.

EIGHT

Best-Case and Worst-Case Scenarios
California 2040

> In the same way that a physical model of a bridge provides a testing ground for different combinations of design and materials, a [social] scenario allows us to model society in the future. We offer here some grounded speculation about the future of [California] society.
>
> *D. Hayes-Bautista, Schink, and Chapa 1988, 1*

IN MY 1988 BOOK, *The Burden of Support,* after dragging the reader through some rather data-thick demographic projections, I described two purpose-fully extreme scenarios as polar possibilities for the California of 2030. The "Worst-Case Scenario" (D. Hayes-Bautista, Schink, and Chapa 1988, 1–10) presented a vivid *Blade Runner*-like dystopia, in which the half of the state that was Latino had been bludgeoned into a permanent underclass by the economic demands of a pampered, retired non-Hispanic white baby-boom population who lived protected by gated communities and laws that out-lawed "un-American" cultural activities. Chillingly, as California stumbled through the 1990s of recession, riots, fire, earthquake, and anti-immigrant propositions (see chapter 5), it appeared as if the state were determined to achieve that worst-case scenario.

In order to provide some symmetry, I also had offered a weakly written "Best-Case Scenario." Without much conviction, I tried to argue that somehow things would work out for the better by 2030, but I don't believe I convinced many, including myself, that a felicitous end was attainable. Still under the influence of the dysfunctional minority model (see chapter 3), I did not see how Latinos could contribute to making the state produc-tive and competitive in the twenty-first century. As a result, that best-case scenario did not ring true the way the worst-case one had.

Shortly after *The Burden of Support* was published, I had an epiphany in my wife's office at the UCLA School of Nursing (see chapter 3): I realized that the data indicated tremendous Latino strengths in behavior and health. With a pang of regret, during the 1990s I wished that I had those data when I wrote the best-case scenario, for I could have written a more believable scenario, one that built on the strengths that a growing Latino population offers the state, rather than the vague, Pollyannaish hope that everyone would be happy in the end.

Now, fifteen years after *The Burden of Support,* I see clearly how to achieve the best-case scenario for 2040: investment in Latino strengths. As in my previous book, I offer here two polar-opposite scenarios as alternative futures for California by 2040.

CALIFORNIA 2040: BEST-CASE SCENARIO

Halfway through her second term, Governor María Isabel Rodriguez de Smith mounted the steps of the restored gold-rush-era capitol in Sacramento on a crisp November day just before Thanksgiving and loudly rang a bell to announce to all Californians, and to the world, that the state, once again, had lived up to its designation as "The Golden State"; the California economy of 2040, if considered separately from the rest of the United States, had become the world's second-largest economic unit. The sum total of goods and services generated by the state's productive labor force and entrepreneurs had just surpassed its remaining European competitor. Japan's economy was a distant fifteenth and losing stature; that country had lost more than one-third of its population since the millennium, falling from 132 million in 2000 to barely 85 million in 2040. The governor was also pleased to announce that Mexico, for nearly forty years the state's number-one trading partner, had ascended to the number-five economic position worldwide.

Aware of the importance of sports to the state, she also reported that in the regional rivalries, the UCLA soccer team had defeated cross-town rival USC by two goals to one, and in the Bay Area, UC Berkeley once again had lost the "ax" to Stanford, whose goalie had put up a spirited defense even though the Cardinal played with two strikers in the penalty box for nearly the entire second half. She added a humorous note by reminding her listeners that, when she had been a child, a football had two points, but the ball had now become "globalized."

These accomplishments did not come easily. Rather, they were the product of nearly forty years of intensive policy work and public investment that had built on the demographic foundation formed in the year 2000: the public decision to invest in a future workforce and society that shortly would be half Latino, so as to ensure California's prosperity throughout the twenty-first century.

From the opening bell of the twenty-first century, corporate America understood the importance of the Latino market. Bottom-line results were impossible to dismiss, and increasingly, those businesses that had geared their products, services, and communications to the Latino market had reaped rewards. Corporation after corporation, business after business, moved out of Latino-market denial and into acceptance, and their profiles improved, even during periods of cyclical business slowdowns in the rest of the country. Cutting-edge technologies and their attendant industries still were centered in the state. The breakthrough that led to new industries was in "bio-cultural" technology, and it began with health sciences applications. For decades, researchers on the East Coast had followed the will o' the wisp of the Human Genomics Project, but had not yet been able to develop large-scale applications that were covered by most insurance plans; the costs of therapy were still too great and the benefits too elusive.

Medical science in California, meanwhile, had broken away from the "big iron" approach that required billions of dollars; instead, it had embraced what was on its doorstep, understanding and making available to all the benefits of the Latino Epidemiological Paradox. In the first decade of the century, public medical schools, backed by the National Institutes of Health, focused on culturally driven alternative medicine, pouring hundreds of millions of dollars into understanding the relationships between culture, behavior, and health. Assisted by their academic connections to a Mexico-California university consortium, researchers were able to specify the combination of diet, family, health beliefs, philosophy, activity, and society that had allowed Latinos to live five years longer than non-Hispanic whites and thirteen years longer than African American Californians during the twentieth century.

Their research had two effects. The first was a dramatic improvement in the state's overall health profile. Each year, more than fifty thousand non-Hispanic white and African American Californians, who otherwise would have died of heart disease, cancer, and stroke, lived to enjoy their families and friends, due to a much longer life expectancy. As the result of applying the lessons to the beginning of the life cycle, infant mortality had plunged, and so too had smoking, drinking, and drug use. In the world picture, the California population had the best health profile, far better than imploding Japan and aging, decrepit Sweden.

The second effect was to stimulate a renaissance in indigenous studies. The unique outlook on life that had helped create the outstanding health profile had its origins in Native American philosophies, as well as the Iberian cultures. In order to better understand these worldviews, their development, and their influence on health, interest in things indigenous and Iberian skyrocketed. Courses in languages in addition to Spanish—Náhuatl, Chumash, Maya, Navajo, and Mixtec, among others—proliferated, so that Californians could come to their own conclusions about these ancient philosophies. Public interest in ancient life in the Americas pushed an explosion of research and coursework about pre- and postcontact life. These interests were no longer polite expressions of multicultural tolerance; they reflected a deeply rooted desire to understand the indigenous roots of twenty-first century California life, which had resulted in better health profiles.

To facilitate the new health research, a consortium was formed between the University of California campuses, the California State University system, the community college system, and universities in Mexico, to identify and create an intellectual framework appropriate for a state whose school-age children were nearly 50 percent Latino. A binational blue-ribbon panel examined the intellectual history of both Latin American and Atlantic American universities, visited scores of campuses and programs throughout the Americas, and talked with literally thousands of parents, community leaders, and business leaders. In addition to European and indigenous social bases, the panel also looked at African-origin contributions and Asian-Pacific Islander influences in the creation of Latin American civil society. After five years of investigation and deliberation, the panel released its recommendation for higher-education efforts in the state. The panel's report outlined the content areas that an "educated person" graduating from the state's universities ought to have mastered: knowledge in literature from the chronicles of Chimalpahín to William Faulkner, historical readings from the *Popol Vuh* to Churchill's speeches, philosophy from the musings of the poet-king Nezahualcoyotl to the questions of Socrates, social theory from Bartolomé de las Casas to Wittgenstein, music appreciation from Mexican baroque to Aaron Copeland, theater from Sor Juana Inés de la Cruz to Shakespeare, art from the murals of Bonampak to the murals of Diego Rivera and East Los Angeles.

Most important, the panel recommended that students in grammar and high school be given a thorough grounding in the history of California. No longer were the indigenous substrates to be seen as mere collectors of acorns, but rather as part and parcel of the formation of civil society. No longer were Latinos treated as a colorful footnote to the state's history; they were to be seen as a major pillar in the erection of the state's social structure. African Americans were no longer seen as latecomers, but as an integral part of the history of the state, present and contributing from the very day the state entered the modern period. And the Asian and Pacific Islander presence was not confined to exotic Chinatowns and Koreatowns but was far more widespread and historic than most had realized. And, of course, the westward thrust of Atlantic Americans, past and present, formed an important core. In short, the panel recommended that an educated Californian of the twenty-first century should be thoroughly familiar with the major threads of California society.

For the first time since the postwar era (1950–70), the state's educational system began to resonate with the values and stories of the emergent civil society. Parents no longer felt locked in battle with an unresponsive school and university system, but rather felt validated and supported, and they joined with large educational systems in the most important effort of the new century, assuring the maximum educational achievement of the state's children, over half of whom happened to be Latino. Intellectually stimulated for the first time, these students found themselves motivated to achieve, wanted to learn more, wanted to accomplish more.

Finally supported in their aspirations by the schools and universities, Latinos' educational attainment skyrocketed, and by 2020 the educational differential between U.S.-born Latinos and their Atlantic American and Asian/Pacific Islander schoolmates had been eliminated. As these educated Californian youngsters entered the state's economy, their effects were immediately felt. The midlevel knowledge positions—customer service, programming, movie-set design—now were filled by state residents, and employers no longer had to resort to unreliable guest-worker programs, constantly in jeopardy due to international dramas.

More important, the state's economy, which had come to rely on pure brainpower and imagination as the world's entertainment and technology capital, was invigorated by an injection of highly educated young workers and executives who had been trained to take advantage of the diversity in the state's population. Films and theater that drew on the diverse roots of the state's history also found acceptance in overseas markets, as the world's stories and tales were by then an integral part of California's culture. Singers who could glide from one language to another found their worldwide sales remarkably enhanced. Designers who could easily read cultural trends around the world developed a reputation for being six months ahead of the rest of the world in clothing, furniture, housewares, and food.

Thanks to the ever-expanding economy, the retirement of the largely non-Hispanic white baby boomers was made secure. Public retirement plans such as CalPERS and private trusts were fed by the state's economic growth. Bulging state coffers made possible the provision of benefits beyond those mandated by federal Social Security laws. So great was the dollar volume of the economy that the Department of Health Services finally was able to offer universal health insurance by 2015. In California, no one would have to do without access to medical care.

As Latino and Asian/Pacific Islander patterns of family formation became the norm—extended families with multiple generations and relations living on one parcel—housing became more dense and concentrated. While the state's population had increased, the number of housing units needed shrank, relieving pressure on the state's remaining open lands. The suburbs actually shrank back to their urban centers, leaving farmland once again open for pastoral pursuits. A network of ultrahigh-velocity mag-lev trains stitched the densifying cores together, whisking passengers from Sacramento to Bakersfield in forty-five minutes, to Los Angeles in another forty-five minutes, and all the way to the border with Mexico in yet another forty-five-minute segment.

The high-speed trains sped through bountiful fields that no longer required pesticide use, as integrated pest management had become the norm. In fact, the state consumed far less energy than it had forty years earlier, in part because of increased consumer awareness about the high costs of energy, and in part because the Third Terrorist War had taught the folly of relying on expensive energy that was easily hijacked by disgruntled fundamentalists. Renewable energy sources, wind turbines, and wave-generators captured the bounteous energy nature had bestowed on the state. Water, the precious liquid, was used far more wisely, as agriculture and industry, finally forced to pay market prices for it, suddenly learned how much they had been wasting and how much could be conserved.

By 2040, the region's Californio identity, the twenty-first century rebirth of the once-promising Yankee-Latin society (1830 to 1880), was nearly universally shared by its residents. Outside the state, analysts remarked on the pronounced Californio accent and vocabulary, and dark-skinned, almond-eyed blondes were very much in demand around the country. The look and sound of California was distinctive and desired. The California Cuisine II fad, sometimes referred to as Mexi-terranean, had swept the country. Tasty, although somewhat spicy, it was reputed to add years to one's life as well as pep to one's step. Designer tequila bars were to be found even in Des Moines, Iowa. A minor market had developed in Mexican baroque and classical music in larger urban areas, while a rock en español oldies wave took the country by storm.

As the lead society in the lead economy, California blazed new trails, linking culture and economics with a style that the rest of the globe admired and tried to imitate. Life was good and promised to get better.

CALIFORNIA 2040: WORST-CASE SCENARIO

Pursued by a tenacious pack of reporters, Governor Peter Billington III dodged through patches of smoke to the last fire hydrant left standing in Sacramento, the state's capital. While retired firefighters demanding that their pensions be funded waved placards and jeered, he gave the spigot a mighty wrench and looked on with dismay as no water issued forth. Only blocks away, house after house exploded into flames, joining a fiery front that stretched from Sacramento to Truckee. Half the state was on fire, and there was no water to extinguish it.

Cornered by microphones and cameras, he turned to face his tormentors, and snarled, "See what your famous diversity has done to this state. We are lost, and it's all *their* fault. My grandfather, Pete Billington, tried to save our state; my father, Pete Billington II, tried to save our state; and I tried to save our state, but you all undercut me. Humph! Diversity, indeed! Well, now you can have your diversity. I quit! I resign as governor." He grasped the lower rungs of a rescue ladder that dangled from a helicopter overhead, and as he was pulled away from the conflagration, he parted with the phrase that would mark his contentious, highly unsuccessful tenure as governor, "This state is impossible. Only a fool would try to govern a state whose population is half Latino."

At the start of the twenty-first century, California seemed poised on the brink of greatness. In spite of Silicon Valley's woes, the rest of the state's economy was doing amazingly well and had just surpassed that of France to become the number-five economy worldwide. Yes, there had been some troubling signs—in a national comparison of student science ability, California had placed dead last. Public schools had been woefully underfunded and underperforming for thirty years. The star University of California system still had its stellar collection of Nobel Prize winners, but they had all come from the post–World War II generation of scholars and researchers—no new generation had been prepared by the state's educational system to follow in their footsteps. The infrastructure was in a sad state, too. Freeways were crowded, airports were jammed, the water system was taxed to the limit, and energy supplies had become erratic. But as 2001 began, the state had huge surpluses in its budget, no new divisive initiative was on the ballot, and agriculture and Hollywood were still mainstays of the economy. It looked as if California could shake off its lethargy and prepare itself to be a leader for the twenty-first century. Few could have foreseen that, forty years later, the state was to become the poster child of the dysfunctional U.S. economy.

Yet, in a matter of months, the state—its public institutions and its private economy—was reeling. The budget surplus had been turned into a budget deficit in a matter of months by a perfect storm of events. The national recession of 2001 had hit the high-tech industry at a vulnerable moment, and high-flying Silicon Valley had been humbled by massive layoffs and shuttered companies. The resulting plunge in net worth experienced by stockholders rippled out into the rest of the weakened economy, commercial real estate fell in value, and even home prices shuddered. The dry-up in retail sales created a staggering loss in sales taxes, which, coupled with the ruinous energy contacts signed during the energy crisis of 2001, left the state with a budget deficit most optimistically estimated at $25 billion—more pessimistically at $50 or $75 billion. No one provided vision or leadership to move out of the crisis, and partisan wrangling stalled resolution. The Republicans refused any budget proposal that did not have massive tax cuts, and the Democrats refused any that did not have massive tax increases. With lawmakers unable to agree on a state budget proactively, budgetary decisions were made by default. Lack of funding caused deep cutbacks in education and health. Most public health clinics and hospitals were closed, and public schools doubled up, in the hopes that these were only temporary measures.

The Second Terrorist War, launched after 2010, made these temporary cutbacks permanent, and a sudden public clamor for security set new budget priorities. In order to provide a public sense of control over possible terrorists in its midst, the federal government instituted a ID card requirement. All persons in the country had to submit to a rigorous background check, and, if they passed, they were required to carry a nonforgeable, fingerprint-embossed ID card at all times. As California had a larger proportion of immigrants than any other state, jittery citizens, egged on by Governor Pete Billington under the banner of "Save Our State from Terrorism," passed an initiative shortly thereafter that demanded even tighter restrictions. The Cal-ID included complete credit and medical histories in addition to immigration status, including an "iris scan," and this card had to be presented before being permitted entry to any public library, hospital, school, or even parking lot. Court battles raged for years as to whether ID security should extend to the use of public streets and sidewalks. Security kiosks had sprung up wherever people congregated, in shopping malls, in front of office buildings, and even at the entrances to public parks and beaches. Staffing these kiosks and other forms of constant patrol was expensive, and security expenditures soon consumed around 45 percent of state and local budgets. Still, some people felt jittery and insecure.

A ballot initiative the next year provided the promise of relief. To cut off terrorists at their source, all immigrants, regardless of area of origin, would no longer be eligible to use any public service. Backers of the initiative promised that this would mean fewer children in schools, fewer patients in public hospitals, fewer people applying for driver's licenses, and fewer requests for police and fire services. So, a provision of the measure permanently slashed state and local expenditures by 30 percent—the percentage of the state that was of immigrant origin—on the premise that lower demand for services would result in budget savings, which in turn could pay for the increased security.

The burden of anti-immigrant legislation fell most heavily on Latino populations. While Latino children (zero to fourteen years) were largely U.S. born (95.9 percent at the beginning of the century), their parents (twenty to thirty-nine years) were largely immigrant (63.4 percent when the century began) (U.S. Bureau of the Census 2000a). U.S.-born children, a lower court decided, could attend public schools and use public services, but their parents were expressly forbidden to be involved in those public services in any way, shape, or form. If U.S.-born Latino children wanted to go the library, for example, the immigrant parents could take them on private transportation but could not accompany them on public buses; they could park in a private lot but could not use the public parking lots; they could even walk on the sidewalk but were forbidden to step onto the public grounds of the library. The same restrictions applied to schools, parks, swimming pools, public hospitals, or any other public facility. Political figures argued that the laws were not discriminatory; after all, the U.S.-born Latino children were not barred from services, only their parents. The fact that a parent might not want to allow a six-year-old to ride alone on a bus to go to a library did not seem to be important to anyone but Latino parents.

Concerns for security had slammed shut the borders with Mexico, the state's former main trading partner. Businesses on the California side found themselves with drastically reduced customer traffic. The San Diego Padres, for example, found attendance cut by two-thirds, as Mexicans could not cross the border to attend games. On the Mexican side, the security concerns tied up traffic going into the United States for hours, sometimes days. Concern about terrorists hiding bombs in television sets or cars manufactured in Mexico meant every such item had to be disassembled, under the eyes of a U.S. employee, then reassembled in a secure room. This security concern caused such a slowdown in the importation from Mexico that maquiladoras shut down their production lines, throwing hundreds of thousands of people out of work.

Concerned for their security after the indecisive Second Terrorist War, aging baby boomers sought safe enclaves, far from the festering urban cores that teemed with foreign-looking populations. Farther and farther out into the virgin farmlands, farther out into the desert, farther up the foothills, they built small, safe, gated villages, with constant security patrols guaranteeing no dangerous strangers would enter. Thanks to the development of secure Internet connections, they were able to telecommute to their jobs in the centers of finance and film.

Their maids, nannies, gardeners, and personal-care attendants, however, had to commute for hours from the increasingly dense urban cores, for they could not afford to buy, or even rent, housing anywhere close to their employers. Expensive private toll roads were built parallel to the old public freeways. Thanks to rigid contractual language, CalTrans, the agency responsible for the state's roads and highways, was forbidden to make any improvement that might compete with the private toll roads, so the old freeway system, built from 1950 to 1970, deteriorated. Heavy trucks pounded away at sixty- and seventy-year-old surfaces, and the jam-packed cars driven by poor Latinos slowly squeezed between potholes and six-trailer land-trains at fifteen miles per hour. Parallel to them, affluent retired baby boomers zoomed along on the private toll roads; their senior-discount pass made the trip from Fresno to Bakersfield, which would cost younger drivers more than $85, practically free. Buses and subway trains postponed maintenance and finally gave out. They were replaced, not with newer vehicles, but with private pirate vans that filled the vacuum. Operating without oversight or scrutiny, they did not require a Cal-ID card for entry, but they also could charge whatever the market could bear and ran free of any safety obligations. The death toll in these gypsy vans was horrendous, but, inevitably, nearly all the accident victims did not have the latest Cal-ID card and should not have been in the state anyway. Who knows? They could have been terrorists.

After 2021, the largely non-Hispanic white baby boomers were retired in great numbers. Former teachers, police, sheriffs, firefighters, administrators, and other civil servants departed the public payrolls in droves and streamed into various retirement funds, such as CalPERS. The systems that supported these retirement possibilities were already suffering from 30 percent cuts imposed more than a decade earlier and talked of declaring bankruptcy in the face of a tidal wave of retirees. Such talk frightened the already insecure retirees. They found a champion in the person of Pete Billington II, son of Governor Pete Billington I, candidate for governor in 2022.

Shortly after taking office, he addressed the economic insecurity plaguing the retiring baby boomers by proposing a state initiative to guarantee the pension of any retired person, whether from public or private employment. By constitutional amendment, the pensions of retired baby boomers took precedence over any other expenditure—education, health, transportation, water—except security. His popularity soared in the non-Hispanic white electorate. By 2025, more than 85 percent of the state's budget was dedicated, by law, to pension guarantees and security. The modest 15 percent remainder was available for education, health, and other services.

With the drastic reduction in education expenditures, the preparation level of Latinos, already low to begin with, dropped even lower than its 2000 levels, as public schools and universities were forced simultaneously to make severe cutbacks in teaching activities and to raise fees and tuition drastically. Those who could afford it—largely the non-Hispanic white and Asian/Pacific Islander populations—forsook the public system and enrolled their children in elite private schools. Fewer Latinos graduated from public high schools; fewer still attended college. Instead, discouraged by overcrowded classes and inattentive, permanent substitute teachers, they drifted out into the job market and were herded into short-term jobs as home health workers, where they were paid very low wages and provided with almost no benefits.

Over the years, the percentage of Latinos without health insurance grew to 40 percent, then 50 percent, then 60 percent, and finally topped out at 85 percent. Unable to pay exorbitant out-of-pocket fees to physicians who would rather treat the lucrative, well-insured baby boomers, Latino patients flooded the public clinics and hospitals. Continuing a trend, after 2000 the number of Latino physicians graduating from the state's medical schools shrank, until the last one finished in 2023, after which there were no more Latino physicians produced in the state. In many barrios, there were more than 100,000 persons for every one physician. Hepatitis, tuberculosis, and salmonella ran rampant. Meanwhile, in Beverly Hills, there was one physician for every 45 people, and the miracles of superplastic surgery kept the residents looking and acting younger every year.

Despairing of finding sufficiently well-trained researchers and workers, high-tech industries had been leaving California since 2000, seeking places, such as North Dakota, with a highly educated workforce. Financial activities followed them out of the state. Even the remaining light manufacturing, plagued by energy and water shortages and clogged freeways, moved into Arizona, Nevada, and Idaho. Pete Billington II won reelection by a landslide in 2026, promising to be ever more vigilant in "saving our state" from the grasp of foreign-looking Latinos who just might be terrorists.

The dynamics that assured California's downward spiral were in place by 2030; the inadequate water, energy, and transportation infrastructure could not physically support twenty-first-century industry. For nearly forty years, California public schools had been at the bottom of the nation in performance, and two entire generations of children, 70 percent of whom happened to be Latino, had gone through their desultory preparation. Not surprisingly, less than 20 percent managed to graduate from the dumbed-down high schools.

The state's universities were no longer the place for cutting-edge research but were perceived around the world as second-rate institutions. As a result, competitive graduate and undergraduate students preferred to be educated in other areas, and the formerly elite University of California had far more spaces available than students who chose to study there. Still, given the colossal failure of public education, less than 10 percent of these students were Latino. The Latino physician shortage had worsened, to the point that the California Latino Medical Association announced that there was better medical care to be found in Haiti than in Latino areas of California.

New corporations based on new technologies increasingly located outside the state. The state had lost the technological edge it once possessed, and new patents were rarely issued to state inventors.

Between 2021 and 2040, the death spiral increased. With nearly all public expenditures guaranteed to security, especially after the Third Terrorist War, and to pension benefits for the retired baby boomers, public systems ground to a near halt. A vestigial school system functioned mainly to provide a raison d'être for the large pensions still being paid out; they had ceased being functional educational establishments decades earlier. Public roadways were essentially unusable, having been beaten to pieces by 2020. Trucks had to pay exorbitant fees to use the private roads, which increased the cost of goods and services. This made the state uncompetitive, compared to other states, and more businesses located outside its borders. Inside the state, poorly paid Latinos found the prices of basic goods constantly increased. Energy, when it was available, was so expensive that most Latino households could afford to have only one light bulb on at night. The California water system, built nearly a century earlier, between 1950 and 1970, had been inadequate for decades. A glass of water in a restaurant cost half a day's wages for those at the minimum wage level. Senior citizens, of course, were able to get water free for the asking.

The police and prison systems were the only public entities that functioned well at all. The fact that one out of every three Latino males spent at least one year in prison before reaching age thirty only frightened the remaining non-Hispanic white baby boomers into demanding even greater levels of protection. And the desperate conditions in the barrios spawned new "criminals," often guilty of no more than theft of a gallon of water or a pound of unground wheat.

2040 was the twelfth year of the La Niña cycle. Years had passed since the last measurable rainfall. Even damp coastal fog was but a memory. A rash of mysterious fires had broken out in urban areas. Schools, parks, city halls, and other public buildings were the first to be torched. Lives were not endangered because most of the buildings had not been operational for decades. But the symbolism, the attack on American institutions, inflamed the electorate, which demanded even higher levels of protection. No one seemed to notice, but each cycle of police and tribunal crackdown was followed by a new cycle of mysterious fires. Outside the state, no one much cared; California, for all its size and resources, had also managed to rank dead last among all the other states in terms of economic activity. No one else cared if California sank or swam. Slowly, it sank.

Most probably, California of 2040 in real life will contain elements of both the best-case and the worst-case scenarios. The goal is to have more elements of the best-case rather than of the worst-case scenario. In many ways, the difference between a best case and a worst case is in our hands, for the major variable separating the two possibilities is Latino educational achievement; that one fact alone will make all the difference by 2040.

LATINO EDUCATION: DEAD-END OR BUMP IN THE ROAD?

The major difference between the best-case and worst-case scenarios is the educational attainment of Latinos, who comprise more than 50 percent of all children born in the state since 2001, and who will comprise more than

50 percent of the new entrants to the labor force by 2017. In a way that eludes the vision of most policymakers, the fortunes of California in the twenty-first century will ride on the backs of today's Latino grade-school children. There are reasons for optimism and reasons for despair. By 2020, the die will have been cast—permanent optimism or permanent despair.

As we have seen, during the past sixty years, Latinos have largely operated at the bottom end of the state's economy. A Latino middle class has emerged recently, and Latino businesses seem poised for take-off. Yet long-term trends in education are troubling. For the past sixty years, Latino adults, twenty-five years and older, have had a far lower educational level than non-Hispanic whites, African Americans, and Asian/Pacific Islanders. Although this lower level has not yet translated into dysfunctional behaviors typical of the urban underclass, it is worrisome. Is the relatively lower level of educational attainment a temporary "bump in the road" that can be overcome quickly? Or does it represent a dead end, not only for Latinos, but also for the state in which they soon will be the dominant population?

Although Latino educational attainment has consistently lagged behind that of any other group, there is a major difference, often unnoticed, between U.S.-born and immigrant Latino educational levels. Immigrant Latinos who arrived in the 1965–90 period generally had around nine years of education. Arriving as young adults, rarely as children, their goal was not to attend school in the state but to join the workforce. Thus the educational level of immigrants rose somewhat in the ten years from 1990 to 2000, but even then only 38.6 percent of immigrant Latino adults had graduated from high school (see Figure 18 on page 97). It is not likely that immigrant Latino educational levels will rise significantly in the future, as that population now largely consists of middle-aged adults who immigrated fifteen to thirty years ago, when they were young.

Of greater concern is the educational level of U.S.-born Latinos. While quite a bit higher than the immigrant Latino levels—almost three-fourths (70.8 percent) graduated from high school—U.S.-born Latino educational levels show a long-term trend that should concern all. The college graduation gap is even greater than the high school gap, and of more concern to an economy increasingly dependent on a highly educated workforce. Barely 12.8 percent of U.S.-born Latino adults have graduated from college in 2000, a far lower percent than African Americans (23.6 percent), non-Hispanic whites (34.8 percent), and Asian/Pacific Islanders (43.2 percent U.S. born and 44.3 percent immigrant). Only 5.7 percent of immigrant Latino adults have graduated from college (see Figure 36).

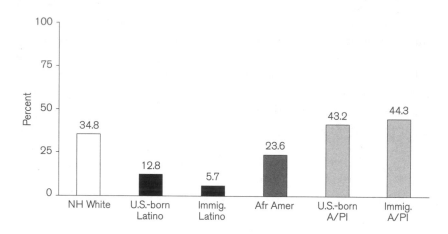

Figure 36. College Graduation (Bachelor's+), Adults 25+, California, 2000.
Source: U.S. Bureau of the Census 2000a.

The elite campuses of the University of California are the principal training ground for students who wish to continue on to graduate and professional education. In addition, they are charged with a basic research mission for the state. Stated bluntly, Latinos have *never* been proportionately represented in the university's student body. The fairest comparison base is the high school graduate population. Figure 37 shows the percentage of graduating high school seniors who were Latino and the percentage of Latinos enrolling in UC campuses from 1992 to 2000. While the percentage of Latinos in each year's high school graduating class rose, from 29 percent in 1992 to 33 percent in 2000—and has been projected to rise to 44 percent by 2010 by the California Department of Finance (2001a)—the percentage of Latinos enrolling as undergraduates in the UC campuses has actually declined, from 16 percent in 1994 to 13 percent in 2000. If Latino students are to be proportionately represented in the University of California, their numbers will need to triple or quadruple there by the end of the decade.

The lack of UC undergraduate representation is not merely an issue of numbers and fairness. It is, instead, about the growing mismatch between the needs of a society moving into a knowledge-based economy and the preparation of the growing, soon-to-be largest segment of the population to fill those needs. The Latino physician shortage provides a good illustration of this mismatch. From 1948 to 1973, the state's medical schools combined, growing from four to eight during that period, managed to educate,

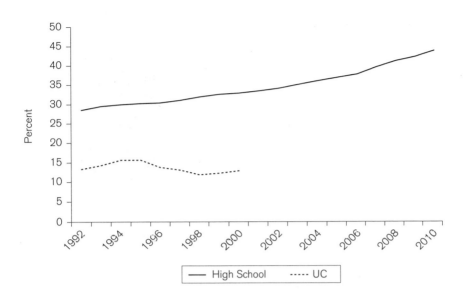

Figure 37. Latinos as Percentage of High School Graduates and Percentage of UC Enrollment, 1992–2010. Sources: CA DOF 2001a; 1992–95 (Regents of the University of California 1997–98); 1996–2000 (Regents of the University of California 2001).

on average, one or two Latino physicians every year. Thanks to intensive efforts in the 1970s, partially the result of Chicano-generation students, the number of graduating Latino medical students rose to an average of about fifty a year (D. Hayes-Bautista, Hsu, Hayes-Bautista, Stein et al. 2000, 733). Yet the number was stuck at about fifty per year during the 1980s and early 1990s. Meanwhile, the Latino population has grown considerably. By 1999, the 3,578 Latino physicians represented 4.8 percent of the total 74,345 physicians licensed to practice in the state. Yet Latinos made up nearly one-third of the state's population (30.4 percent). In terms of a ratio of population-per-physician, there were 335 non-Latino patients for every non-Latino physician. There were, however, 2,893 Latino patients for every Latino physician (see Figure 38).

There is no reason, of course, why non-Latino physicians cannot take care of Latino patients. However, non-Latino physicians, by and large, choose not to serve Latino populations, choosing instead to practice in non-Latino areas and choosing not to learn to communicate with their patients in Spanish in their offices. Data from our recent survey of Latino

Figure 38. Population per Physician, Non-Latino and Latino, California, 1999.
Sources: CA DOF 1998; D. Hayes-Bautista 2000.

physicians (D. Hayes-Bautista 2000) show that, compared to non-Latino physicians:

Latino physicians are more than three times as likely to have their office in a heavily Latino-populated zip code area (40 percent or more Latino);

78.8 percent of Latino physicians speak Spanish, compared to 2.6 percent of non-Latino physicians. (UCLA Institute for Social Science Research Data Archives 1996)

Some heavily Latino areas of California have very few physicians of any kind practicing in them. The city of Bell, for example, has only twenty-two physicians for its 112,944 residents. The surest way to have physicians practicing in shortage areas is to educate and train Latino physicians (Firebaugh 2002). The question is one of access to care, not affirmative action.

Under current medical-school policy, however, the Latino physician shortage will worsen over the next twenty years. This is due to the fact that, since 1992, the number of Latinos matriculating in first-year classes in the five University of California medical schools has fallen by about one-third. Figure 39 shows the annual first-year matriculation figures: the number of Latinos has dropped, from a high of ninety in 1992, to a low of forty-six in 2001. Unless Latino enrollments are substantially increased, very quickly, the Latino physician shortage will worsen. The population-to-physician ratio will become more lopsided, increasing from 2,893 to one in

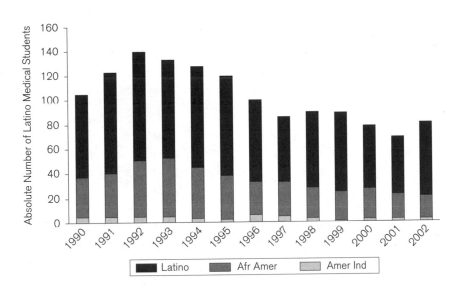

Figure 39. Underrepresented Minority First-Year Medical School Matriculations, University of California Schools, 1990–2002. Sources: 1990–2000 (Medical Student Diversity Task Force 2000); 2001–02 (UCOP 2002).

1999 to 3,317 to one by 2010 and 4,044 to one by 2020 (D. Hayes-Bautista, Hsu, Hayes-Bautista, Stein et al. 2000). Meanwhile, in other parts of the state, there appears to be a physician surplus, and some providers are reported to be leaving the state. Chances are low that any of those surplus physicians will voluntarily move their practices to Latino neighborhoods.

The Latino physician shortage is but one indicator of the problems in store for the state from lack of investment in Latino educational success. Similar shortages are seen in other health professions (dentists, optometrists, nurses, pharmacists, and so on) and in other professions (attorneys, engineers, social workers, teachers, and so on). The state can ill afford to train professionals who then leave the state to practice elsewhere, but it seems unwilling to train professionals who will apply their skills here, where there is the most demand.

To compound the situation, the state has not kept itself competitive in educational infrastructure investment. In the 1950s, California was one of the nation's leaders in educational input and output. As recently as 1964, California ranked fifth in per-pupil spending (Public Education 1998). The Master Plan for Higher Education guaranteed a college-level slot for every student, the university system was a marvel, and Nobel Prizes rolled in.

TABLE 7
Educational Attainment for Adults 25+, California, 2002 (%)

	Non-Hispanic White	Latino Immigrant	Latino U.S.-born	A/PI Immigrant	A/PI U.S.-born	African American
High school grad.	92.7	38.6	76.7	85.7	93.3	87.8
College grad.	34.8	5.7	12.8	44.3	43.2	23.6

SOURCE: U.S. Bureau of the Census 2000a.

During the 1990s, however, California ranked near the bottom of any national comparison, of input or output, in reading scores, SAT scores, and high school graduation. During the 1980s and 1990s, the state built far more prisons than it did schools. Unfortunately, this disinvestment in education occurred at precisely the moment that Latino populations grew tremendously, and Latino children currently educated are in a system far less capable than the one that educated the baby boomers in the 1950s and 1960s.

On a positive note, one dynamic missed in making static comparisons between different ethnic groups is the fact that Latino children have acquired educational levels far superior to those of their immigrant Latino parents. It is common to interpret the consistently higher Asian/Pacific Islander educational levels as indicative of some unknown cultural factors at work. Yet, a more pedestrian, less exotic explanation is that immigrant Asian/Pacific Islander parents arrive with already high educational levels, exceeding those of non-Hispanic white adults. Their U.S.-born Asian/Pacific Islander children merely maintain already high levels. In the meantime, U.S.-born Latino children move up rapidly from the low levels of their parents, to levels that begin to approach, but do not yet match, Asian/Pacific Islanders' and other groups' levels. Table 7 shows the trend for adults twenty-five years and older in California for 2000.

U.S.-born Latinos have vastly improved over the educational attainment of the immigrant Latino generation (largely, the parents of the U.S.-born), and they are around twice as likely—98.7 percent—to graduate from high school (76.7 percent, compared to 38.6 percent, high school graduates) and 124.6 percent more likely to graduate from college (12.8 percent, compared to 5.7 percent, college graduates). U.S.-born Asian/Pacific Islanders, however, do not demonstrate such high levels of improvement. They barely have improved—8.9 percent—over their parents' high school graduation rates (93.3

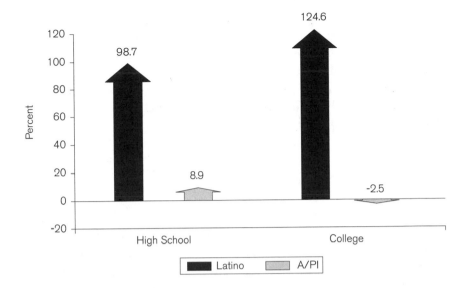

Figure 40. Percent Improvement of the U.S.-born over Immigrant Educational Levels, Latino and A/PI, Adults 25+, 2000. Source: U.S. Bureau of the Census 2000a.

percent, compared to 85.7 percent, high school graduates) and actually are slightly less likely—2.5 percent—to graduate from college, compared to immigrant Asian/Pacific Islanders (43.2 percent, compared to 44.3 percent, college graduates).

The advantage that immigrant Asian/Pacific Islander parents give their U.S.-born children is that, as immigrants, they arrive with far higher educational levels than those achieved by non-Hispanic whites; while 44.3 percent of immigrant Asian/Pacific Islanders arrive with a college degree, only 34.8 percent of non-Hispanic white adults have achieved that level of college graduation. Thus, even though U.S.-born Asian/Pacific Islanders do not achieve to the level of their immigrant parents, it is not surprising that they achieve higher levels than largely U.S.-born non-Hispanic whites.

Immigrant Latino parents, only 5.7 percent of whom have a college education, generally do not provide this advantage to their children. The schools their children attend do not prepare them well, sometimes offering no Advanced Placement classes at all. Private schools and private tutoring for SAT review courses usually are beyond their economic reach. Nonetheless, their U.S.-born Latino children have improved vastly over the levels of their immigrant parents (see Figure 40). Thus, while they have not yet achieved their Asian/Pacific Islander classmates' levels of college graduation, they have improved remarkably over their parents' levels, making giant strides in educational attainment, while U.S.-born Asian/Pacific Islanders do worse than immigrant Asian/Pacific Islanders. Latino students are capable of tremendous increases in educational attainment over those of their parents. They simply do not start with many parental advantages. Our educational systems do not build on the tremendous educational increase from the parents' to the children's generation. Instead, when the bar for admissions to the prestigious University of California is raised (for example, by giving extra grade-point credit for Advanced Placement courses), these educational aspirations are thwarted.

Another major factor separating the worst-case from the best-case scenario is Atlantic American accommodation to diversity. After 2010, the baby boomers will begin leaving the labor force, and the remaining working adults will be, increasingly, Latinos. If Latino educational achievement can be successfully addressed, the post–2010 period looks quite good. If it is not, then the future looks bleak indeed, for the needs of "graying society" may well outweigh the needs of the younger population. The response to Latino educational issues will be conditioned by Atlantic American reactions to an increasingly diverse population. If a more Puritan model is followed, the state will not manage its diversity well, and the stage will be set for ongoing cultural conflict. If, on the other hand, diversity is approached from a Quaker-like stance, there is every reason to see a brighter future.

With respect to both of these factors, the state's direction is in the hands of the state's electorate today and for the next decade, until around 2015. To update Marx's observation on the making of history, humans "make their own history, but they do not make it under circumstances chosen by themselves, but under circumstances directly found, given, and transmitted from the past" (Carper and Carper 1991, 209). California can make its history by realizing that the time is now, and the conditions can be voted upon. The best legacy the state can give its future generations is a well-educated workforce, which will happen to be predominantly Latino. "Only in an act of the present can we make present the past, as well as the future" (Fuentes 1988, 89).

REFERENCES

PUBLISHED REFERENCES

Acuña, Rodolfo. 1972. *Occupied America: The Chicano's struggle toward liberation.* San Francisco, CA: Canfield Press.

American College of Physicians—American Society of Internal Medicine. 2000. *No health insurance? It's enough to make you sick—Latino community at great risk.* By Melinda L. Schriver. In the American College of Physicians home page [cited 2002–2003]. Philadelphia, PA, and Washington DC: American College of Physicians—American Society of Internal Medicine, 1996–2003. Available at: http://www.acponline.org/uninsured/lack-contents2.htm

Anuario estadístico de los Estados Unidos Mexicanos, 1997. 1998. Aguascalientes, Mexico: Instituto Nacional de Estadística, Geografía e Informática.

Balderrama, Francisco E., and Raymond Rodríguez. 1995. *Decade of betrayal: Mexican repatriation in the 1930s.* Albuquerque: University of New Mexico Press.

Baltzell, E. Digby. 2001. *Puritan Boston and Quaker Philadelphia: Two Protestant ethics and the spirit of class authority and leadership.* With a new introduction by the author. New Brunswick, NJ, and London: Transaction Publishers. (Orig. pub. 1996.)

Barabak, Mark Z. 1997. Anti-bilingual drive's tone is key for Latinos. *Los Angeles Times,* Oct. 16.

Barrera, Mario. 1990. *Beyond Aztlan: Ethnic autonomy in comparative perspective.* South Bend, IN: University of Notre Dame Press.

Bellah, Robert N. 1996. *Habits of the heart: Individualism and commitment in American life.* Berkeley: University of California Press.

Berger, Peter L., and Thomas Luckmann. 1966. *The social construction of reality: A treatise in the sociology of knowledge.* New York: Anchor Books.

Boeta, Jose Rodulfo. 1977. *Bernardo de Gálvez.* Temas españoles, 543. Madrid: Publicaciones Españolas.

Bolton, Ralph. 1981. Susto, hostility and hypoglycemia. *Ethnology* 20, no. 4: 261–76.

Braudel, Fernand. 1988. *The identity of France: History and environment.* Translated by Siân Reynolds. New York: Harper and Row.

Brown, E. Richard, Ninez Ponce, Thomas Rice, and Shana Alex Lavarreda. 2002. *The state of health insurance in California: Findings from the 2001 California health interview survey.* Los Angeles: UCLA Center for Health Policy Research.

Brownstein, Ronald. 1992. Clinton: Parties fail to attack race divisions. *Los Angeles Times,* May 3.

California Center for Health Statistics. 1999. *California life expectancy: Abridged life tables by race/ethnicity for California, 1995–97.* Prepared by Carmen Harms and C. Jane McKendry. Sacramento: California Department of Health Services.

———. 2002. *Birth records—Years 1994, 1999, 2000, 2001.* In California Department of Health Services home page [updated Oct. 25, 2002; cited Apr. 22, 2003]. Sacramento: California Department of Health Services. Available from http://www.applications.dhs.ca.gov/vsq/default.asp

California Coalition for Immigration Reform (CCIR). n.d. Our borders are out of control. Huntington Beach: California Coalition for Immigration Reform. Photocopy.

California Department of Finance (CA DOF), Demographic Research Unit. 1998. Race/ethnic population projections with age and sex detail, 1970–2040. In California Department of Finance home page [updated June 5, 2003; cited 2002–2003]. Sacramento: California Department of Finance. Available from http://www.dof.ca.gov/HTML/demograp/Race.htm; link to http://www.dof .ca.gov/newdr/1998.txt

———. 1999. Race/ethnic population estimates: Components of change, California counties, July 1970–July 1990. In California Department of Finance home page [updated June 5, 2003; cited 2002–2003]. Sacramento: California Department of Finance. Available from http://www.dof.ca.gov/html/ demograp/eth70–90.htm; link to http://www.dof.ca.gov/html/demograp/ Race7090.xls

———. 2001a. California public K–12 enrollment projections by ethnicity, history and projection, 2001 series. In California Department of Finance home page [updated June 5, 2003; cited 2002–2003]. Sacramento: California Department of Finance. Available from http://www.dof.ca.gov/html/demograp/

K12ethtb-cp.htm; link to http://www.dof.ca.gov/html/demograph/K12 Ethtb.xls

————. [2001b]. Race/ethnic population estimates: Components of change, California counties, Apr. 1990 to July 1999 [cited 2002–2003]. Sacramento: California Department of Finance. Available from http://www.dof.ca.gov/ HTML/DEMOGRAP/Race/Calif.xls

California Department of Health Services (CA DHS). 1989. *Vital statistics of California, 1987*. By David W. Mitchell, William A. Avritt, Kenneth W. Kizer, and Clifford L. Allenby. Sacramento, CA: Department of Health Services and Welfare Agency.

————. 1996. *Vital statistics of California, 1994*. By Kathryn Riedmiller, Sandy Ficenec, Robin Jones, C. Jane McKendry, Anthony Oreglia, Rod A. Palmieri, and George B. (Peter) Abbott. Sacramento, CA: Department of Health Services.

————. 1998. *Deaths, death rates and age, Table 5–15* [cited May 30, 2003]. California: Department of Health Services. Available from http://www.dhs.ca .gov/hisp/chs/OHIR/vssdata/1998data/chapter5/5–15–1998.xls

————. 2000a. *Age-adjusted perinatal and infant mortality rates for single births by race/ethnicity of mother, California birth cohorts, 1990–1997, 1999 (By place of residence)* [cited 2002–2003]. Available from http://www.dhs.ca.gov/hisp/chs/ OHIR/vssdata/2000data/00Ch4Excel/6Reorg.xls

————. 2000b. *Birth cohort file 2000*. CD-ROM. Sacramento: California Department of Health Services, Center for Health Statistics.

————. 2000c. *Birth statistical master file 2000*. CD-ROM. Sacramento: California Department of Health Services, Center for Health Statistics.

————. 2000d. *Death statistical master file 2000*. CD-ROM. Sacramento: California Department of Health Services, Center for Health Statistics.

————. 2001a. *Birth statistical master file 2001*. CD-ROM. Sacramento: California Department of Health Services, Center for Health Statistics.

————. 2001b. *Vital statistics of California, 1998*. Prepared by Kathryn Riedmiller and Kamal Bindra. Sacramento: California Department of Health Services.

————. 2002a. *California's infant mortality rate, 2000*. By Sandy Ficenec. Sacramento: California Department of Health Services, Center for Health Statistics.

————. 2002b. *Death statistical master file 2002*. CD-ROM. Sacramento: California Department of Health Services, Center for Health Statistics.

————. 2003. *Deaths, death rates and age-adjusted death rates for 18 major causes of death by race/ethnicity. California 1990–1998*. Table 5–15 [updated May 6, 2003; cited May 30, 2003]. Sacramento: California Department of Health Services. Available from http://www.dhs.ca.gov/hisp/chs/ohir/vssdata/1998data/ PDFCh_5/5–15–1998.pdf

California Department of Industrial Relations, Division of Fair Employment Practices. 1964. *Californians of Spanish surname: Population, employment, income, education*. San Francisco: California Department of Industrial Relations, Division of Fair Employment Practices.

California Economic Development Agency. 1962. *California statistical abstract, 1962*. Sacramento: Economic Development Agency of the State of California.

California Employment Development Department (CA EDD). 1986. *Socio-economic trends in California, 1940–1980*. Sacramento, CA: Department of Health Services and Welfare Agency.

Camarillo, Albert. 1984. *Chicanos in California: A history of Mexican Americans in California*. San Francisco: Boyd and Fraser.

Cano Sánchez, Angela, Neus Escandell Tur, and Elena Mampel González. 1984. *Gaspar de Portolá: Crónicas del descubrimiento de la Alta California, 1769*. Barcelona: Universitat de Barcelona.

Carper, N. Gordon, and Joyce Carper. 1991. *The meaning of history: A dictionary of quotations*. New York: Greenwood Press.

Caughey, John Walton. 1934. *Bernardo de Gálvez in Louisiana, 1776–1783*. Berkeley: University of California Press.

Center for the Study of Latino Health and Culture (CESLAC), UCLA. 2000. *Latino profiles study report: American dream makers*. Los Angeles, CA: United Way of Greater Los Angeles.

Chavez, Leo R. 2001. *Covering immigration: Popular images and the politics of the nation*. Berkeley: University of California Press.

Chavez, Linda. 2001. Just another ethnic group. *The Wall Street Journal*, March 14.

Clark, Margaret. 1959. *Health in the Mexican-American culture: A community study*. Berkeley: University of California Press.

Cook, Sherburne F., and Woodrow Borah. 1971. *Essays in population history: Mexico and the Caribbean*. Vol. 1. Berkeley: University of California Press.

Cuevas, Mariano, comp. and ed. 1914. *Documentos inéditos del siglo XVI para la historia de México*. Mexico City: Museo Nacional de Arqueología, Historia y Etnología.

Dana, Richard Henry. 1986. *Two years before the mast*. Edited with an introduction by Thomas Philbrick. New York: Penguin Books.

Daniels, Roger. 1990. *Coming to America: A history of immigration and ethnicity in American life*. New York: HarperPerennial.

Davila, Arlene. 2001. *Latinos, Inc.: The marketing and making of a people*. Berkeley: University of California Press.

Elizondo, Virgilio P., and Timothy M. Matovina, eds. 1998. *Mestizo worship: A pastoral approach to liturgical ministry*. Collegeville, MN: Liturgical Press.

Feinstein's TV Attack on Immigration. 1994. *Los Angeles Times*, July 10.

Fischer, David Hackett. 1989. *Albion's seed: Four British folkways in America*. New York: Oxford University Press.

Fonner, Edwin. 1975. Mortality differences of 1970 Texas residents. Master's thesis, School of Public Health, University of Texas.

Forbes, Jack D. 1968. Race and color in Mexican-American problems. *Journal of Human Relations* 16, no. 1 (first quarter): 55–68. Also printed in Ogletree, Earl J., and David Garcia, comps. 1975. *Education of the Spanish-speaking urban child: A book of readings.* Springfield, IL: Charles C. Thomas.

Fuentes, Carlos. 1988. How I started to write. In *The graywolf annual five: Multicultural literacy,* ed. Rick Simonson and Scott Walker, 83–111. St. Paul, MN: Graywolf Press.

García Sáiz, María Concepción. 1989. *Las castas mexicanas: Un género pictórico americano.* [Mexico City]: Olivetti.

González-Portillo, Patricia A. 2001. Segregación de niños de origen mexicano. *La Opinión* (Los Angeles), Apr. 16.

Gordon, Milton Myron. 1964. *Assimilation in American life: The role of race, religion, and national origins.* New York: Oxford University Press.

Grebler, Leo, Joan Moore, and Ralph C. Guzman. 1973. The ebb and flow of immigration. In *An introduction to Chicano studies,* comp. Livie Isauro Duran and H. Russell Bernard, 209–27. New York: Macmillan.

Griswold del Castillo, Richard. 1979. *The Los Angeles barrio, 1850–1890: A social history.* Berkeley: University of California Press.

———. 1980. The del Valle family and the fantasy heritage. *California History* 59, no. 1: 2–15.

Gutiérrez, Yolanda. 2000. México se perfila como primer socio commercial de EU. *La Voz de Michoacán* (Morelia, Mexico), Sept. 22.

Harrington, Michael. 1993. *The other America: Poverty in the United States.* New York: Macmillan Publishing Company.

Harrison, Lawrence E. 1985. *Underdevelopment is a state of mind: The Latin American case.* Lanham, MD: Center for International Affairs, Harvard University, and University Press of America.

Hayes-Bautista, David E. 1978. Latino health conditions: Policies for future research. Paper delivered at the annual meeting of the American Public Health Association, Oct. 16, Los Angeles, CA.

———. 1996. *The health of California's public: A chartbook.* Woodland Hills: The California Endowment and California HealthCare Foundation.

———. 1997. *The health status of Latinos in California.* Woodland Hills: The California Endowment and California HealthCare Foundation.

———. 2002. The Latino health research agenda for the twenty-first century. In *Latinos: Remaking America,* ed. Marcelo M. Suárez-Orozco and Mariela M. Páez, 215–35. Berkeley: University of California Press.

Hayes-Bautista, David E., and Jorge Chapa. 1986. Latino terminology: Conceptual bases for standardized terminology. *American Journal of Public Health* 77, no. 1: 61–68.

Hayes-Bautista, David E., Paul Hsu, María Hayes-Bautista, Delmy Iñiguez, Cynthia L. Chamberlin, Christian Rico, and Rosa Solorio. 2002. An anomaly within the Latino epidemiological paradox: The Latino adolescent male mortality peak. *Archives of Pediatric and Adolescent Medicine* 152: 480–84.

Hayes-Bautista, David E., Paul Hsu, María Hayes-Bautista, Robert M. Stein, Patrick Dowling, Robert Beltran, and Juan Villagomez. 2000. Latino physician supply in California: Sources, locations, and projections. *Academic Medicine* 75, no. 7: 727–36.

Hayes-Bautista, David E., Paul Hsu, Aidé Pérez, and Mariam Iya Kharamanian. 2003. The Latino majority has emerged: Latinos comprise over 50 percent of all births in California. Los Angeles, CA: Center for the Study of Latino Health and Culture.

Hayes-Bautista, David E., Aída Hurtado, R. Burciaga Valdez, and Anthony C. R. Hernandez. 1992. *No longer a minority: Latinos and social policy in California.* Los Angeles, CA: UCLA Chicano Studies Research Center Publications.

Hayes-Bautista, David E., Delmy Iñiguez, and Cynthia L. Chamberlin. 2001. *LAUSD enrollment 1966–1998: Decline, then recovery, while the city grew.* Los Angeles. CA: Center for the Study of Latino Health and Culture, UCLA.

Hayes-Bautista, David E., and Gregory Rodriguez. 1996. LA county's answer for racial tensions: Intermarriage. *Los Angeles Times,* May 5.

Hayes-Bautista, David E., Werner O. Schink, and Jorge Chapa. 1988. *The burden of support: Young Latinos in an aging society.* Stanford, CA: Stanford University Press.

Hayes-Bautista, David E., Werner O. Schink, and María Hayes-Bautista. 1993. Latinos and the 1992 Los Angeles riots: A behavioral sciences perspective. *Hispanic Journal of Behavioral Sciences* 15, no. 4: 427–48.

Hayes-Bautista, David E., Werner O. Schink, and Gregory Rodriguez. 1994. *Latino immigrants in Los Angeles: A portrait from the 1990 census.* Los Angeles, CA: Alta California Policy Research Center.

Hefner, Paul. 1994. Prop. 187 exposed cultural clash: Swelling Latino numbers, assimilation, costs of illegals became campaign issues. *Daily News of Los Angeles,* November 14.

Hollenbach, David. 1995. Virtue, the common good and democracy. In *New communitarian thinking: Persons, virtues, institutions, and communities,* ed. Amitai Etzioni, 143–53. Charlottesville: University Press of Virginia.

Humphreys, Jeffrey M. 2000. Buying power at the beginning of a new century: Projections for 2000 and 2001. *Georgia Business and Economic Conditions* 60, no. 4 (July–Aug.): 14.

Hurtado, Aída, David E. Hayes-Bautista, R. Burciaga Valdez, and Anthony C. R. Hernandez. 1992. *Redefining California: Latino social engagement in a multicultural society.* Los Angeles, CA: UCLA Chicano Studies Research Center Publications.

Immigration and Naturalization Service (INS). 1991. *Statistical yearbook of the Immigration and Naturalization Service, 1990.* Washington DC: U.S. Government Printing Office.

———. 1992. *Statistical yearbook of the Immigration and Naturalization Service, 1991.* Washington DC: U.S. Government Printing Office.

———. 1993. *Statistical yearbook of the Immigration and Naturalization Service, 1992.* Washington DC: U.S. Government Printing Office.

———. 1994. *Statistical Yearbook of the Immigration and Naturalization Service, 1993.* Washington DC: U.S. Government Printing Office.

———. 1995. *Statistical yearbook of the Immigration and Naturalization Service, 1994.* Washington DC: U.S. Government Printing Office.

———. 1996. *Statistical yearbook of the Immigration and Naturalization Service, 1995.* Washington DC: U.S. Government Printing Office.

———. 1997. *Statistical yearbook of the Immigration and Naturalization Service, 1996.* Washington DC: U.S. Government Printing Office.

———. 1998. *Statistical yearbook of the Immigration and Naturalization Service, 1997.* Washington DC: U.S. Government Printing Office.

———. 1999. *Statistical yearbook of the Immigration and Naturalization Service, 1998.* Washington DC: U.S. Government Printing Office.

Jacoby, Tamar. 2001. *Someone else's house.* New York: Free Press.

Jordan, Terry G. 1993. *North American cattle-ranching frontiers: Origins, diffusion, and differentiation.* Albuquerque: University of New Mexico Press.

Kahl, Joseph A. 1974. *The measurement of modernism: A study of values in Brazil and Mexico.* Austin: University of Texas.

Kay, Margarita Arftschwager. 1977. Health and illness in a Mexican American barrio. In *Ethnic medicine in the Southwest,* ed. Edward H. Spicer, 99–158. Tucson: University of Arizona Press.

Kowsky, Kim. 1995. Welcome to Mr. G's, the final frontier for smokers' rights. *Los Angeles Times,* Mar. 18.

Latino Coalition for a New Los Angeles and the Latino Futures Research Group. 1993. *Latinos and the future of Los Angeles: A guide to the twenty-first century.* Los Angeles, CA: Latino Coalition for a New Los Angeles.

León-Portilla, Miguel. 2000. *Tonantzin Guadalupe: Pensamiento náhuatl y mensaje cristiano en el "Nican Mopohua."* Mexico City: Fondo de Cultura Económica.

Letters. 2001. *Los Angeles Times Magazine,* Aug. 5.

Lewis, Oscar. 1959. *Five families: Mexican case studies in the culture of poverty.* New York: Basic Books.

———. 1965. *La vida: A Puerto Rican family in the culture of poverty.* San Juan, Puerto Rico, and New York: Random House.

Lopez, Robert, and Rich Connell. 2000. Special report: The Class of '89: Journeys into the new Los Angeles. *Los Angeles Times,* June 27.

López Austín, Alfredo. 1980. *Cuerpo humano e ideología: Las concepciones de los antiguos nahuas.* Serie antropológica, 39. Mexico City: Universidad Nacional Autónoma de México, Instituto de Investigaciones Antropológicas.

Los Angeles County Department of Health Services (LAC DHS). 1989. *Vital statistics of Los Angeles county, 1985.* Los Angeles, CA: Programs Coordination and Support Services, Data Collection and Analysis Division.

Los Angeles County, Internal Services Department (LAC ISD). 1992. *Impact of undocumented persons and other immigrants on costs, revenues and services in Los Angeles county.* Los Angeles, CA: Internal Services Department.

Los Angeles Times Poll. Study 281: L.A. After the Riots; Charter Change, May 9–12, 1992. Results Summary. 1992a. Compiled by Rob Cioe. In *Los Angeles Times* home page [cited June 9, 2003]. Available from http://www.latimes.com/extras/timespoll/stats/pdfs/281ss.pdf

Los Angeles Times Poll. Study 300: L.A. Six Months After the Unrest, October 9–14, 1992. Results Summary. 1992b. In *Los Angeles Times* home page [cited June 9, 2003]. Available from http://www.latimes.com/extras/timespoll/stats/pdfs/300ss.pdf

Los Angeles Times Poll. Survey #346: California, Early October 1994. 1994a. Compiled by John Brennan, Karen Wada, Susan Pinkus, Roger Richardson, Jill Milburn, Claudia Vaughn, Cecelia Barrera, and Rob Cioe. In *Los Angeles Times* home page [cited June 9, 2003]. Available from http://www.latimes.com/extras/timespoll/stats/pdfs/364ss.pdf

Los Angeles Times Poll. Survey #348: California, Late October, 1994. 1994b. In *Los Angeles Times* home page [cited June 9, 2003]. Available from http://www.latimes.com/extras/timespoll/stats/pdfs/348ss.pdf

Los Angeles Times Poll. Survey #389: Exit Poll: The General Election, November 5, 1996. 1996. In *Los Angeles Times* home page [cited Jan. 8, 2004]. Available from: http://images/latimes/com/media/acrobat/2003–07/8598114.pdf

Los Angeles Times Poll. Survey #413: Exit Poll: California Primary Election, June 2, 1998. 1996. In *Los Angeles Times* home page [cited Jan. 8, 2004]. Available from: http://images/latimes/com/media/acrobat/2003–07/8628666.pdf

Los Pobladores: The Founders of the City of Los Angeles. 1981. Bronze plaque at El Pueblo de los Angeles State Historic Park, Los Angeles. Dedicated Sept. 4.

Madsen, William. 1964. *Mexican-Americans of South Texas.* New York: Holt, Rinehart and Winston.

Martinez, John J. 2001. *Not counting the cost: Jesuit missionaries in colonial Mexico—A story of struggle, commitment, and sacrifice.* Chicago, IL: Jesuit Way.

Mason, William Marvin. 1998. *The census of 1790: A demographic history of colonial California.* Ballena Press Anthropological Papers, 45. Menlo Park, CA: Ballena Press.

Matovina, Timothy M. 1998. Liturgy, popular rites and popular spirituality. In *Mestizo worship: A pastoral approach to liturgical ministry,* ed. Virgilio P. Elizondo and Timothy M. Matovina, 81–91. Collegeville, MN: Liturgical Press.

Matovina, Timothy M., and Gerald E. Poyo, eds. 2000. ¡Presente! U.S. Latino Catholics from colonial origins to the present. American Catholic Identities. A Documentary History, 8. Maryknoll, NY: Orbis Books.

Mazón, Mauricio. 1984. The zoot-suit riots: The psychology of symbolic annihilation. Mexican American Monographs, 8. Austin: University of Texas.

McDonnell, Patrick J. 2001. Brash evangelist. Los Angeles Times Magazine, July 15, 14–17, 35–36.

McKeever Furst, Jill Leslie. 1995. The natural history of the soul in ancient Mexico. New Haven, CT: Yale University Press.

McWilliams, Carey. 1949. North From Mexico: The Spanish-speaking people of the United States. Philadelphia, PA: J. B. Lippincott Co.

———. 1968. The Mexicans in America: A student's guide to localized history. New York: Teachers College Press.

Mead, Lawrence M. 1991. The new politics of the new poverty. The Public Interest 103 (spring): 3–20.

Medical Student Diversity Task Force. 2000. Special report on medical student diversity. Prepared for University of California President Richard C. Atkinson. Oakland: University of California, Office of the President.

Menchaca, Martha. 2001. Recovering history, constructing race: The indian, black and white roots of Mexican Americans. Austin: University of Texas.

Monroy, Douglas. 1990. Thrown among strangers: The making of Mexican culture in frontier California. Berkeley: University of California Press.

Moore, Joan W., with Alfredo Cuellar. 1970. Mexican Americans. Englewood Cliffs, NJ: Prentice-Hall.

Moore, Joan W., and Raquel Pinderhughes, eds. 1993. In the barrios: Latinos and the underclass debate. New York: Russell Sage Foundation.

Moreno Toscano, Alejandra, Armando Cisneros, Carlos Aguirre, and Yolanda Terán. 1983. Atlas histórico de México. Mexico City: Siglo Veintiuno Editores.

Morrison, Peter A. 1993. Goodbye past, hello future: California's demographic shift. Los Angeles Times, Sept. 13.

Murray, Charles. 1984. Losing ground: American social policy, 1950–1980. New York: Basic Books.

National Association of Latino Elected and Appointed Officials (NALEO). 2002a. 2002 Latino election handbook. Los Angeles, CA: NALEO Educational Fund.

———. 2002b. 2002 National directory of Latino elected officials. Los Angeles, CA: NALEO Educational Fund.

National Institutes of Health (NIH), Office of Research on Minority Health. 2000. New web site provides information about the NIH minority health initiative [cited Aug. 10, 2000]. Available at http//www.nih.gov/news/pr/apr2000/od-14.htm

National Review. 1992. Vol. 44, no. 11. June 8.

Navarro, Armando. 1995. *Mexican American youth organization: Avant-garde of the Chicano movement in Texas.* Austin: University of Texas.

Nunis, Doyce B. 1998. Alta California's Trojan horse. In *Contested eden: California before the gold rush,* ed. Ramon Gutierrez and Richard J. Orsi, 299–330. Berkeley: University of California Press.

Nuño, Ismael Navarro. 1999. Que Dios guíe sus manos. In *Healing Latinos: Realidad y fantasía,* ed. David E. Hayes-Bautista and Roberto O. Chiprut, 159–69. Los Angeles, CA: Cedars-Sinai Health System and the Center for the Study of Latino Health and Culture, UCLA.

Ogletree, Earl J., and David Garcia, comps. 1975. *Education of the Spanish-speaking urban child: A book of readings.* Springfield, IL: Charles C. Thomas.

Ortego, Philip D. 1971. Education and the Chicano: Moctezuma's children. In *Voices: Readings from* El Grito, *a journal of contemporary Mexican American thought.* Berkeley, CA: Quinto Sol Publications.

Perlman, Janice E. 1976. *The myth of marginality: Urban poverty and politics in Rio de Janeiro.* Berkeley: University of California Press.

Public Education: California's Perilous Slide. 1998. *Los Angeles Times,* May 17.

Puig, Claudia. 1993. Latino radio surge: A coming of age. *Los Angeles Times,* Jan. 7.

Rainwater, Lee, and William L. Yancey. 1967. *The Moynihan report and the politics of controversy, a trans-action social science and public policy report.* Cambridge, MA: MIT Press.

Ramos, George. 2000. Veterans win O.K. of statue to honor Latino war heroes. *Los Angeles Times,* Apr. 5.

Regents of the University of California. 1997–98. Applications, admissions, and enrollments for California first-time freshmen by ethnicity: Fall terms 1992 through 1996. In the University of California Office of the President Information Digest home page [updated Apr. 10, 1998; cited June 23, 2003]. Oakland: Regents of the University of California. Available at http://www.ucop.edu/sas/infodigest98/toc.html; link to http://www.ucop.edu/sas/infodigest98/pdf/PAGE10.pdf

———. 2001. First-time freshman application flow by ethnicity by year: Fall 1996–Fall 2000. In the University of California Office of the President Information Digest home page [updated June 7, 2002; cited June 23, 2003]. Oakland: Regents of the University of California. Available at http://www.ucop.edu/sas/infodigest98/toc.html; link to http://www.ucop.edu/sas/infodigest02/pdf/ido2aaep25.pdf

Rendon, Armando. 1970. La raza—Today, not mañana. In *Mexican-Americans in the United States: A reader,* comp. John H. Burma, 307–24. Cambridge, MA: Schenkman Publishing Company and Canfield Press.

Romo, Ricardo. 1983. *East Lost Angeles: History of a barrio.* Austin: University of Texas.

Rosales, F. Arturo. 1997. *Chicano! The history of the Mexican American civil rights movement.* 2nd rev. ed. Houston, TX: Arte Público Press.

Rosenberg, H. M., J. D. Maurer, P. D. Sorlie, N. J. Johnson, M. F. MacDorman, D. L. Ho, J. F. Spitler, and C. Scott. 1999. Quality of death rates by race and Hispanic origin: A summary of current research, 1999. *Vital and Health Statistics. Series 2; Data Evaluation and Methods Research* 128 (Sept.): 1–13.

Rowan, Helen. 1970. A minority nobody knows. In *Mexican-Americans in the United States: A reader,* comp. John H. Burma, 295–306. Cambridge, MA: Schenkman Publishing Company and Canfield Press.

Royce, Josiah. 2002. *California, from the conquest in 1846 to the second vigilance committee in San Francisco: A study of American character.* Introduction by Ronald A. Wells. Santa Clara, CA: Santa Clara University.

Ruiz de Burton, María Amparo. 2001. *Conflicts of interest: The letters of María Amparo Ruiz de Burton.* Edited by Rosaura Sanchez and Beatrice Pita. Houston, TX: Arte Público Press.

Sahagun, Louis. 2000. LA unified gets dismal ratings from public. *Los Angeles Times,* Apr. 11.

Sahagun, Louis, and Doug Smith. 2000. Whatever his legacy, Cortines jolted district. *Los Angeles Times,* June 30.

Samora, Julian, with Jorge A. Bustamante and Gilbert Cardenas. 1971. *Los mojados: The wetback story.* Notre Dame, IN: University of Notre Dame Press.

Sánchez-Albornoz, Nicolás. 1974. *The population of Latin America: A history.* Translated by W. A. R. Richardson. Berkeley: University of California Press.

Sandler, Martin W. 2001. *Vaqueros: America's first cowmen.* New York: Henry Holt and Co.

Santa Barbara County, California. County Recorder's Office. 1859. Marriage book, 1859. In microfilm "Marriage books, 1850–1859: Declaration of marriages, # 7—1884. Book A-B, 1850–1882," reel 1, item 2.

Santa Maria Times. 1882. Vol. 1, no. 12. July 8.

Saunders, Lyle. 1954. *Cultural difference and medical care: The case of the Spanish-speaking people of the Southwest.* New York: Russell Sage Foundation.

Schorr, Lisbeth B., with Daniel Schorr. 1988. *Within our reach: Breaking the cycle of disadvantage.* New York: Anchor Press/Doubleday.

Sego, Eugene B. 1998. *Aliados y adversarios: Los colonos tlaxcaltecas en la frontera septentrional de Nueva España.* San Luis Potosí, Mexico: El Colegio de San Luis, Gobierno del Estado de Tlaxcala, and the Centro de Investigaciones Históricas de San Luis Potosí.

Sherwood, Ben. 1995. For Pete Wilson, his political ambition is never blind. *Los Angeles Times,* July 23.

Skelton, George. 1997. California and the West: A wake-up call for GOP about a wide-awake giant. *Los Angeles Times,* Dec. 15.

Slatta, Richard W. 1997. *Comparing cowboys and frontiers.* Norman: University of Oklahoma Press.

Sorlie, Paul D., Eric Backlund, Norma J. Johnson, and Eugene Rogot. 1993. Mortality by Hispanic status in the United States. *JAMA* 270, no. 20 (Nov. 24): 2646–68.

Spragens, Thomas, Jr. 1995. Communitarian liberalism. In *New communitarian thinking: Persons, virtues, institutions, and communities,* ed. Amitai Etzioni, 37–51. Charlottesville: University Press of Virginia.

Starr, Kevin. 1973. *Americans and the California dream: 1850–1915.* New York: Oxford University Press.

———. 1990. *Material dreams: Southern California through the 1920s.* New York: Oxford University Press.

Strategy Research Corporation. 1994. *The Hispanic market handbook.* Miami, FL: SRC HQ Office.

UCLA Institute for Social Science Research Data Archives. 1996. *Census of population and housing, 1990 (U.S.): PUMS A sample 5% sample.* File: CEN90.PUMSACA. [Updated June 6, 2003]. Los Angeles, CA: UCLA Institute for Social Science Research Data Archives. Available for download only from http://www.sscnet.ucla.edu/issr/da/index/framei.htm

United States Bureau of the Census. 1880. *Tenth census of the United States, 1880.* Microfilm Roll 1880 T-9, 81. *California,* vol. 13. Washington DC: National Archives and Records Administration. A Microfilm Publication.

———. 1933a. *Fifteenth census of the United States: 1930.* Abstract of the Fifteenth Census of the United States. Washington DC: U.S. Government Printing Office.

———. 1933b. *Fifteenth census of the United States: 1930. Population,* Volume II. *General report: Statistics by subjects.* Washington DC: U.S. Government Printing Office.

———. 1952. *Census of the population: 1950.* Volume II. *Characteristics of the population: Number of inhabitants, general and detailed characteristics of the population.* Part 5. California. Prepared under the direction of Howard G. Brunsman. Washington DC: U.S. Government Printing Office.

———. 1997. Selected characteristics of the foreign-born population by year of entry and selected countries of birth: 1996. Data from the 1996 March Current Population Survey (CPS), Table 6. Electronic format no longer available. Transcript stored at CESLAC. Comparable data from the Bureau of the Census currently is available at http://www.census.gov/population/socdemo/foreign/cps1996/tab0211.txt and http://www.census.gov/population/soc demo/foreign/cps1996/tab0213.txt

———. 2000a. *Current population survey: Basic monthly.* In United States Bureau of Labor Statistics home page [updated Mar. 18, 2003; cited 2002–2003]. Available at http://www.bls.census.gov/cps/; link to http://www.bls.census .gov/cps/cpsbasic.htm

————. 2000b. *Current population survey: March supplement.* In United States Bureau of Labor Statistics home page [updated Mar. 18, 2003; cited 2002–2003]. Available at http://www.bls.census.gov/cps/; link to http://www.bls.census.gov/cps/ads/adsmain.htm

————. 2001a. *Census 2000 summary file 1 (SF 1): 100 percent data.* Map TM-P001H, *Persons who are Hispanic or Latino (of any race): 2000.* In United States Census Bureau home page. Washington DC: U.S. Bureau of the Census. Available from http://www.census.gov/main/www/cen2000.html; link to http://factfinder.census.gov/servlet/ThematicMapFramesetServlet

————. 2001b. *Census 2000 summary file 1 (SF 1): 100 percent data.* Table P8. *Hispanic or Latino by race.* In United States Census Bureau home page [updated Oct. 31, 2002; cited June 5, 2003]. Washington DC: U.S. Bureau of the Census. Available from http://www.census.gov/main/www/cen2000.html; link to http://factfinder.census.gov/servlet/DTTable?_ts = 73918485921

United States Department of Commerce (US DOC). 1975. *1972 survey of minority-owned business enterprises: Minority-owned businesses. Spanish origin.* Washington DC: U.S. Department of Commerce.

————. 1980. *1977 survey of minority-owned business enterprises: Minority-owned businesses. Spanish origin.* Washington DC: U.S. Department of Commerce.

————. 1986. *1982 survey of minority-owned business enterprises: Minority-owned businesses. Hispanic.* Washington DC: U.S. Department of Commerce.

————. 1990. *Census of population and housing, 1990. Summary tape file 3 on CD-ROM (California).* Prepared by the U.S. Bureau of the Census. CD-ROM. Washington DC: U.S. Bureau of the Census.

————. 1991. *1987 economic censuses: Survey of minority-owned business enterprises. Hispanic.* Washington DC: U.S. Department of Commerce.

————. 1996. *1992 economic census: Survey of minority-owned business enterprises. Hispanic.* Washington DC: U.S. Department of Commerce.

United States Department of Health, Education, and Welfare (US DHEW). 1979. *Health status of minorities and low income groups.* Prepared by Melvin H. Rudov and Nancy Santangelo. Washington DC: U.S. Government Printing Office.

United States Department of Health and Human Services (US DHHS). 1985a. *Health status of minorities and low income groups.* Prepared by Melvin H. Rudov, Jeanne A. Klingensmith, Nancy Santangelo, and Margaret W. Pratt. Washington DC: U.S. Government Printing Office.

————. 1985b. *Report of the secretary's task force on black and minority health.* Vol. 1. Washington DC: U.S. Department of Health and Human Services.

————. [1998]. *Eliminating racial and ethnic disparities in health.* Washington DC: U.S. Department of Health and Human Services, Initiative to Eliminate Racial and Ethnic Disparities in Health [updated Nov. 13, 2000; cited June 16, 2003]. Available at http//www.raceandhealth.hhs.gov/sidebars/sbinitOver.htm

United States General Accounting Office (US GAO). 1990. *The urban under-class: Disturbing problems demanding attention.* Washington DC: U.S. General Accounting Office.

University of California, Office of the President (UCOP). 2002. Medical school first-year class enrollments, 2000 through 2002. Underrepresented minorities (URM) and other Hispanics/Latinos. In University of California Office of the President Academic Advancement home page [cited June 23, 2003]. Oakland: University of California, Office of the President, 2002. Available at http://www.ucop.edu/acadadv/datamgmt/meddata/; link to http://www.ucop.edu/acadadv/datamgmt/lawmed/med-enrolls.pdf

Vallejo, Mariano G. 1838. *Bótica general de los remedios esperimentados.* Sonoma de la Alta California: Impreta del Gobierno.

Villagrá, Gaspar de. 2001. *Historia de Nuevo México.* Edited by Mercedes Junquera. Crónicas de América, 22. Madrid: Dastin.

Voices of Citizens Together (VCT). 1995. Why Los Angeles county is broke. Full-page advertisement in the *Los Angeles Daily News,* July 16.

Weber, Max. 2001. *The Protestant ethic and the spirit of capitalism.* Translated by Talcott Parsons. Introduction by Anthony Giddens. London and New York: Routledge.

Weidenbaum, Murray. 1990. The war on poverty is up to the individual. *Los Angeles Times,* Sept. 23.

Weintraub, Daniel M. 1994. Crime, immigration issue helped Wilson, poll finds. *Los Angeles Times,* Nov. 9.

Whisler, Kirk, and Octavio Nuiry. 1996. *The complete Hispanic media directory.* Newport Beach, CA: ADR Publishing.

Whitman, Walt. 1907. The Spanish element in our nationality. In *Complete prose works: Specimen days and collect, November boughs and good bye my fancy.* Boston, MA: Small, Maynard and Co.

Whitmore, Thomas M. 1992. *Disease and death in early colonial Mexico. Simulating Amerindian depopulation.* Dellplain Latin American Studies, 28. Boulder, CO: Westview Press.

Wilkie, James W., Eduardo Alemán, and José Guadalupe Ortega, eds. 2001. *Statistical abstract of Latin America,* vol. 37. Los Angeles: UCLA Latin American Center Publications, University of California.

William C. Velásquez Institute (WCVI). 2000. *WCVI phone survey of Latino registered voters, California, N = 560. September 27–October 4, 2000 +/-4.1%.* In the William C. Velásquez Institute Polling Data home page [cited 2002–2003]. San Antonio, TX, and Los Angeles: William C. Velásquez Institute. Available at http://www.wcvi.org/latino_voter_research/polling_data.html; link to http://www.wcvi.org/latino_voter_research/polls/ca_total_n560.html

Williams, Ron L., N. J. Binkins, and E. J. Clingman. 1986. Pregnancy outcomes among Spanish-surname women in California. *American Journal of Public Health* 76: 387–91.

Wilson, William J. 1987. *The truly disadvantaged: The inner city, the underclass and public policy.* Chicago, IL: University of Chicago Press.

Word, David L., and R. Colby Perkins. 1996. *Building a Spanish surname list for the 1990's—A new approach to an old problem.* U.S. Bureau of the Census, Population Division, Technical Working Paper no. 13 (Mar. 1996). Washington DC: U.S. Bureau of the Census.

UNPUBLISHED REFERENCES

Bancroft Library, University of California, Berkeley. 1767–1822. Provincial State Papers. 14 volumes. Archives of California. Part of the Hubert Howe Bancroft Collection [microfilm].

———. 1799. Mariano Guadalupe Vallejo Documentos para la Historia de California. Certificate of the examination and approval of Manuel Gutiérrez de Quixano in the art of surgery, Feb. 28, 1799, by José Ignacio García Jove, José Francisco Rada, and Joaquín Pío Antonio de Eguía y Muró. C-B 28:6 (2 exp.).

Belmont High School Alumni Project. 2000. Survey conducted by the *Los Angeles Times* Poll, Oct. 18–Dec. 17, 1999. Data obtained via personal communications by Ray Enslow, June 7, 2000, and Jan. 8, 2004.

Center for the Study of Latino Health and Culture (CESLAC), Arthritis 2001, 3: U.S.-born Latino males. Focus group conducted by María Hayes Bautista. Jan. 26. Transcript stored at CESLAC.

CESLAC Arthritis 2001, 10: Immigrant Latina females. Focus group conducted by María Hayes-Bautista. Sept. 7. Transcript stored at CESLAC.

CESLAC, Chicano Health Movement (CHM) 1999, 1: Latino dentist. Individual interview by Valerie Talavera-Bustillo. June 25. Transcript stored at CESLAC.

CESLAC CHM 1999, 2: Latina health administrator. Individual interview by Valerie Talavera-Bustillo. July 6. Transcript stored at CESLAC.

CESLAC CHM 1999, 3: Latino surgeon. Individual interview by Valerie Talavera-Bustillo. Mar. 24. Transcript stored at CESLAC.

CESLAC CHM 1999, 4: Latino hematologist. Individual interview by Valerie Talavera-Bustillo. June 19–27. Transcript stored at CESLAC.

CESLAC CHM 1999, 5: Latino health administrator. Individual interview by Valerie Talavera-Bustillo. June 23. Transcript stored at CESLAC.

CESLAC CHM 1999, 6: Latino medical researcher. Individual interview by Valerie Talavera-Bustillo. Feb. 10–11. Transcript stored at CESLAC.

CESLAC CHM 1999, 7: Latina program administrator. Individual interview by Valerie Talavera-Bustillo. Feb.–May. Transcript stored at CESLAC.

CESLAC CHM 1999, 8: Latina pathologist. Individual interview by Valerie Talavera-Bustillo. July 1. Transcript stored at CESLAC.

CESLAC CHM 1999, 9: Latino family physician. Individual interview by Valerie Talavera-Bustillo. Mar. 4, 8. Transcript stored at CESLAC.

CESLAC CHM 1999, 10: Latino family physician. Individual interview by Valerie Talavera-Bustillo. June 22. Transcript stored at CESLAC.

CESLAC CHM 1999, 11: Latino elected official. Individual interview by Valerie Talavera-Bustillo. July 1. Transcript stored at CESLAC.

CESLAC CHM 1999, 12: Latino health law attorney. Individual interview by Valerie Talavera-Bustillo. June 29. Transcript stored at CESLAC.

CESLAC CHM 1999, 13: Latino ophthalmologist. Individual interview by Valerie Talavera-Bustillo. March 19. Transcript stored at CESLAC.

CESLAC Diabetes 1997, 1: Immigrant Latina. Individual interview by María Hayes-Bautista. Jan. Transcript stored at CESLAC.

CESLAC Diabetes 1997, 2: Immigrant Latina. Individual interview by María Hayes-Bautista. Feb. 1. Transcript stored at CESLAC.

CESLAC Diabetes 1998, 5: Immigrant Latinos. Focus group conducted by María Hayes-Bautista. Dec. 17. Transcript stored at CESLAC.

CESLAC, Edward R. Roybal Institute for Applied Gerontology (Roybal), at California State University, Los Angeles, 1997. Roybal Immunization Consortium for Older Adults (RICO) Survey. Data set on computer diskette. Stored at CESLAC.

CESLAC Health Definitions 1999, 7: U.S.-born Latino college students. Focus group conducted by María Hayes-Bautista. July 29. Transcript stored at CESLAC.

CESLAC, Mexican American Grocers Association (MAGA) 1995, 1: Latina executive, food and beverage. Individual interview by María Hayes-Bautista. Jan.–Feb. Transcript stored at CESLAC.

CESLAC MAGA 1995, 2: Latino executive, processed meats. Individual interview by María Hayes-Bautista. Jan.–Feb. Transcript stored at CESLAC.

CESLAC MAGA 1995, 3: Latino executive, soaps and detergents. Individual interview by María Hayes-Bautista. Jan.–Feb. Transcript stored at CESLAC.

CESLAC MAGA 1995, 4: Latino executive, banking; with interpolations by NH white female colleague of interview subject. Individual interview by María Hayes-Bautista. Jan.–Feb. Transcript stored at CESLAC.

CESLAC MAGA 1995, 5: Latino executive, consumer products. Individual interview by María Hayes-Bautista. Jan.–Feb. Transcript stored at CESLAC.

CESLAC MAGA 1995, 6: Latino executive, food industry. Individual interview by María Hayes-Bautista. Jan.–Feb. Transcript stored at CESLAC.

CESLAC MAGA 1995, 7: Latino executive, food and beverage. Individual interview by María Hayes-Bautista. Jan.–Feb. Transcript stored at CESLAC.

CESLAC MAGA 2003: Steve Soto. Individual interview by David E. Hayes-Bautista. Jan. 9. Transcript stored at CESLAC.

CESLAC, Mexican American Legal Defense and Education Fund (MALDEF) 1997, 1: NH Whites. Focus group conducted by María Hayes-Bautista. Apr. 9. Transcript stored at CESLAC.

CESLAC MALDEF 1997, 2: NH Whites. Focus group conducted by María Hayes-Bautista. Apr. Transcript stored at CESLAC.

CESLAC MALDEF 1997, 3: NH White, evangelical young adults. Focus group conducted by María Hayes-Bautista. Apr. 12. Transcript stored at CESLAC.

CESLAC MALDEF 1997, 4: NH Whites. Focus group conducted by María Hayes-Bautista. Apr.–May. Code sheet stored at CESLAC.

CESLAC MALDEF 1997, 5: NH Whites. Focus group conducted by María Hayes-Bautista. Apr.–May. Transcript stored at CESLAC.

CESLAC MALDEF 1997, 6: NH Whites, middle age. Focus group conducted by María Hayes-Bautista. Apr.–May. Transcript stored at CESLAC.

CESLAC MALDEF 1998, 1: U.S.-born Latino blue collar workers. Focus group conducted by María Hayes-Bautista. July 21. Transcript stored at CESLAC.

CESLAC MALDEF 1998, 2: U.S.-born Latino professionals. Focus group conducted by María Hayes-Bautista. July 13. Transcript stored at CESLAC.

CESLAC MALDEF 1998, 3: Immigrant Latinos. Focus group conducted by María Hayes-Bautista. July 7. Transcript stored at CESLAC.

CESLAC MALDEF 1998, 4: Immigrant Latinos. Focus group conducted by María Hayes-Bautista. July 28. Transcript stored at CESLAC.

CESLAC MALDEF 1998, 5: NH Whites. Focus group conducted by María Hayes-Bautista. June 22. Transcript stored at CESLAC.

CESLAC MALDEF 1998, 6: NH Whites. Focus group conducted by María Hayes-Bautista. July 15. Transcript stored at CESLAC.

CESLAC Social Attitudes Survey 2000. Population-based survey conducted by telephone by the UCLA Survey Research Center, Juarez and Associates, and CESLAC, under the supervision of David E. Hayes-Bautista and Paul Hsu. SPSS files stores at CESLAC.

CESLAC, United Way (UW) 1998, 1: U.S.-born Latinos, high school only. Focus group conducted by María Hayes-Bautista. Oct. 7. Transcript stored at CESLAC.

CESLAC UW 1998, 2: U.S.-born Latinos, some college. Focus group conducted by María Hayes-Bautista. Oct. 21. Transcript stored at CESLAC.

CESLAC UW 1998, 3: U.S.-born Latinos, some college. Focus group conducted by María Hayes-Bautista. Oct. 27. Transcript stored at CESLAC.

CESLAC UW 1998, 4: U.S.-born Latinos, high school only. Focus group conducted by María Hayes-Bautista. Oct. 28. Transcript stored at CESLAC.

CESLAC UW 1998, 5: Immigrant Latinos. Focus group conducted by María Hayes-Bautista. Oct. 14. Transcript stored at CESLAC.

CESLAC UW 1998, 6: Immigrant Latinos. Focus group conducted by María Hayes-Bautista. Oct. 10. Transcript stored at CESLAC.

CESLAC UW 1998, 7: Latino civic leaders. Focus group conducted by María Hayes-Bautista. Oct. 29. Transcript stored at CESLAC.

CESLAC UW 1998, 8: Latino business leaders. Focus group conducted by María Hayes-Bautista. Oct. 30. Transcript stored at CESLAC.

Bustamante, Cruz. 1999. Personal communication, May 30.

Firebaugh, Marcos. 2002. Personal communication, June 17.

Guerra, Fernando J. 2003. Personal communication, June 6.

Hayes-Bautista, Catalina Mercedes Ixcotl. 2003. Personal communication, May 8.

Lopez-Williams, Ruth. 2002. Personal communication, Nov. 1.

United States Bureau of Labor Statistics (US BLS). 2002. Consumer Expenditure Survey, Standard Error Table. Table 1701, "Housing, tenure, type of area, race of reference person, and Hispanic origin of reference person." Unpublished data estimates. Washington DC: U.S. Bureau of Labor Statistics.

Los Angeles Times: Belmont High follow-up, 11, 170; del Valle, 200; and Proposition 187, 127, 134; and Proposition 227, 138; after Rodney King riot, 125; Salazar death, 42; Spanish-language newspaper, 109; Wilson campaign, 126, 127

Lummis, Charles Fletcher, 200

Luther, Martin, 203

MacArthur Park, 169–70

majority: African American urban, 118; Latino population, 59, 72, 202

MALDEF. *See* Mexican American Legal Defense and Education Fund

males, labor-force participation, 74–75, 75 *fig*, 77, 96–98, 98 *fig*

Manpower Development Training programs, 62

market, 102–10, 176, 204; in best-case scenario, 210, 213–14; food industry, 9, 53, 90–93, 102–4; "gazelle" corporations, 105; Minority-Owned Businesses, 109; South Central Los Angeles stores, 123. *See also* consumption; economics; Latino market

marriages. *See* family orientation; intermarriage, ethnic/racial

Martínez, Leandro, 196

Marx, Karl, 228

Marxism, 44

Mason, William Marvin, 22, 191–92

McLean, Robert, 18

media: all over Latin America, 107, 201; image of Latinos in English language, 3, 11, 72, 112, 114, 128, 145, 165, 166; Latino adolescent market, 172–73; in Spanish language, 1–2, 9, 15, 108–9, 201. *See also* advertising; billboards; publications; radio; television

medical schools: baby bust and, 70; in best-case scenario, 210; Chicano students, 50–51; Latin American-trained physicians and, 53, 54, 55; Latino population, 53, 223, 224–25; minorities underrepresented, 225 *fig*; UC system, 49–50, 69, 70, 72, 222–23, 225 *fig*; in worst-case scenario, 218. *See also* physicians, Latino

Mendez, Sylvia, 27–28

Mendez v. Westminster, 28

"Message from Hispanic Americans" (MALDEF), 10–11, 148–49, 157, 160–69

mestizaje (ethnic mixing), 6–7, 22–23. *See also* intermarriage, ethnic/racial

mestizo, 22–26, 29, 63, 190–91; Catholics, 190–91, 194, 195–96. *See also* Californios

Mexican American Grocers' Association (MAGA), 90–91, 93, 102–4, 140

Mexican American Legal Defense and Education Fund (MALDEF), 46; American identity studies, 149–60; injunctions vs. anti-Latino initiatives, 129, 140; "Message from Hispanic Americans" ad, 10–11, 148–49, 157, 160–69

Mexican American War/Treaty of Guadalupe Hidalgo (1848), 24, 25, 26, 29, 198

Mexican Problem, 1

Mexicans, 5, 26, 155; American identity, 10, 151–52, 155–60; and Chicanos, 7; colonizing (beginning 1769), 5, 16, 191–92; deportation era, 6, 9, 17–19; ethnic diversity, 4–5, 6–7, 22–25, 29–32, 116, 191–92; gold rush, 196; immigration (1970–90), 6, 7, 8, 10, 11, 51–56, 116; Mexican Problem, 1; and naturalization, 140; as race, 6–7, 29, 30 *table*, 31–32; Southwest, 24, 25, 191–92. *See also* immigrant Latinos

Mexican schools, 1, 27–28, 32

Mexico: in best-case scenario, 209, 211; California statehood (1820s), 193; Chicano reception in, 48; dance, 108; death rates, 83; Gross Domestic Product (1975–90), 91; immigration from diverse places in, 29–32, 116, 191–92; Independence, 23, 196, 197, 198; languages, 33, 34; Mexican American War/Treaty of Guadalupe Hidalgo (1848), 24, 25, 26, 29, 198; music, 107–8; population (pre-1492), 20, 21 *fig*; poverty, 59; Revolution (1910), 16; War of Independence (1810–21), 23; in worst-case scenario, 12, 216–17. *See also* Mexicans

Office of Health Resources Opportunity, Health Resources Administration, 66
Office of Minority Health, 66–67
La Opinion, 109
organizations: Chicano, 46, 47, 50, 70; deportation-era Latino, 42; NCHO, 39, 50–51. *See also* clubs

Pacific Islanders, 5; in best-case scenario history studies, 212; birth rates, 95, 201; educational attainment, 221, 226–27; family orientation, 213; intermarriage, 205; population (2040), 202; poverty levels, 63; and Proposition 187, 128; vs. Proposition 209, 136; and Proposition 227, 137
Parsons, Talcott, 34
peer groups, Latino adolescent, 172–73
Philadelphia Plan, 67
physicians, Latino: heart transplant, 187; immigrants (1970s), 53–55; oldest medical license in California, 192; population per, 218–19, 224–25, 224 *fig;* shortage, 13, 53, 222–25; in worst-case scenario, 13, 218–19. *See also* health care; medical schools
Pico, Pío, 197–98
Pico Union, 169
Plessy v. Ferguson, 28
pochos (U.S.-born), 48. *See also* U.S.-born Latinos
police brutality: toward Chicanos, 46–47; toward Rodney King, 122
politics, 59–68, 145; Chicano, 44–45, 47, 55; Democratic Party, 138, 141; electoral polarization of whites from others, 9, 126–38, 142; Latino Legislative Caucus, 2, 10; Latino officeholders, 10, 142–43, 143 *fig,* 200; Latino power, 2, 10, 143–47; Latino revolutionary figures, 44–45; Latino vote, 4, 9–10, 128, 136, 137, 138–43, 146, 156; leftist, 44–45, 55; minority, 61; and NCHO, 50; Proposition 209, 136, 139; Proposition 227, 3, 9, 119, 137–38, 139; Republican Party, 127, 136–37, 138–39, 141; social activism (1965–75), 38–49. *See also* discrimination; laws; Proposition 187

population: America (pre-1492), 20–21; baby boom, 40, 69, 71; baby bust, 69–70, 116; bracero, 52; California African American and Latino, 62; California caste creep (1790), 22; California Latino (1769–1850), 16; California Latino (1910–65), 16, 17 *table,* 18–19, 19 *fig,* 93; California Latino (1940–2040), 1–3, 2 *fig,* 13, 70–72, 201–2; California Latino (1960s), 39, 93; California Latino (1970), 93–94, 94 *fig;* California Latino (1975), 93; California Latino (1990), 94; California Latino (2000), 94, 94 *fig;* California Latino (2004), 181; California losing (1990s), 122; California poverty (1960–2000), 65 *fig;* Chicano activists, 49; Chicanos born in U.S., 43; Latino adolescent, 172; Latino college and university, 41, 50, 56, 222; Latino growth (1970–75), 55, 70–71; Latino immigrants (1950), 52; Latino majority, 59, 72, 202; Latino male labor force, 74–75, 75 *fig,* 98; Latino medical school population, 53, 223, 224–25; LAUSD enrollment (1969–94), 131–32; LBA, 110; Los Angeles Latino, 16, 41, 72, 120–21, 121 *fig,* 132–34, 133 *fig,* 172, 202; naturalizing, 140–41, 141 *fig;* per physician, 218–19, 224–25, 224 *fig;* poor, 61; Proposition 187 and, 128, 134; South Central Los Angeles, 120–21, 121 *fig;* southern California Latino (1800s), 195; southern California Latino (1998), 176; undocumented immigrants, 132–34, 133 *fig;* U.S.-born and immigrant Latinos, 19, 131 *fig,* 180; U.S. Mexican (1930), 30 *table;* welfare, 76 *fig. See also* birth rates; death rates; demographics; immigration
poverty, 59–68; California (1960–2000), 65 *fig;* California Latinos (1990 and 2000), 97 *fig;* culture of, 59–61; and dysfunctional behavior, 78, 96; and health, 65, 66; and Latino family orientation, 76–77; Latino immigrants

restrictive covenants, 1, 28, 69, 119
retirement: baby boomers, 71, 212–13,
    217–18, 219, 228; in best-case scenario,
    212–13; in worst-case scenario, 217–18,
    219
retro-assimilators, 9, 111–13, 115, 205
Revolution: American, 198; Mexican
    (1910), 16
revolutionary figures, Latino, 44–45
riots, urban America, 41, 58; and culture of
    poverty, 60–61; minority image rising
    from, 7–8, 58, 60, 124–25. *See also*
    long hot summers (1965–69); Los An-
    geles riots
Royce, Josiah, 28
Ruiz de Burton, María Amparo May-
    torena, 198–99

Salazar, Ruben, 42
Sanchez, Joe, 90
San Francisco: Chicano moratorium, 45,
    49; University of California Medical
    Center, 49–50, 69, 70
San Gabriel Spanish-American League, 200
San Jose State University, Latino student
    population, 41
Santa Barbara: Californios, 16, 194, 195–97;
    early elementary school (before 1796),
    192; Latinos in Carpinteria schools,
    27; "Old Spanish Days," 16; Pablo de
    la Guerra street, 26; Plan de Santa
    Bárbara, 46; University of California,
    83
Santa Fe, New Mexico, 13
Saunders, Lyle, 35
Saxon, David, 69–70
Schink, Werner, *The Burden of Support:
    Young Latinos in an Aging Society*
    (with Hayes-Bautista and Chapa), 3,
    71–72, 78–79, 208–9
scholarships: CHAMA, 54; hometown as-
    sociations, 111
schools: barrio, 40–41; in best-case sce-
    nario, 211–12, 220–21; California Mas-
    ter Plan for Higher Education, 40,
    225–26; California's national ranking
    (1950s-90s), 169, 225–26; Chicano ac-
    tivism on quality of, 46; early elemen-

tary (before 1796), 192; Latino gradu-
    ation rates, 40, 53, 63, 96, 97 *fig*,
    170–71, 221, 224–25; Latinos feeling
    different from non-Hispanic whites,
    40–41, 153; Los Angeles Unified
    School District (LAUSD), 11, 45, 114,
    131–32, 169–71; Mexican, 1, 27–28, 32;
    Proposition 187 vs. Latinos in, 126,
    130–32, 134; segregated, 1, 6, 27–28,
    32, 42; Spanish language prohibited,
    1, 3, 9, 15, 119, 137–38; in worst-case
    scenario, 12–13, 214–15, 217, 219,
    220–21. *See also* bilingual education;
    colleges; dental schools; educational
    attainment; high schools; medical
    schools; universities
Schorr, Lisbeth, 68
security: in worst-case scenario, 215–17,
    219, 220. *See also* military; police bru-
    tality; wars
segregation, racial/ethnic, 6, 14–15, 29, 40,
    54, 61–62; Chicanos protesting, 7, 46;
    housing, 1, 6, 16, 28, 60, 69, 119; laws
    creating, 23–24n, 25–31, 205; military,
    18, 42; school, 1, 6, 27–28, 32, 42;
    swimming pools, 1, 14, 32. *See also*
    barrios; discrimination
Shils, Edward, 34
slaves, from Africa, 21
Sleepy Lagoon trial, 36
smallpox, 21, 190
social activism (1965–75), 38–49. *See also*
    Chicanos; civil rights; politics
social behaviors: urban underclass, 61, 62,
    74–78, 88, 96, 98–100, 104. *See also*
    civil society; dysfunctional minority
    image; family orientation; health;
    labor force; Latino social behaviors;
    middle class; religion
social programs, 124; for minorities, 8, 58,
    61, 62, 87–88; poverty, 8, 41, 61, 62,
    67, 68, 75–76, 87–88, 99 *fig*; prenatal
    care, 84, 86–87, 126; undocumented
    immigrants and, 126, 130, 133; urban
    renewal, 120; in worst-case scenario,
    216. *See also* welfare
La Sociedad Hispano-Americana de Bene-
    ficencia Mutua, 198

Ueberroth, Peter, 124, 125
underclass. *See* poverty; urban underclass
unemployment: California, 121–22; me
  decade/greed decade (1980s), 68;
  urban underclass, 74
unions, labor, 42, 45, 49, 50
United Farmworkers, 45, 50
United Way of Greater Los Angeles, survey,
  102, 135–38, 158–60
universities: baby bust and, 69–70; in best-
  case scenario, 210, 211; Chicano rebellion (1960s), 7, 44–45, 49–51; Chicano
  studies, 45, 46, 112–13; graduates,
  220–21, 221 *fig;* Latino admissions,
  12–13, 41, 222, 223 *fig;* on minorities
  and dysfunction, 69; in worst-case
  scenario, 218, 219. *See also* colleges;
  dental schools; medical schools; University of California system
University of California system, 69–70,
  221–22, 228; and affirmative action,
  136; Berkeley, 41, 56, 69, 192; in best-
  case scenario, 211; Latinos enrolling,
  222, 223 *fig;* medical schools, 49–50,
  69, 70, 72, 222–23, 225 *fig;* San Francisco Medical Center, 49–50, 69, 70;
  Santa Barbara, 83; Systemwide Health
  Sciences Committee, 70; in worst-
  case scenario, 12–13, 214, 219. *See also*
  UCLA
University of Wisconsin, Race and Poverty
  Institute, 61
Univision, 109
Unz, Ron, 137–38
urban areas: African American majority,
  118; in best-case scenario, 213; housing, 9, 118, 119–21, 213; Latinos on city
  councils, 142; middle class flight, 9,
  118–20, 122, 169–70; minorities, 7–8,
  58, 60, 61; school rankings, 169; in
  worst-case scenario, 217. *See also* inner
  city; Los Angeles; riots, urban America; urban underclass
urban underclass, 58, 61, 68; African
  American classified as, 58, 61; Belmont High, 170; Chicano, 62; His-
  panic/Latino classified as, 58, 64, 89;
  market and, 104; and social behaviors,

61, 62, 74–78, 88, 96, 98–100; South
  Central Los Angeles riots (1992) and,
  124–25; in worst-case scenario, 208.
  See also dysfunctional minority image;
  poverty; welfare
U.S.-born Latinos: age, 131 *fig;* and American identity, 9, 152–55, 158, 159–60, 159
  fig. 173–74, 177–78; anti-Latino initiatives and, 9–10, 128, 131, 135–41; baby
  boomer, 18, 19–20; barrio-born, 19, 39;
  behavioral differences from immigrant
  Latinos, 96–102, 98 *fig,* 112–16; confusion over Latino identity, 9, 113–18; educational attainment, 12–13, 96–99,
  101, 170–71, 221, 226–28, 227 *fig;* focus
  groups, 10, 11, 14–15, 112–15, 134–39,
  144–74; languages, 101, 111–14, 165, 166,
  174; market, 119; on "Message from
  Hispanic Americans" ad (MALDEF),
  162, 165–69; *pochos,* 48; population
  compared to immigrant Latinos, 19,
  131 *fig,* 180; responses to immigrant
  Latinos, 110–17, 146–47; retro-assimilators, 9, 111–13, 115, 205; school children,
  131; in worst-case scenario, 12–13, 216.
  See also Californios; Chicanos
U.S. Bureau of the Census, 5–6, 29–32, 52,
  132. *See also* population

Valdez, Robert, 72, 137
Valens, Richie (Ricardo Valenzuela), 19
Vallejo, Mariano G., 192, 198
values: American, 150; middle class, 8,
  10–11, 162–63, 171; modern vs. tradi-
  tional, 34–35. *See also* family orienta-
  tion; work ethic
Velasquez, Alec, 56–57
Velásquez Institute survey, 141
Vietnam War, 42, 45
Vila, Jayme, 196
Villa, Pancho, 44–45
violence: music and, 108; public image of
  Latinos, 36. *See also* police brutality;
  riots, urban America
Virgin of Guadalupe, 189
Voices of Citizens Together (VCT), 130–31,
  132
Von's, 91–92

Compositor:	Binghamton Valley Composition, LLC
Text:	11.25/13.5 Adobe Garamond
Display:	Adobe Garamond
Printer and binder:	Maple-Vail Manufacturing Group
Indexer:	Barbara Roos
Illustrator:	Bill Nelson